3D PRINTING

3D PRINTING

THE NEXT TECHNOLOGY GOLD RUSH

By Christopher D. Winnan

FUTURE FACTORIES AND HOW TO CAPITALIZE ON
DISTRIBUTED MANUFACTURING

ISBN-13: 978-1494213961
ISBN-10: 1494213966

Manufactured in the United States of America.

CONTENTS

DISCLAIMER vii
ACKNOWLEDGMENTS...viii

INTRODUCTION.. 1

PART I
3D Printing Technology 6
Scanning Technology 25
Modeling Technology 33
Model and 3D Design Resources 52
Freelance Printing, Scanning and Designing 57

PART II
Designing New Products... 69
Niche Markets 74
Untapped Markets 76
Three Pioneering Printers... 79
Miniatures.. 85
Doll's Houses.. 88
Action Figures 92
Gaming Miniatures.. 103
Radio-Controlled Scale Models 114
'Green' Products.. 118
Upcycling 124
Spares 126
Metaphysical 138
Skulls and Bones 142
Pets 145
Custom Items and Works of Art............................... 149
Cosplay.. 152
Health 158
Crafts 162
Miscellaneous Ideas 164
Plastic Covers.. 173

PART III
Overcoming Negativity 176
Some Interesting Analogies....................................... 182
Printing on a Larger Scale 187

Printing Materials..190
Legal Issues...199
The Printed Gun Controversy 206
3D Printing in the Third World..212
The Disruptive Power of 3D Printers.................................218
The Future of 3D Printing - How Far Could All This Go? ...227

PART IV
Appendices..235
About The Author 275

DISCLAIMER

While all attempts have been made to review the information provided in this book, the authors do no assume any responsibilities for errors, omissions, or contrary interpretations of the words or phrases contained within. The information provided in the book is for educational and entertainment purposes. The reader is responsible for his or her own use and the authors does not accept any responsibilities for any liabilities or damages, real or perceived, resulting from the use of this information.

ACKNOWLEDGMENTS

Thanks to Kevin Hayward for his much needed editing skills and the section on Legal Issues.   Thanks also to Hannah Jones for her excellent proofreading skills and to Karick (Karen Reynolds-James) for her tireless formatting abilities. Thanks also to all that was kind enough to allow me to link to their images, especially Tomasz Orzechowski, Co-Founder & Industrial Designer of TO DO Product Design (http://to-do.com.pl/index.html) of whose design of a twenty century modeler work station graces the front cover.

1

INTRODUCTION

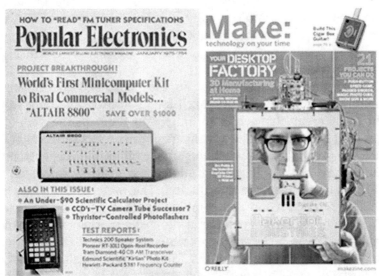

History repeats itself?

If you are reading this, you already know that 3D printers are bringing about a revolution in manufacturing. Much like the industrial and computer revolutions, these amazing new machines will completely transform the face of manufacturing, distribution and consumption. But, for the moment, that is all just rhetoric, until current printer owners get up, lead the way and show where all the profits lie. Resolutions are improving and costs are decreasing all the time. Did you know for example, that 3D printing was used to create the suits of armour in *Iron Man* and the Aston Martins in the latest Bond movie? Even so, some people worry that we are still in the 'spend a lot or be disappointed' early-adopter stage. The real question that most people want answered is this: "Can I make a buck from these machines?" and the answer is a resounding yes, not only a buck, but probably a couple of hundred bucks a day and maybe even a lot more. This exciting new technology is destined to provide all kinds of exciting new opportunities and employment.

If you have an interest in 3D printers at the moment, then you should be looking at yourself as the twenty-first-century counterpart of pioneers like Bill Gates and Steve Jobs, from the early computer home-brew clubs. It was guys like these who first thought about how to monetize this technology, and went on to be the earliest IT billionaires. If 3D printers really are the beginning of a game-changing new technology, then there are going to be plenty of billionaires made on the way, maybe even the world's first trillionaire, who knows?

3D printing is a technology on the cusp, and therefore it is essential that you be fully prepared for its arrival. The only way to profit from great changes is to anticipate them in the very early stages, and be ready to take advantage of the opportunities that they create. We are still at the beginning phase today, but major technical advances are already heralding enormous business opportunities. This book is not just idle speculation. The material here has been meticulously researched and combined with a uniquely specialised knowledge of overseas manufacturing, niche markets and emerging economies. I was lucky enough to spend much of the nineties in Seoul, observing the largest of the Asian Tigers transform itself into an industrial powerhouse. The following decade was spent in the Peoples' Republic of China, observing the dragon wake from it centuries of slumber. Most recently, I have been on numerous trips to Myanmar, exploring the key strategic regions of the Burma Road and the Indian Gulf. As a well-established guide book writer, I am in a very good position to document these areas, opening up paths for other entrepreneurs and investors to follow. In this book I will be focusing not on one particular geographical area, but one specific technology, that of additive manufacturing, better known as 3D printing.

Since the 3D printer patents expired in 2009, I have been watching this field with great interest. Home-brew tinkerers and hacker-space gizmologists have quietly been bringing the designs and capabilities of these amazing new machines up to a level where they are almost ready to hit the mainstream. Back in the seventies, it took more than five years before personal computers found their first killer app, and another ten years before they were able to crack the home market. Kurzweil's law of accelerating returns demonstrates very clearly that the coming paradigm shift to digital manufacturing will take place even faster than the seismic events of the previous digital revolution. The average Joe still has only a very vague idea of what 3D printing actually is, let alone its capabilities, its financial applications and its massive game changing potential. If you want to play a role in the next industrial revolution, you will need to be a good three steps ahead of everybody else, who are just now waking up and paying attention to what 3D printing is all about.

This book is much more than a brainstorming of random ideas that might eventually come into effect sometime in the next decade. I have actively tried to steer clear of all the usual type of fantasy, tea-leaf predictions, 'move into toilet paper and become a billionaire' thinking. This book is about opportunities and markets that exist right now. This is not some cyberpunk fantasy of vague speculation, but a detailed overview of everything that is relevant and important in the 3D printing industry. Even now, this is a vast field, with new changes taking place every single day. It will undoubtedly affect many areas of our everyday lives with accordingly immense social impacts. This book shows you how to successfully anticipate these developments, and how to surf the crest of this technological tsunami, while everybody else is swallowed up and swept away.

At the same time, this book is not a specialist MBA in digital entrepreneurship. I have researched and presented the most relevant material available, but at the same time this is not a book about niche marketing or online business. I have obviously touched on these areas, as they will undoubtedly play an important role, but this is not a dummies guide to setting up a 3D printing business in the age of the internet. There are plenty of books out there about online selling and internet marketing. If you are savvy enough to see that another industrial revolution is about to take place, then it is also a fair bet that you already know how to make tools like eBay, Etsy and Facebook work for you. To this end, I am happy to share with you as much as I currently know about the current state of digital manufacturing, but I will not be teaching you how to suck eggs.

While there are already hundreds, if not thousands of books out there on starting and running a successful internet business, this book is something else completely. This is a collection of cutting-edge knowledge that has not yet been compiled elsewhere. In fact, parts of it are so specialised, that you would be hard pushed to find large chunks of it just about anywhere. Despite their explosive implications, few people are writing in any detail about the digital rights management of physical objects, or the enormous varieties of scale in the miniatures market, or state of the art advances in mixed-mesh modelling. Few apart from the most avid collectors appreciate the field of 1/6 scale military figures as an emerging art form, or the industrial applications of complex geometries and spiral vortices, or even the rapid miniaturisation that is taking place in the arena of autonomous robotics. All of these subjects are covered here, clearly explaining their close relationships with 3D printing.

For me personally, the most fascinating aspect of 3D printing is not the current state of play, but those amazing possibilities that are opening up in areas that we simply have not previously been able to explore with current technology. These include the enormous potential of areas such as implosion propulsion, mass personalisation and virtual object manipulation. 3D printing is not just an isolated technological breakthrough, but one that will affect an entire spectrum of fields, from design to development to distribution. Perhaps most interesting of all will be the environmental impacts of these developments. Could 3D printing usher in an age of practical sustainability that we as a planet now so desperately need? Read on and find out all this and more in the following chapters.

PART I

A Technological Primer

2

3D Printing Technology

Remember the Altair 8800?
Source: http://en.wikipedia.org/wiki/Altair_8800

The Altair was a pretty primitive and useless computer by today's standards, but it was really the first personal computer. For most people, it would have been impossible to predict all the ways personal computers have since changed our lives, and only the real enthusiasts could see what lay ahead of them. Those enthusiasts turned out to be visionaries like Steve Jobs, Bill Gates and Larry Ellison. They had the ideas that they were the first sparks, the kindling that set the fires ablaze. They also became some of the richest men on the planet.

In the early 1980s, prices for top-end Apple or IBM-type machines were in the $1,000-$1,500 range, or about $2,200-$3,000 at current prices. 3D printers are, if anything, cheaper. Ultimaker started in May 2011 and sells its current version for about $1,600. Erik de Bruijn, the Dutch founder, was recently quoted as saying "It's been a real roller coaster, you know, starting a company,". "But we've sold thousands already. It's amazing how many people want this technology."

Much of the budget movement is open-source, and works with standard computer-aided design packages, including some that are available free on the Web. Early computers, by contrast, certainly were not open source, and this is having an enormous impact on their rapid growth and development. In fact, one of the main reasons that these machines are developing so exponentially, is because of this open source ethos, which has allowed them to evolve quickly in terms of build footprint, print resolution and materials used. Someone in Macedonia might be optimising the software, while another in Mumbai is improving the physical extruder head, and someone else in Singapore is posting how-to-build guides on Youtube. All of them are linked informally and instantaneously through forums, IRC channels and the usual instant comms/social networks. For those of you saying "I want one", there are 3D printer users' groups that can help you build or assemble machines that you buy as a kit. For example, a 3D printer users' group meets every other Monday evening in the London Hackerspace. The meetings are to help people with all stages of building and running a 3D printer. And if you do not happen to live in London or some other large metropolis, then building a 3D printer from video instructions on Google video is now a perfectly viable option.

Additive manufacturing, as 3D printing is also known as, is not actually a 'new' technology. It is simply now coming into the public consciousness, and being more widely publicised. 3D Systems co-founder, Chuck Hull, invented stereolithography in 1986, and the company remains to this day one of the markets' largest players, along with Stratasys and Z Corp. Prices for commercial 3D printers range from $15,000 to more than $300,000. At the other end of the scale, personal 3D printers requiring DIY assembly, now sell for as little as $500, whereas five years ago the lowest-priced printer was at least $15,000.

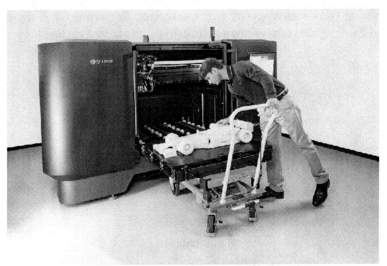

A High End Objet1000 Printer

The open source development of 3D printers began in 2009. Before then, the technology was under patent, and there was little incentive for home users to become involved. The RepRap project (short for replicating rapid prototyper) was founded in 2005 by Dr. Adrian Bowyer, a senior lecturer in mechanical engineering at the University of Bath in the UK. It began with a paper written in February 2004 that discussed a method of fabrication available to the masses and which could evolve in an autonomous fashion. To date, the RepRap project has released four 3D printing machines: "Darwin", released in March 2007, "Mendel", released in October 2009, "Prusa Mendel" and "Huxley" released in 2010. Developers have named each after famous biologists, as 'evolvability' was a key part of the concept when the first RepRap was released into the wild. While they are not meant to compete with the top end commercial machines, the development and democratisation of the technology is running hand-in-hand with new models and paradigms for designing, collaborating, and funding. There are many fast-growing 'cottage industries' forming around this technology—the funding is often crowd-sourced, and the retail is web-based. Overheads are minimal, and the ethos is collaborative rather than competitive. The 'old model' was all about buying up new technologies in order to sit on them and prop up outdated systems "(I mention no corporations by name, but I am sure that we can all think of a great many)." 3D printing is quickly becoming more than simply a technology—it is morphing into a movement and a mindset. For some, it is as much about finding alternatives to capitalism as it is about technology.

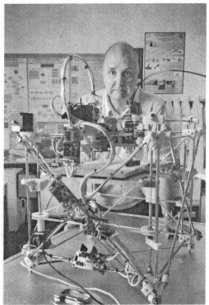

The Reprap and its Proud Father

All this may sound utopian, but it is hard not to be taken by the general enthusiasm. Today we all benefit immensely from open source software—all these free Unix and Linux programs powering and streaming through the Net. Now, imagine for a moment a world with open source hardware. Come up with a really great product, and you can share it with the world—to be hacked and modified by the people who actually use it, warranted against obsolescence by the irrepressible nature of human ingenuity.

I personally believe that open source is a future inevitability. If you are designing a post-printable product that does not have this kind of hackability and community, then you are suddenly a stegosaurus or a T-Rex, or some other obscure soon-to-be-extinct dinosaur. Out there in the technological undergrowth is a species of pathetically small furry mammals, but they have hackability and community, and they will be out exploring the cosmos when the only remaining evidence of your existence lies deep in the fossil record.

Current domestic 3D printers are perhaps 'toys' in the same way that a dot-matrix printer was an expensive toy of its time, but things are moving fast. Just fifteen years ago most of us could not afford a printer of any kind, then inkjets quickly became affordable, and now laser printers are standard in many homes. Back in the late eighties, the company for whom my father worked bought one of the first desktop lasers, and the price was well into five figures. Just twenty years later, a friend ordered three desktops for his company, and the supplier sent him a small laser printer as a freebie.

Most consumer 3D printers available at the moment use a manufacturing process in which layers of plastic are deposited layer by layer, building up to form the required shape of the final object. This begins with a software process, developed by Stratasys, which processes a .stl file (stereolithography file format), mathematically slicing and orienting the model. It then converts the 3D images into a digital pattern, made up of many thin horizontal layers. If required, support structures are automatically generated, whereby the machine dispenses two materials – one for the model and one for a disposable support structure. Technically speaking this is known as FDM extrusion or fused deposition modelling. A plastic filament is unwound from a coil and supplies material to an extrusion nozzle which can turn the flow on and off. The technology was first developed by S. Scott Crump in the late 1980s, and then commercialized in 1990. The term fused deposition modelling and its abbreviation to FDM are trademarked by Stratasys Inc. The exact equivalent term, fused filament fabrication (FFF), was coined by the members of the RepRap project to give a phrase that would be legally unconstrained in its use. Despite the fancy names, these are robotic hot glue guns. By extruding a thin line of plastic onto a printable surface, they build layer upon layer of plastic on itself until the item is completely constructed. It is easiest to think of squeezing a line of toothpaste onto a toothbrush, then continuing to squeeze toothpaste out on top of the toothpaste already on the toothbrush. This layering of material is what 3D printers are all about.

Some machines work by laying down a strand of acrylonitrile butadiene styrene (ABS) polymer from a heated nozzle. ABS is best known as the plastic from which Lego bricks are made. Other 3D-printer makers have chosen to "go green", using a biodegradable compound called PLA or polylactic acid, a plastic made from food starch, perhaps more familiar to us as the polymer that makes our milk go clumpy once it is affected by bacteria. These two types of plastics have become the most popular choices as they do not give off the kind of toxic fumes that make the work place smell like a KKK meeting. A multitude of other plastics are now becoming available, including polycarbonates, polycaprolactones, polyphenylsulfones and waxes, each with different trade-offs between strength and temperature properties.

The technology is not just limited to resin modelling. Polycarbonate, chocolate, food safe silicone rubber, clay, ice and cake frosting can also be printed with slightly altered extruders. Apart from plastic extruding machines, there are also printers that use a powder technique whereby print heads - like the ones in everyday inkjet printers - deposit glue in the desired pattern. The glue bonds grains of powder into the desired shape, and the base on which the object is produced, descends gradually as each layer of glued powder is added. When complete, the object lies within a cube of powder and has to be dug out. The surplus can then be recycled for future use.

Some printers are equipped with multiple "extruders" (the part that puts the plastic down). But generally, they only come with one, so that if you want multicoloured parts, they have to be assembled outside the printer. The machines also suffer from some limits on resolution, or the thickness of the layers of plastic. Generally, that is about 200 microns, or 0.2 millimetres, which is not a lot, but enough to give the pieces a rough "feel" that must be sanded down. The resolution of the newer homemade 3D printers is now down to 75 microns, which is getting close to the limits of the plastic. At this resolution you can no longer see the layered formation.

Objet, one of the higher end printer companies in Israel, has now merged with Stratasys, and so it looks like the first generation of industrially polished, non-home-brew machines is just around the corner. The Objet Connex500 printer is a good example of this, as evidenced by some stunning, if tiny, incredibly detailed prints. It can print incredibly small models at a 16 micron resolution, with flourishes so subtle that they are hard to notice at a glance, even printing with up to 14 different materials at the same time.

And then of course, there is the home-brew community itself. Many hobbyists have barely whetted their appetites with Makerbots and Repraps, and we are now seeing geographically diverse internet communities springing up all over the web, each doing their best to push the boundaries of what their machines can achieve.

While there are undoubtedly other competitors, it will be very interesting to see how this race develops and who will be the early front runners. Will it be the early pioneers intent on staying the course, will big IT move in en masse, or will it be a Linux type distributed community that makes the key breakthroughs?

Whatever happens, 3D printers are already here in their primary incarnation, and it is up to us as pioneers to make the best use of the equipment possible. If you do not have the latest cutting edge model capable of 1080 resolution, and are still experimenting with a self-built rep rap, then do not worry, there are still plenty of opportunities for all. The real beauty of the evolving printers is that to some extent, users are able to print off their own upgrades. A quick search on Youtube will bring up a growing number of videos where users print components and designs that they have downloaded from the internet, to create a newer and better model of their existing machines.

3D Printers Currently Available

The main reason that I was loathe to add a chapter to the previous edition of this book about 3D printers currently on the market is that I knew that it would become dated very quickly. There are clearly some absolute geniuses pushing the envelope of this technology, but at the same time, there is no guarantee that any of them will survive. It is the Wild West right now, and although there are people out there starting viable businesses, many fear that once the kinks have been worked out by these young entrepreneurs, the industry giants will simply step in and it will be hello Black and Decker Bot or Sony Sinterengine.

Already we are seeing the Edison effect manifest itself. Just as indisputable evidence shows that Edison was in no way the inventor of the movie camera or the light bulb, every third grader on the planet will tell you an entirely different story. I suppose this is what happens if you listen to third graders. We are already seeing some larger than life characters in the 3D printing field, claiming to be sole inventors, even taking the developments of the open source community and claiming them as their own proprietary intellectual property. The rule of karma may even now be dictating the inevitable backlash that these people deserve.

Regardless of these developments, I feel that it is unfair to write a book about the opportunities associated with 3D printing without at least a brief introduction to a selection of the machines that are currently out there. The main problem here is that, even when publishing through kindle, whatever I write here is going to be at least a few months old by the time you to read this. In 3D printing, that is an awfully long time. With this caveat in mind let us look at just half a dozen of the players operating at the time of writing.

While there is abundant information all over the Net about the various models currently available, by far the best place to get up close and personal with these devices is a hobbyist exhibition, such as the recent Maker Faire. In an insanely crowded and cacophonic pavilion devoted entirely to 3D printers, the hype surrounding this explosive technology was palpable, and it felt that half of the American population was in attendance, in order to find out what all the buzz was about. Unsurprisingly, the number of 3D printing companies showcasing their products has increased every year since the first New York Maker Faire in 2010, when there were just three companies. In 2011 five businesses participated and in 2012 more than twenty companies, as well as dozens of ancillary businesses selling software, parts and other supplies, were in attendance. A Maker Faire is an extremely organic scene. Inventors, creators, and engineers from all walks of life have their gadgets, science projects, and creations on display for all to see, and they range from downright amazing to completely bizarre.

Perhaps the biggest surprise from this years event was that Makerbot Industries, the company that much of the media has already branded market leader at the entry level, turned out to be the biggest disappointment. The New York-based company started selling printer kits in April 2009, 5,200 of which were, as Makerbot's co-founder and CEO Bre Pettis says, "in the wild" by August 2011. After receiving a whopping $10 million worth of venture capital, and then upsetting most of their customers by moving almost immediately to a proprietary format, their newest fourth-generation printer, the Replicator 2 is now one of the most expensive units at $2800. The company has more than 150 employees and has now opened a store in lower Manhattan. Some attendees stated that the printed objects they had on display were some of the worst of the show. Apparently the software is very tricky to implement and operate, even for someone that is technically minded.

Fortunately, there are already many new players on the field including Solidoodle, Up!3D, Ultimaker, and Tinkerines. The Tinkerines Ditto was one of the long shots at the New York Faire that impressed many. Some claimed that it produced the best objects, and at $900 in kit form or $1400 assembled, it was amazing bang for the buck. Tinkerines is new to the scene, so they do not yet have a dual-nozzle head, nor do they yet support ABS plastic (the necessary heated base is still being developed). Eugene Suyu, from Vancouver, the twenty-four-year-old co-founder, studied design at Simon Fraser University in British Columbia. Tinkerine, which he founded with friend Andy Yang, has already produced a couple of models of its 3D printer, the Ditto. The acrylic version showcases an aesthetic sense as much as solid engineering. "With one or two companies the pricing was generally pretty high, but now with so many new people entering the market, the prices for these printers are starting to flatline," said Suyu.

For even the most basic model of printer, be prepared to spend at least $500-$700, and that is if you do all of the part sourcing and assembly yourself, including soldering the electronics. The reprap.org forum and wiki are excellent resources, although they have become a little slower recently thanks to all the new interest in the subject. There is also #reprap IRC channel on freenode, again with a very helpful and inviting community.

Most companies sell their products online, or at hobbyist events like Maker Faire, but the first two US stores have now opened, which is perhaps an indication of things to come. Diego Porqueras raised $167,410 (after asking for $42,000) in May 2012 on Kickstarter, and set up Deezmaker in his Pasadena garage. After being overwhelmed with orders, Porqueras opened the first 3D printer store on the West Coast and retails a stripped-down version of his Bukobot printer for $599. The most fertile breeding grounds for this new technology are unsurprisingly crowdsourcing (online funding platforms) websites such as Kickstarter and Indiegogo. Kickstarter has seen some thirty 3D printer related projects, while Indiegogo has had another dozen projects seeking funds.

Up to his neck in $50,000 of credit-card debt, Brook Drumm, a California-based web designer, turned to Kickstarter, in order to raise the $25,000 that he needed to launch his 3D project. To Drumm's amazement, just twenty-four hours after submitting his pitch, the project reached its goal. Thirty days later, the Printrbot had been inundated with $830,827 from 1,808 backers, surpassing his wildest expectations.

http://www.kickstarter.com/projects/printrbot/printrbot-your-first-3d-printer

Printrbot's most affordable model costs just $400 and was designed to be the simplest 3D printer yet, an all-in-one kit that can be assembled and printing in a couple of hours. Drumm assembles all the electronics, the hot end, and puts the connectors on all the motors and components, so that there is no soldering required. This is the printer that a child could put together. The Printrbot borrows from many great designers in the open source 3D printer world, with linear bearings, smooth drill rods, a lasercut print bed, a manufactured PCB heated bed, and of course, the latest open source software.

Atlanta-based Hyrel 3D had 73 backers pledge $152,942 above their original $50,000 goal in their latest Kickstarter campaign for a pre-assembled steel and aluminium 3D printer, that uses precision linear rails for all three axes. It features a hot-swap interchangeable mounting system and a quick filament change system, allowing users to easily replace and replenish a filament. Options include an expandable build area pack going from 150x150x200 mm to 200x200x200 mm, and an expansion slot and electronics for a second "Hot-Head" extruder. The basic printer including a single extruder head and a build area of 150x150x200 mm is sold for $1,395, while a pre-assembled model with dual extruders, a build area of 200x200x200 mm, and an ultrasonic wash tank costs $3,500

There are two advantages of having a dual extruder system. The first allows the standard 3mm filament to be printed in two different colours. Second, dual extruder systems which use an ABS/PLA combination allows the user to create shapes which cannot be made with a single extruder. In this case, the PLA is used as a supporting "filler" base material where the ABS prints on top of it. At the end of a print, the PLA can be dissolved in an ultrasonic wash tank, leaving the ABS part intact. The Hyrel also features a hot-swap interchangeable mounting system. Both extruder heads can be removed and replaced in less than a minute, even if the tips are operating at the extruding temperature.

Hyrel 3D is also in the process of developing a full-colour 3D printer. The next generation 3D printer will have red, green and blue colour extruder heads, and will blend the colours so that they can then be printed at any opacity. There will be full control of the texture, shading and overall colour. The full-colour 3D printer is still in development and price will be in the $5,000 range. It is expected to be released in the third quarter/autumn of 2013. Although we already have full-colour 3D printers in the market, such as the ZPrinter 650 (5 print heads, including black) and ZPrinter 850 from 3D Systems, which are capable to print 390,000 colours, the price of $60,000+ is just too expensive for individuals and small business units. Hyrel 3D's effort in developing full-colour 3D printer could possibly bring quality colour 3D prints to the masses very soon. At the high end of the hobbyist scale is the Form 1 from Formlabs:

http://www.kickstarter.com/projects/formlabs/form-1-an-affordable-

professional-3d

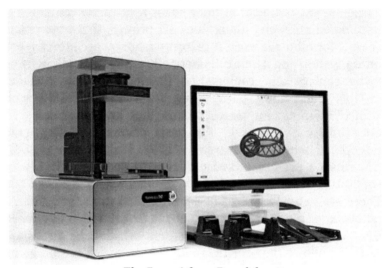

The Form 1 from Formlabs

Pre-order machines were priced at $2,699, although actual market pricing has not yet been released. Even so, the Formlabs' Form 1 printer raised almost as much cash in its first day as the Printrbot did for its entire campaign. The machine utilises stereolithography, reaching layer thicknesses and feature sizes that are a major step ahead of what is possible with the FDM extrusion-based processes common to MakerBot's Replicator and homebrew RepRap designs. Stereolithography (SL) is the oldest 3D printing system and was developed by Chuck W. Hull (co-founder of 3D Systems) in 1986. A laser is used to draw on the surface of a liquid plastic resin that hardens a layer at a time, when exposed to a certain wavelength of light. This is also referred to as digital light projection (DLP). Parts created this way are very accurate, require minimal post processing and are ideal for use as master patterns for vacuum casting.

Until now, SL has been one of the most expensive 3D printing processes. With pricey lasers and high-precision optical components, SL 3D printers could easily cost tens or even hundreds of thousands of dollars. The results of this new incarnation are impressive: the Form 1 can print layers as thin as 25 microns (0.001 in) with features as small as 300 microns (0.012 in) in a build volume of 125 x 125 x 165 mm (4.9 x 4.9 x 6.5), enabling the printer to turn out objects that are 5 inches wide and about 6.5 inches tall. Plastic is not deposited on a build platform; instead, parts are extracted from a gooey pool of resin. To put this in perspective, the Form 1 resolution is four times higher than the new MakerBot Replicator 2 (100-micron layer thickness), and is on par with professional grade systems. This means it can print complex geometries with exquisite details and beautiful surface finishes. Form 1 uses low-cost blu-ray lasers to cause a light-sensitive liquid polymer material to harden, the same kind found in high-definition DVD players. The laser, steered by a pair of mirrors, passes over one layer of liquid, telling it which areas need to "become" the object, and then a platform lifts the object up slightly, and the laser adds another layer. For the X and Y axes, resolution is defined by the DLPs resolution, so it is possible to achieve quite high quality with off the shelf equipment. In fact, there is only one moving axis. Everything else is fixed. With a decent M8 (1.25mm) lead screw and a 1/16 micro stepping stepper motor users can achieve 2560 steps per millimeter.

Because of the nature of the chemicals used in the process, SLA models can be translucent. They are not optically clear, so we will not be printing ourselves new spectacles just yet, but the semi transparent qualities do bring a new palette of options for designers, and electronics whizzes will be able to do amazing things with clear resin and LED lighting.

The Formlabs project was started by an expert team of MIT engineers and design students who, as researchers at the MIT Media Lab, were lucky to experience the best and most expensive fabrication equipment in the world. With initial seed funds provided by Eric Schmidt of Google, they have already built and tested seven generations of prototypes. The Form 1 has an anodised aluminium housing that gives it a respectable, serious look, quite different from the plywood-clad, low-cost homebrew printers.

Apart from the higher initial cost, one of the other major disadvantages is the higher cost of the resin. Current estimates put it at about $149 per litre, which makes it is approximately three times more expensive than Makerbot-style extrusion printing. This works out at about 10 cents per gram, allowing users to print 7-800 cubic centimeters with a single kilogram of resin. The other major drawback is speed, currently taking several hours even for a small object.

DLP printers which use the power of light to impact the printable resin material and set it in place are proving very popular as one route of development. In mid-2012, the B9Creator DLP Printer also hit its Kickstarter funding goal in just one day. The company sought only $50,000 on the social venture capital site and yet, to date, has received pledges for over half a million, and anyone who put in more than $2,375 has now had a complete unit delivered.

One disadvantage that is rarely mentioned is that these UV curing epoxies, urethanes and polyesters can cause sensitization in some people. Some are worse than others, depending mainly on the monomers used. Once they cure, they are fairly inert however, but when one is handling raw uncured resin, gloves should ideally be used.

In the meantime, new designs are coming thick and fast. The Rostock, for instance, has moved away from the box shape typical of most 3D printers. Initially developed by Johann Rocholl, it differs in that it uses three arms that are attached to three vertical axes, each independently driven by stepper motors. Often known as a Delta because of its triangular shape, not only is this a sexier printer in terms of looks, but it has a much faster Z axis movement than the threaded rods of a traditional 3D printer designs. These severely limit the speeds to about 200-400 mm/min speeds, but with a Delta, speeds of up to 40000 mm per minute are quite feasible. The extruder pump attaches to the frame, not the extruder head, allowing for much improved speed and accuracy, in fact the mass of the end effector with two hotends is less than 150g. It uses six diagonal rods with universal joints, and all of these are fully printable. Other advantages include being able to use the tilt of the extruder to produce smoother layers and super round circles. Unlike most other 3D printers, the Rostock can also be re-purposed as a "pick and place" circuit-board assembler, because the arms are not restricted to horizontal movement. Apart from this high-speed positioning, a delta has significantly fewer parts (fewer than 200 not including washers, nuts and SMD-mounted electronics), and therefore a much lighter and simpler set up. These massive improvements have the 3D printer community very excited. One commentator on Hackaday put it best when he wrote "Sorry, could you repeat that? I couldn't hear you over the sound of my brain melting and flowing out my ear holes!!"

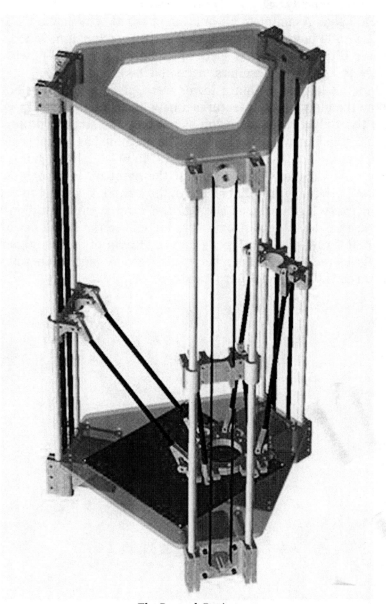

The Rostock Design

A small team from PartDaddy, an engineering company that makes machine parts in Goshen, Indiana is working on the Rostock Max, an open-source 3D printer based on Johann's original prototype. Their design is being funded as a Kickstarter project, and they have quickly raised $21,567, well in excess of their original $10,000 goal. A complete kit in lasercut wood is available for $949, while $1,500 buys a fully assembled acrylic version. Innovations will include UltiMachine's new electronics board, the RAMBo, with the ability to run two extruders, a heated bed, and up to 5 stepper motors, all located within a lower wrap piece around the bottom hiding the electronics. It features a new linear motion design which uses t-slot aluminium extrusion as not only the structural member, but also the linear bearing surface. The machine has an approximate build volume of 10" in diameter and 13" in height although it is only set up for 1.75mm filament only at the moment. In recognition of Johann's original inspirational design the company is going to donate $5 for every kit purchased through this campaign. In addition they will also be donating $2 from every kit sold to the developer of the REPETIER software developer (Marcus Littwin of Germany), and to the developer of the super fast slicing/gcode generation software known as SLIC3R (Alessandro Ranellucci of Italy).

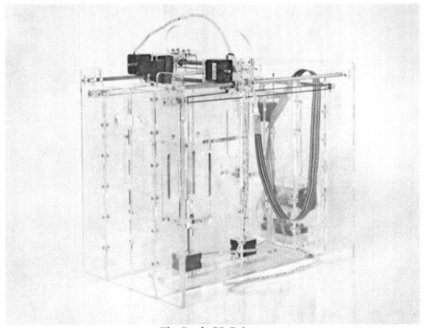

The Pwdr 3D Printer

In a move to encourage experiments and innovations in powder-based rapid-prototyping, The University of Twente have developed the Pwdr, an open source powder-based rapid prototyping machine. The machine is ready to use both the 3DP as the SLS process with minimal adaption, although the printer is currently prepped for 3DP. Could desktop laser sintering for the masses be on the horizon?

The machine has very reasonable specifications for a introductory version – 96 dpi and Z-axis layer thickness of 50 microns, with a build speed of about a minute per layer, and a maximum build size of 125 mm cubed. The Pwdr Model 0.1 consists of chassis, tool head and electronics, all of which can be sourced off-the-shelf, in any local hardware and electronics stores, totalling less than €1000 ($1200). The building process requires moderate electronics skills and might be the perfect starting point for DIY enthusiasts. The software used to control the Pwdr machine is available for download and, as would be expected, is based on open source tools like Arduino and Processing.

Thanks to the 'evolvability' of the open source machines, we are now seeing not only new designs but upgrade kits for existing designs. One such project is the Ultra-Bot 3D Printer, which utilizes the "vitamins" from the Makerbot Cupcake, with numerous important improvements. For $349 the kit includes a new set of Printrboard electronics that are relocated inside the inner bottom plate, high precision stepper motors for better build quality and resolution of the parts, and an elimination of the Z axis parts on top of the printer that are moved to the lower portion of the Cupcake. Finally the build area is increased to 5"x 6 1/2" x 7 1/2" (127x165x191 mm).

The FDM form of 3D printing is actually only the first stage of additive manufacturing and just as we are now seeing the first DLP printers hitting the market, it is very likely that we will soon see even more advanced methods reach the hands of hobbyists and home users.

Selective Laser Sintering (SLS) is a polymer additive manufacturing technique where a low power laser is used to sinter (not fully melt) powder particles together, layer by layer. This process, which uses a directed CO_2 heat laser was developed and patented by Dr. Carl Deckard at the University of Texas in the mid-1980s, The most common and useful material used is nylon powder and apparently, adding ground glass gives even greater strength for performance and durability. Other materials include ceramic, glass powder and metals (direct metal laser sintering) such as steel, titanium, silver and gold. These developments are very exciting for designer makers but the technology has yet to fall in price in the same way as FDM.

The process of 'Electron Beam Melting' (EBM) melts metal powder in a high vacuum and is distinguished from metal sintering techniques, by producing parts that are extremely strong because they are fully dense and free of any voids. It was developed by Arcam AB. Electrons tend to scatter off gas molecules and expensive, inconvenient vacuum chambers are still required for this process to work.

As more affordable laser systems with higher power, more accurate beam steering, and better focusing optics were developed, SLM or selective laser melting was born. Like EBM, the powder material is fully melted during fusion, but the SLM laser does not require vacuum to function. It only requires that an inert argon or nitrogen atmosphere is used in the work area to prevent oxidation. SLM parts have one very large heat affected zone and so this method of manufacture creates huge thermal stresses that are not yet fully understood. Even so, NASA's Marshall Space Flight Centre in Huntsville, Alabama, has 3D printed nickel alloy rocket engine parts using SLM. The part will be used on the J-2x engine for the largest rocket ever built, known simply as the Space Launch System. A part such as this J-2x manifold would not be milled on a CNC machine because the forces required to remove metal would warp and destroy a part this thin. Before SLM, it would have to be fabricated as a weldment from its component parts. Its curved and flaring nozzles would first be stitched together from sheet metal, than bent, and tacked to the main body. Welding introduces non-uniform stress points or "heat affected zones" at the weld sites, and makes failure modes less predictable. It is beyond human skill to manually reproduce parts like this to the required tolerances. It would therefore have to be made using automated bending machines and robotic welders, which take considerable time to program and set up.

While I have focussed here on the DIY movement, it is inevitable that innovations from industry and academia will soon begin filtering down into the DIY machines. At the moment the UK seems to be setting the pace. The University of Southampton has just opened a state-of-the-art rapid prototyping facility, while 2011 saw the development of an EPSRC Centre for Innovative Manufacturing in Additive Manufacturing, which is led by the University of Nottingham. Another facility to open last year was the £2.6million Centre for Additive Layer Manufacturing (CALM) at the University of

Exeter, who quickly went on to develop the world's first ever 3D chocolate printer.

A new "China 3D Printing Technology Industry Alliance" has been established at the Beijing University of Aeronautics and Astronautics. Apart from establishing new industrial standards, the group will also investigate the opening of an advanced manufacturing park, a national 3D printing technology research and development base and an industrial demonstration base in China.

The Obama Administration is putting $30 million into the new 'National Additive Manufacturing Innovation Institute' (a 3D printing institute to you and me), to be located in Youngstown, Ohio, at the heart of the so-called American "Rust Belt" region of the Midwest. NAMII is a public-private partnership with a massive consortium of forty companies, nine research universities, five community colleges and eleven non-profit organizations. Word is that this will be the first of fifteen "centers of excellence" with the purpose of advancing and promoting 3D printing technologies to help U.S. industry become more competitive. The 3D printing institute will receive $30 million in federal funding and $40 million from private industry. The institute is being developed under a $1 billion Obama administration initiative: the NNMI (or National Network for Manufacturing Innovation). The Obama program has charged the NCDMM (or National Center for Defense Manufacturing and Machining) with managing the new institute. This last part makes it clear to all that although a public-private partnership, this institute is going to be headed by the U.S. military. Such technology could create human organs, bones or body parts tailored for specific patients. Journalists attending a press event related to the announcement at UC Irvine's Rapid Tech Lab were shown a skull replica that belonged to a soldier who was injured in Afghanistan. A scan of the skull was sent digitally across the globe to UC Irvine's lab, which printed an exact replica and sent it Fed-Ex to a doctor, who then used the printout to design the plates and procedure that eventually saved the soldier's eyesight. A month later, the soldier was back on active duty with 20/20 vision. Despite the feel good story presented to the press, the technology also has the potential to speed up and cut the costs of manufacturing robots or military weapons, but as Tony Stark was not present, they shied away from demonstrating any mass destruction capabilities and focussed instead on medical examples.

Even so, the first of the $2.8 million mobile 3D printing labs—each a twenty-foot shipping container holding the latest manufacturing tools—was deployed to Afghanistan in July, according to Military.com. Two engineers can work together to create parts from plastic, steel and aluminum on the fly. They represent the new effort by the Rapid Equipping Force to deliver battlefield equipment as fast as possible to soldiers in the loneliest outposts.

3

Scanning Technology

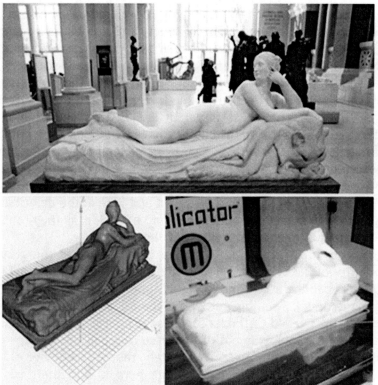

3D printed remixes of masterpieces commissioned by the metropolitan museum of art—'reclining naiad', by Antonio Canova, 1819-24

Just as a 2D inkjet printer requires a flat bad scanner and some reliable OCR (optical character recognition) software to capture a page of text and then reprint it, a 3D printer requires a similar input device before it can reproduce a physical object. 3D scanners analyze a real-world object to collect data on its shape and colour. The collected data can then be used to construct digital, three-dimensional models.

A number of different technologies currently exist, each with their own limitations, advantages and costs. Optical technologies for example, encounter many difficulties with shiny, mirrored or transparent objects. For most situations, a single scan will not produce a complete model of the subject. Multiple scans, even hundreds, from many different directions are usually required to obtain information about all sides of the subject.

Scanners generally fall into two camps: Contact machines that probe the object through physical touch, and non-contact scanners that emit some kind of radiation such as light, ultrasound or x-ray and then detect its reflection. Triangulation 3D laser scanners use laser light to examine the environment, but due to the high speed of light, calculating the round-trip time is difficult, and the accuracy of the distance measurement is relatively low. Triangulation range finders are exactly the opposite. They have a limited range, but their accuracy is relatively high, in the order of tens of micrometers. In conoscopic systems, a laser beam is reflected through a conoscopic crystal and projected onto a CCD. Structured-light 3D scanners project a pattern of light on the subject and look at the deformation, adding the advantages of both speed and precision, as they can scan multiple points, or even entire field of view all at once.

Interest in 3D scanning is on the rise because of the growing popularity of 3D printing. With printers like MakerBot, Form1, and RepRap becoming accessible to many, simple scanning solutions are in great demand. Scanning and digital modification are the best way to obtain the needed CAD data for these printers, but most scanning equipment is a long way out of the price range of the average non-professional 3D printer user. Fortunately, though, a number of tools are coming that will help the average person with their wish to design a product.

A number of web based scanning services have emerged in order to satisfy the growing 3D printer market. At the moment, the leader of these seems to be Autodesk's 123Dcatch. No doubt, it will soon be commonplace to see numerous apps that will use a standard smart phone in conjunction with a stepper-motor driven revolving stand. Just as we did not see home DJs remixing mash ups until people were able digitally manipulate audio with a sampler, we cannot expect the same kind of remixing to take place with 3D models until .stl files become a little more ubiquitous.

The Metropolitan Museum of Art recently held an event to make 3D scans and prints of works from throughout the museum (see the picture above). Attendees used digital cameras and Autodesk's 123Dcatch to generate 3D models, and then printed those using MakerBot Replicators. They might seem a bit crude at first (especially when compared to an expensive laser scan) but keep in mind that these were untextured 3D models produced from photographs, using free software.

Here's how it works: take photos of your item on a neutral background. Rotate around the object, snapping a photo every 15 or so degrees, from a few different heights: above, below, from the side. It will take about 40-75 photographs for 123D Catch to create a good 3D model. It does not work so well with objects that are very shiny. Upload them to the site, and after a short wait, you will receive an email saying that your model is ready for download. Open the resulting .obj in a 3D modelling program (MeshLab, MeshMixer or Blender, perhaps) to clean it up and export to .stl. A little bit of cleaning up in SolidWorks to add a back face and a level base, and the model is ready for printing. This is all done in about six hours. Autocad have also arranged partnerships with three large 3D printing companies, just in case you do not have your own machine yet.

Another web based scanning service is PHOV, also allowing users to create photo-realistic three-dimensional models from digital photographs. Fun applications include creating your own online avatar, or a detailed statue of yourself. More serious uses are also evolving such as turning ancient artefacts into 3D archaeological archives and locating 3D real estate presentations on virtual globes and then outputting them through a 3D printer.

My3DScanner is yet another free online service that creates 3D models directly from ordinary digital photographs. It is a fully automated, end-to-end, online 3D scanning system that takes digital photographs (or videos) as input and produces 3D computer models (dense colour 3D point clouds and meshed polygonal models) as output without any user intervention. Input pictures do not require calibration and any sort of pre-processing by a user, and the software will turn any camera or mobile phone into 3D modelling device.

The MakerScanner is a completely open source 3D scanner that Andy Barry created at the beginning of his senior year at Olin College of Engineering. Barry now works as a research engineer in the AutoDesk Innovations Lab at the NASA Ames Research Lab. His budget 3D scanner works by sweeping a red laser beam across any object in front of a web cam and is the perfect complement to a MakerBot or other 3D printer. Every one of the scanner's plastic parts can be printed on a MakerBot or other 3D printer. At the MakerBot wiki there is complete documentation for the MakerScanner v0.3.

This technology works for all kinds of digital images, even x-rays. If you happen to have fifty cameras that you can click in sync, you could even obtain 3D captures of very dynamic action shots such as dirt thrown in the air, smoke, a batter in mid-swing, a water balloon bursting, flames etc. You could capture any of those events blurred over a set period and then print them to create something extremely artistic.

This kind of technology is becoming more and more embedded all the time, and already there is a 3D scanner app for the iPhone. Unfortunately, Trimensional: MakerBot Edition is not open source and only advanced users can unlock the 3D Model Export feature in order to create physical copies of scanned objects on a 3D printer, or to import textured 3D scans into popular 3D graphics software. If you are going to try the app then remember that an extremely dark room is required and iPhone screen brightness must be set to maximum.

If you are looking for open source alternatives, then VisualSFM by Changchang Wu at the University of Washington is a great tool for creating 3D reconstructions of photos. It is comparatively easy to use, but extremely difficult to install. 3D reconstruction can be done with just four mouse clicks, and users can even watch dynamic reconstructions, but they also need to install packages, download academic software, and edit and compile source code, before they can get the software running.

Insight3d is an alternative open source piece of software that allows users to create 3D models from photographs. By automatically matching a series of photos, it calculates the positions in space from which each photo has been taken (including the camera's optical parameters) to create a 3D pointcloud of the scene and a textured polygonal model. This application is still in development at the time of writing but looks to be a very useful resource and well worth supporting.

For many, a lack of CAD skills keeps them from printing objects in 3D. Even though tools like Sketchup and Tinkercad reduce this barrier, the falling prices of real-time 3D scanning might be the answer.

Until recently, most programs could only capture one side of an object, which creates a kind of relief sculpture. In order to overcome this limitation, it was possible to take multiple scans but manually merging them has until now been very difficult.

Microsoft has recently announced that it is finally bringing the ability to accurately scan 3D objects to the masses. The company has been working on a software update for its Kinect for Windows motion controller device that would turn it into a 3D scanner to be known as Kinect Fusion 3D.

The software, called "Kinect Fusion", was first developed in 2010 by Microsoft Research in Cambridge, England. In the same year, Adafruit Industries offered a bounty for an open-source driver for Kinect, which has led to some amazing 3D depth map projects.

Kinect for Windows is a PC-based spin-off of Microsoft's wildly successful Kinect motion controller for the Xbox 360, launched in November 2010, which has since gone on to sell over 18 million units. Microsoft was at first wary of hackers repurposing the gaming controller for their own innovative uses, but eventually embraced and now supports development of new uses for the Kinect, and it is now being included in their software development kit.

Kinect Fusion takes the incoming depth data from the Kinect for Windows sensor and uses the sequence of frames to build a highly detailed 3D map of objects or environments. The tool then averages the readings over hundreds or thousands of frames to achieve more detail than would be possible from just one reading. This allows Kinect Fusion to gather and incorporate data not viewable from any single viewpoint.

Due to its low resolution, the current Kinect does not see small objects (anything that is less than about the size of a shoe) but the technology is advancing, and it has been reported that the Kinect 2 will be able to accurately read lips.

Profactor recently released a beta version of free software called ReconstructMe that works a lot like Kinect Fusion. ReconstructMe is a software tool for Windows that also uses the Microsoft Xbox Kinect (or other 3D depth camera that uses the Asus Xtion PRO LIVE) to capture 3D models in real-time and generate a 3D object on a computer in an .stl or .obj file. There are a few downsides to ReconstructMe: the Kinect for Windows isn't supported yet. Right now, ReconstructMe is limited to scanning objects that fit into a one-meter cube and not having a GUI can only operate from the command line, but it looks like the ReconstructMe team is working on supporting larger scans. Currently, the software is Windows only and really RAM hungry (to the point of crashing after a 15 minute scan with 8 GB's of RAM), so you will need a fairly powerful video card as it does the calculations on the GPU. With the default calibration, the resolution has an accuracy of +/- 4mm but there are lenses sold for the Kinect that shorten its range and this should effectively increase the resolution and accuracy slightly.

The best way to scan a person is to have them sit in an office chair, point the Kinect at their head, and then slowly spin them in a circle. Once you have a raw scan, (I suggest using the free version of NetFabb Studio Basic to rotate it) cut away the parts you don't want, and then repair it to make it solid and suitable for 3D printing on your MakerBot. The Ponoko blog has an excellent video explaining the process. You can also place objects on a turntable, like a lazy susan, and spin it by hand. Just make sure that anything ReconstructMe sees within its scanning area all rotates in the same way.

A number of third-party developers including the French startup company, ManCTL, have already developed Kinect 3D scanning software, called Skanect, which is used to scan physical objects and people.

Another option known as KScan3D is a Kinect-based 3D scanning software running on Windows OS allowing users to capture 3D scans with a click of a button. Users can scan, edit, process, and export finalized data in a variety of common file formats such as .obj, .stl, .ply, and .asc formats for visual effects, games, CAD/CAM, 3D printing, online/web visualization, and other applications. KScan3D can be purchased separately or as a bundled package with the Kinect for Windows hardware for $299 and $599.

Developers at Matherix 3Dify have also been trying to turn objects into 3D models with a Kinect sensor, but what they offer is not real-time scanning. What you need to do is simply capture a video of the object and 3Dify automatically builds a 3D model of the object in just a few minutes. For example, this 3D model, (http://matherix.wordpress.com/2012/02/28/getting-started-matherix-3dify-version-0-5/), of a man's face was from a twelve-second video with a processing time of five minutes on an Intel Core2Duo with 2GB memory. This project is still under development. As is an application from Geomagic, who are now working on the technology behind the Microsoft® Kinect™-to-3D print app that is part of 3D Systems' Cubify.com, and will be built on top of popular Geomagic Studio®.

In the meantime, there are still high-end scanners available but at a significant cost. Z Corp offers a line of handheld laser scanners as part of their catalogue, which also includes 3D printers, yet these run into the tens of thousands of dollars. For a peek into the future, it is a good idea to have a look at the professional technology on offer from industry specialists such as Photon, Trimble or Faro. The Faro Focus 3D scanner is a particularly nice example, being the smallest portable 3D scanner so far built with a weight of just 5.0kg, but still costing in the region of $30,000. Using a touch screen, it produces photorealistic 3D colour scans with a range of up to 120m, in 70 megapixels onto a removal SD card, and boasts a battery life of nearly five hours. It has an amazing speed of 976,000 measurement points per second and is used mainly by civil engineers, as well as restoration teams working on heritage buildings. It can even be used by law enforcement forensics teams who need to record entire crime scenes. The new Focus3D is five times smaller than its predecessor and yet is capable of producing incredibly detailed 3D images of complex environments and geometries in only a few minutes. If we recall how quickly the first mobile phone bricks were reduced to the size of a current smartphone, then we can expect the abilities of machines like the Faro to be in our phones and tablets in just a few years. The best place to monitor the rapid development of this technology is the Laser Scanning Forum (www.laserscanning.org.uk/forum/) where nearly five thousand members ranging from mining professionals to keen hobbyists are already discussing this exciting subject.

Apart from automating the process of 3D imaging and 3D printing, 3D data scanned in this way can be used for a wide range other purposes including design, testing, innovation, archiving and prototyping. 3D maps of interiors in particular, will be especially useful to architects designing an ideal working space, and realtors creating walkthroughs of a home. Game developers who make realistic first-person shooters like Call of Duty could use this kind of technology to easily scan buildings to generate maps, instead of designing them from the ground up from pictures. Once everybody has a reasonably detailed scanned image of themselves, it will be much more common to import yourself into a video game. We can also look forward to virtual clothes shops, where you can try on different clothes using your virtual 3D self, comfortably at home with your browser. A number of large retailers are already working on these kinds of solutions. The digitization of the physical world is accelerating and the line between physical and virtual reality will blur even more as the technological change continues.

4

Modeling Technology

The turning gears on this object were printed rather than assembled. Courtesy of Zcorp

While some people still claim that modelling in 3D is an extremely skilled process that cannot realistically be done by the layman, the real problem has more to do with costs than ability. AutoCAD, CATIA, Solidworks etc. retail in the range of hundreds or even thousands of dollars, but it is likely that we will soon see a similar situation develop to the "everyone with a Mac and Photoshop is a graphic designer" paradigm that so democratised desktop publishing. The reality is that with the right motivation and training, CAD expertise is not insurmountable. If you already have the ability to make objects out of clay, Lego or Meccano, then you just need to learn the interface of the CAD program.

Just as 3D printers are evolving very rapidly, so is the software that runs them. Internet forums are full of old school engineers spouting statements that sound very much like the following. "I have twenty plus years 3D design experience using multiple programs and yet I am still learning new stuff every day." This is usually followed by refrains of "CAD is not a very difficult skill to master, you need to spend a lot of time learning, then relearning, then learning more." I can only imagine that accountants use to sound like this before the introduction of spreadsheets. Remember that before VisiCalc, or Lotus123 or Excel, the only way to add up 50,000 numbers was by hand or with a pocket calculator. A spreadsheet now does the same in a fraction of a second. Previously, offices full of book keepers spent their entire careers comparing thousands of numbers on two pieces of adding machine tape, that might have been two hundred feet long a piece. Sorting was impossible. Complex, self-calculating, linking financial models were impossible. The arrival of spreadsheets kickstarted the financial boom of the eighties. This amazing new technology allowed anybody to become a stockbroker, and Gordon Gecko soon acquired god-like status.

In the coming few years, there will be a major simplification of complex CAD programs to make them more accessible for the masses, just as has already happened in music production, Photoshop and website development. Take, for example, Tumblr and how easy it has made creating a well-designed blog. These new arrivals might not completely replace the full versions of the classics, because there is still a great deal of progress to be found in the expertise of the masters often using those programs.

"3D printing is a way to re-envision the manufacturing process," says Brian Mathews, vice-president of Autodesk, the largest maker of 3D design software. Others accuse the $10 billion computer-aided design industry, a sector long ruled by antiquated and expensive software suites, of restricting collective innovation. A new platform is coming of age, and if there is anything to be learned from the history of the computer revolution, it is that when a new platform is established, all technologies on older platforms become endangered species. There is a fundamental shift in technology taking place, perhaps even a second CAD revolution, but this time on the server side. Centralised data, computation and rendering with streamed client connections, where hybrid applications make latency problems a thing of the past.

Conventional thinking suggests that an individual requires at least ten thousand hours of practice to really master a discipline, and with that in mind, you might want to take a look at some of the SolidWorks designers on sites like Fiverr.com, and other micro-tasking sites. The learning curve on most existing CAD CAM software is very steep, and so it is often worth outsourcing the design work. As any student of programs such as Autocad will tell you, it can often take beginners an entire weekend to model their first toothbrush, even when simply following the instructions to model a casting from the book. There are already some fifty or more CAD designers listed on Fiverr.com that are offering their SolidWorks skills for hire. Sometimes five bucks will only pay for half an hour of modeling work, and sometimes you will just have to negotiate as well as you can. For example, one customer recently commissioned a SolidWorks model of Deckard's PKD blaster from the sci-fi classic Bladerunner. Even though it was the smaller snub nosed version, a detailed .stl still cost four Fiverr gigs for a grand total of $20 dollars. Of course, this is a very new market and you might be able to have the same work done in Mumbai or Wuhan for a tiny fraction of the price.

If you do find a good modeler then try to develop a positive, long term relationship with them, as some of these guys might just eventually become the Michelangelo's and Da Vinci's of the 3D printer age. Fiverr.com already has plenty of competitors, and then there are also all the outworker sites such as freelancer.com, elance.com and guru.com. 3D printer forums would also be fertile grounds for these digital artists, as would sites like Pokono and Thingiverse where designers are already posting their best ideas.

Even so, being proficient in these programs can be a real benefit in properly assessing the works of others. If you are able to step through the model from the top, down through the feature manager, to check efficiency, coherence, and sound method, then you will save a lot of trouble when you actually come to print. It might look good as a dumb solid, but as a history-based model, making any future edits could be difficult, and this is what real-world design deals with all the time—continual edits

While better options are slowly emerging from the open source community, it would do no harm to begin familiarizing yourself with a copy of SolidWorks. If you are not familiar with this yet, then start with the company website www.SolidWorks.com/ and then look at the Wikipedia entry, http://en.wikipedia.org/wiki/SolidWorks

At the moment, there is plenty of instructional material out there for those who want to learn the ropes. Here are a few examples of good training materials.

1. Lynda.com—SolidWorks 2012..."SolidWorks 2012 Essential Training [1 DVD + Exercise files]

> Author: Gabriel Corbett
> Duration: 07h 02m
> Released on: 3/7/2012
> Exercise files: Yes

In this course, author Gabriel Corbett shows how to create manufacturing-ready parts and assemblies in SolidWorks 2012. Beginning with simple 2D sketching and the software's sketch-editing tools, the course provides step-by-step instruction on building 3D geometry from 2D sketches. The course covers creating complex 3D objects with the Extrude, Revolve, Sweep, and Loft tools and shows building complex assemblies by mating individual parts together into robust assemblies and structures.

The course shows how to cut and revolve holes into parts and use the Hole Wizard tool to generate industry standard holes like counter bores, counter sinks, and taps. Best practice for designing parts is emphasized throughout the course as well as methods for creating parts faster and easier using equations, mirroring, and patterning tools. The course wraps up with generating manufacturing-ready drawings complete with an itemized Bill of Materials. As a bonus feature, Gabriel shows how to photo render a final design. Exercise files are included with the course.

Topics include:

- Starting a new sketch
- Adding and removing relationships

- Dimensioning a sketch for specific size attributes
- Setting system options, units, and templates
- Drawing polygons
- Drawing circles, arcs, and splines
- Creating offset geometry
- Moving, copying, and rotating elements
- Working with planes, axes, and the coordinate system
- Using Revolve and Loft to create 3D objects
- Trimming with the Revolve, Loft, and Sweep cuts
- Creating smooth and angled corners with fillets and chamfers
- Designing with sketch blocks
- Working with sub-assemblies
- Creating threaded parts
- Integrating Excel to manage design tables
- Adding dimension notations to a drawing
- Rendering an image of a part or assembly

2. Inspirtech—SolidWorks 2009—Fundamentals [1 DVD]

At Inspirtech we understand that learning a new software package can be an overwhelming task. Often times, it is difficult to even know where to begin. So, we have put together a structured course that guides users through the learning process. Inspirtech sets itself apart from the competition with a unique and highly effective holistic approach to teaching. Lessons are filled with engaging examples and exercises that are just enough to inspire confidence, yet not too much to confuse and frustrate the learner. Upon completion of the course, learners will be prepared to challenge the CSWA exam.

Training features:

- Convenient self-paced learning
- Over 8 hours of instructional videos
- 18 project based lessons
- Over 120 examples and exercises
- SolidWorks files included

Table of Contents:

- Lesson 1—Introduction to Parametric Solid Modeling (29:48)
- Lesson 2—Material, Colours & Mass Properties (27:33)
- Lesson 3—Introduction to Parts (28:26)
- Lesson 4—Cut Extrudes and Construction Geo (32:54)
- Lesson 5—Mirrors, Fillets & Trims (31:28)
- Lesson 6—Offsets, Convert Entities & Fillets (34:01)
- Lesson 7—Revolves, Champers & Shells (27:35)
- Lesson 8—Hole Wizards & Sketch Patterns (32:09)
- Lesson 9—Introduction to Assemblies (27:42)
- Lesson 10—Concentric Mates & Physical Dynamics (24:43)
- Lesson 11—Additional Mates & Sub-Assemblies (29:33)
- Lesson 12—Introduction to Drawings (30:49)
- Lesson 13—Additional Views & Dimensions (27:39)
- Lesson 14—Assembly Drawings (29:34)
- Lesson 15—Sweeps (26:58)
- Lesson 16—Lofts (28:50)
- Lesson 17—Feature patterns (17:09)
- Lesson 18—COSMOSXpress (29:33)
- Lesson 19—SolidWorks Motion
- Lesson 20—SolidWorks Toolbox

3. Alex Ruiz—SolidWorks 2010: No Experience Required (2010) [1 eBook (PDF)]

The only continuous, step-by-step tutorial for SolidWorks

SolidWorks is a 3D CAD manufacturing software package that has been used to design everything from aerospace robotics to bicycles. This book teaches beginners to use SolidWorks through a step-by-step tutorial, letting you build, document, and present a project while you learn.

Tools and functionality are explained in the context of professional, real-world tasks and workflows. You will learn the essential functions and gain the skills to use the software at once.

- SolidWorks is a popular design program for manufacturing, and this book introduces it in the context of actually creating an object
- Begins with an overview of SolidWorks conventions and the interface
- Explains how to create models and drawings, create a revolved part and sub assembly, and model parts within a sub assembly
- Explores modification capabilities and drawing and Bill of Materials templates
- Moves on to top-level assembly models and drawings, Toolbox components and the Design Library, mates, export and printing capabilities, and creating renderings
- Includes a glossary, a foreword from the SolidWorks product manager, and downloadable tutorial files

SolidWorks 2010: No experience required and will quickly turn beginners into confident users of SolidWorks.

Publisher: Sybex
Number of Pages: 648
Publication Date: 2010-03-15
ISBN-10 / ASIN: 0470505435
ISBN-13 / EAN: 9780470505434

The SolidWorks Tutorial DVD by Magnitude Engineering Solutions comes with its own menu and media player so there is no instillation required. Just insert the DVD and choose what lesson you want from the menu, and learn at your own individual pace. These tutorials are made by industry professionals who are Certified SolidWorks users and provide the tools to learn and master SolidWorks quickly and easily. The SolidWorks Tutorial includes a total of 194 Video Tutorials, with project part files, audio narration and sample projects.

http://www.magnitudeengsol.com/SolidWorksTutorial.php

The current generation of CAD software may be over-complicated, highly technical and outrageously expensive but that is changing very quickly. Even as I write, there are a number of simple to operate, web based, interoperative programs attracting a great deal of attention, and the venture capitalist funding to match. It now falls to the 3D modelers, of thingiverse.com and other object file innovators to link their creations to this broader movement. At last we are seeing collaboration and interoperability, as well as true volume mesh modelers. Surprisingly, it is still very rare for a designer to have software object that that is outputted in the same way. What follows is an introduction on how this rapidly changing market is shaping up.

The key to the 3D printing revolution, in addition to software, is the ability to learn 3D design. A whole new world opens up when you're not afraid of creating 3D shapes, thanks to 3D printers. 3D design can be a skill we all have, and the abundance of under fifteen-year-old Tinkercad users proves this. We're seeing amazing learning curve on the complexity of 3D models in the Tinkercad community. When technical constraints are hidden and the playground is all you see, creativity bubbles up. With playfulness, growing 3D design skills and good tools, these youngsters will make the next industrial revolution happen.

Tinkercad

Tinkercad is a browser based CAD program that is taking the 3D printer world by storm. The small, two-person Finnish startup received $1 million in venture capital in 2010 to further develop the program. One half of the company, former Google engineer Kai Bachman bought a 3D printer in 2002 but was incredibly frustrated when he tried the various existing 3D CAD programs to drive it. Either they were too complex, or they were too simplistic to create the realistic solid models Bachman envisioned. He therefore decided to create a piece of software to make 3D modelling and design something anyone can do. The target market is Makers, the new enthusiast/hobbyist market snapping up inexpensive 3D printers, most of whom have no formal design background. CAD programs are notoriously difficult to learn, but Tinkercad is trying hard to remedy this, and by all accounts succeeding.

Unlike other web-based drawing programs like Sketchup, Tinkercad requires no download. It is aimed at folks who are beginners to 3D modelling and thus has a simple and intuitive interface, as well as a very low learning curve, allowing folks to easily design something without the CAD package holding them back. The designers have included a few simple thirty minute tutorials designed as 'Quests', using gamification as an interesting way of introducing users to using the software.

The user is presented with a number of quests with learning steps that are small and teach new skills as you progress. At the end of the quests you feel confident with the software Tinkercad and have the ability to actually produce an object. One of the quests involves dice design. You can even make a die that always rolls a six. Another teaches you how to design a printable teddy bear.

Designing in Tinkercad is based on two core concepts:

1. You can add shapes to your design either as solids or holes.
2. You can combine a number of shapes together, forming a new shape. Using these two simple concepts you can build your own almost arbitrarily complex tools to create very interesting designs. Once your design is ready, you can either print it out using one of the printing services with which Tinkercad is integrated, or alternatively download the .stl file for printing on a home printer.

Any design someone makes appears to be public. This means that if you see a design you like you can either copy and edit yourself, or indeed simply download the .stl file to print—or indeed send it off to one of the printing companies Tinkercad uses. We assume that the company is making its money on small commissions every time an item is printed by one of the 3D printing companies it offers.

Technically speaking, the software is designed in Javascript and Go! (a language championed by Google) and is reasonably fast and responsive. To make editing possible, Tinkercad has a large cloud based component and each of the editing operations is executed on hundreds of processor cores in real time. In fact, even if the Tinkercad browser app is a relatively complex component, two-thirds of the codebase is actually on the server side. Tinkercad runs a bespoke geometry kernel that distributes calculations over hundreds of processor cores in a medium sized cluster, which has been designed to scale to thousands of cores. https://tinkercad.com/

SketchUp

SketchUp is a 3D modelling program created by Google for a broad range of applications that has attracted 30 million activations in the past year alone. It is available in free as well as 'professional' versions. In April 2012, Google sold the program to Trimble, a company best known for GPS location services. The free version is missing some functionality of SketchUp Pro, but includes integrated tools for uploading content to Google Earth and to the Google 3D Warehouse, a repository of models created in SketchUp. A new toolbox enables a viewer to walk around and see things from a person's point of view; it adds labels for models, a look-around tool, and an "any polygon" shape tool.

Although SketchUp is not necessarily the best design software for modelling solid objects and 3D printing, it is one of the most popular free 3D design software packages on the planet and has inspired many people to try their hands at design. Sketchup was originally developed for architects, who do not typically need precision greater than 1/16", and so developers designed it to work best with geometry of about 1/16" and larger. Apparently, now it's nearly impossible to fix the problem without redesigning Sketchup from the ground up. While there are many video tutorials online for learning both basic and advanced methods, disadvantages include the fact that SketchUp cannot output the .stl format used by all 3D printers unless a special exporter plug-in is downloaded.

Printing SketchUp models involves file conversion, scale conversion and quite a bit of checking for mysterious things like "watertightness". While SketchUp 8 has added a solidity-checker, there is also a CADspan plug-in that resurfaces models and makes it 'water-tight' or 'manifold', which simply means that the model is a complete enclosure. It also reorients faces when needed.

With demand for rapid prototyping on the rise, companies such as Materialise are coming out with plug-ins to make the SketchUp-to-object printing process easier. This is essentially a wizard: After installation, the plug-in ensures that the model will fit on the printing "plate", indicate areas of glazing (transparency), and even add ready-made elements (like trees) from a collection of "guaranteed-to-print" objects supplied by i.materialise. Once ready, the plug-in allows a one-click-upload of the prepared model for printing.

Sketchups' sale to Trimble has been very beneficial to the 3D printing community. At Google, Sketchup was an odd fit, being based on a language very different from the many web based languages in which Google staff program, and they didn't put a lot of engineering effort into the software. On the other hand, Google made the investment to turn SketchUp into a popular software platform, and Trimble can now capitalize on that brand. They have purchased not only a piece of software but a huge community and the new owners are already capitalising on this. An open source "TestUp" internal testing tool is now available to any developer and the .stl import and export tools that are currently available as open source plug-ins will soon be baked into the main program. In fact, Sketchup will now be released annually, with the next version being called "Sketchup 2013."

http://www.sketchup.com/

Sketchfab

The world is in 3D, but most of the web is still in 2D. Sketchfab is a WebGL-based tool that allows 3D modellers to show objects in glorious 3D with full vantage control, a universal 3D viewer you can embed on any webpage. It is a bit like Youtube, but for 3D files. The project is self-funded and they currently have 2,300 models uploaded to the site. 3D artists can upload models in just two clicks.

Work began on the site two years ago in conjunction with the release of the WebGL standard. With twelve years of experience in the 3D industry, the founders believe it will become the dominant way to display 3D models online, adding "we believe 3D is the next big media, after photos and videos."

The site has a distinct, minimal style and the UI takes a back seat to the interactive views of the model. Visitors can pan, zoom, and rotate objects, and of course leave feedback in the form of likes or comments. Sketchfab supports uploads from the major modelling programs; 3DS Max, Maya, Blender, and Solidworks are all supported.

Sketchfab fills a unique space in the market. Thingiverse is a repository of printable 3D files and GrabCAD is a community and repository of CAD files, targeting mainly engineers. Sketchfab focuses on the display with the ability to display any 3D model online as well as in 3D software.

The product is ambitious, but its newness creates some deficiencies. The site is slow to load, understandable given the size and complexity of some of these models, but noticeable in an age of super-responsive sites and apps. And if you don't have WebGL enabled, you won't be able to interact with the pieces.

The short-term goal is to create the best portfolio site available for 3D designers, but they are keeping their eyes on the rapid development of 3D printers and scanners.

Sketchfab is the first web service to publish interactive 3D content online in real-time without plug-ins. The free service does not require any third-party application installed on either the client side or the server. All Sketchfab needs is for the end-user to be running a WebGL compatible browser. When WebGL was being discussed a few years ago as the next generation of browser technology, there was both a sense of "oh yeah!" and "so what?" that accompanied the discussion. Sketchfab is showing the value of having a standard platform for 3D graphics display.

To share a model, upload it to the Sketchfab site; a free account is required. The Sketchfab server will process it and put it on display. To display it at another web site, copy the provided embed code; the process is the same as embedding a YouTube video. Sketchfab users are free to remove models at any time. To upload models with textures, pack all the files in a .zip file before uploading. Sketchfab is a great tool for 3D artists who previously had 2D portfolios on CG communities like Deviantart. Now they can be viewed in full 3D. http://sketchfab.com/

Sunglass

Sunglass is a new browser-based collaboration tool for 3D design. Sunglass is one part interactive 3D viewer and mark-up tool, one part social design space, and one part interoperability option. One or several users can share an existing 3D design model.

It used to be that only powerful desktops could run CAD software, collaboration was a nightmare, and software could cost anywhere between $5,000 to $50,000. Two Massachusetts Institute of Technology (MIT) graduates — Nitin Rao and CEO Kaustuv DeBiswas are hoping to shake up the existing $10 billion CAD industry. Sunglass is launching a cloud-based way to create, edit, and share 3D designs, like a Google Docs for CAD. All of the heavy-duty processing work happens on the company's servers, while the user end is browser based, powered by WebGL and HTML5, with full Dropbox integration for storing 3D files. It's also compatible with over forty file formats, so stubborn designers can still open up your projects in their preferred programs.

"There are 10 million designers just like us looking to engage with each other in a flat world," co-founder and CEO Kaustuv DeBiswas said recently. "Products are now built for global consumption so why can't they be designed via global collaboration?" His partner Rao says he has been driven by the cost of existing design software and how it's too expensive for emerging countries.

At the moment Sunglass isn't a 'proper' CAD system as such but a way to convert 3D CAD designs into B–REP models (surfaces defined by boundary representation) and then holding them in an online webGL–based environment for sharing. In time, tools and applications will become available to enable a wide range of 'things' which can be done to and with models. In its current guise it is focusing on the sharing aspect. Sunglass users can simultaneously access a single 3D model and suggest tweaks through text chat, voice chat or even a sketch tool for marking suggestions.

The company is also building an API to let designers share their most useful tools with others. The company is planning the world's first 3D app store to offer the tools. Previously, designers would have to buy entire software suites to gain access to a single tool. The most basic version of Sunglass is free and then designers can pay for extra apps or add-ons. At the same store, designers can buy one-off 3D models from others. Unity, which has a 3D gaming engine that powers titles like Shadowgun, has a store where game developers can buy 3D effects and models from other developers.
https://sunglass.io/ (https://sunglass.io/)

OpenSCAD

OpenSCAD is software for creating solid 3D CAD objects, but it is not an interactive modeller. Instead, it is something like a 3D-compiler which reads a script file that describes the object, and renders the 3D model from this file. It is basically a programming language for 3D models, and while it does not have the traditional graphical interface of AutoCAD, OpenSCAD is able to create very complex parts with only a few lines of code. OpenScad appeals especially to experienced coders and programmers. There are thread models and other libraries available at wikibooks.org.

OpenSCAD provides two main modelling techniques: constructive solid geometry, (CSG, taking 3D primitives and stretching, scaling, and intersecting them to create a 3D shape), or extrusion from a 2D outline. Besides .dxf files, OpenSCAD can read and create 3D models in the .stl and .off file formats. Quite a few

RepRap parts were designed in OpenSCAD, and the lightweight interface and open source nature means it is generally a good tool for designing 3D print items. It uses Computational Geometry Algorithms Library (CGAL) as the basic Computational Solid Geometry engine, taking care of details such as intersection, difference and Minkowski sums. The results can be rendered into 3D .stl files. It uses OpenCSG and OpenGL for fast previewing of models.

In the 3D Printing world it seems to have been quite difficult to put text onto designs. Fonts are a nightmare, there are undoubtedly rights issues and it has all been a headache so far. OpenScad overcomes this problem by use of a third party add-on tool known as a Nameplate Generator. If you do want to edit OpenSCAD parts in your browser, there is always OpenJsCAD, an OpenSCAD interpreter written entirely in Javascript. http://www.openscad.org/

To3D

To3D is a new and open source beta 3D mechanical modeller. Not only does it focus on 3D designs, but it also attempts to simplify the effort of keeping track of and sharing designs with other people. Existing tools are very good at modelling parts, and then making assemblies from those parts, but they are not so good at starting a design at the concept or layout stage and developing detailed parts, without a lot of redundant work and loss of control. Today's tools are also quite complex, can be labour intensive to use and require a lot of training. This presents a problem for the occasional user who requires a system that is intuitive and easy to learn. Keeping track of all the files that are created can also be a drain on time and focus, so To3D is trying to remove the burden of data management by creating far fewer files than other CAD systems. The system is web based and therefore platform independent.

The designers had their Eureka! Moments when they discovered that a local college was requiring all students to have an iPad for school. This spoke strongly to them of the realization that the world is changing, and they needed to consider what that meant for the engineering community. To reduce its computing footprint, heavy lifting is done in the cloud on multiple servers, graphics and other data is sent to the browser in the smallest chunks possible as the design is added to or changed. http://www.to3dnow.com/home.aspx

Blender

Blender is a fantastic open source 3D modeling, animation, shading and rendering package but not one that is really suited to 3D printing applications. In fact many people now feel that the Blender Foundation shot themselves in the foot by releasing their fourth open source short movie called Tears of Steel, a short that mixed 3D digital content with live action and was produced using only open source software. Despite these commendable attributes, the lameness of the acting and the plot distracted from the quality of the CGI making it a poor tech demo, resembling VFX animation and coming across as very fake.
http://www.blender.org/

MeshUp

The Meshup Teabunny

Uformia recently launched a new project called MeshUp, with many powerful and interesting functions such as mesh mixing and the ability to design a one- or two-sided shell volume, then combine it with micro-structures to create lightweight yet structural objects for 3D printing. Mesh models tend to have all kinds of problems such as cracks, holes and self-intersections. This is due to a disconnect between the real world being represented and the modelling software's attempts to represent real, volumetric, complex and "messy" objects by only surfaces.

This makes for a very dynamic, painless and playful modelling experience, as they demonstrated by combining two of the most iconic 3D models in CG, the Stanford Bunny and the Utah Teapot. Both polygonal models are automatically converted to functional volumes so that the Teapot can simply be moved to another part of the Bunny and the two maintain a union while keeping the resulting model watertight at all times. Unfortunately the system is very computationally intensive and can be slow for complex objects, if you do not have a multi-core computer.

The project was funded on Kickstarter but only just achieved their funding targets, and I suspect this might have been because the product is not open source and their rewards were not very well thought through. 153 backers pledged $28,082, ensuring that they just scraped past the $25,000 goal, even though some thought that it might not make it at all. For $25 all backers receive is a MeshUp t-shirt or an .stl model of the MeshUp Teabunny. Even at $50, backers were only offerered a small physical copy of the Teabunny, and it required a cool $100 to receive a fully featured copy of MeshUp. If they had made the price a quarter of this, and promoted it through the 3D printer forums, I am sure that they would have reached their target far more quickly. The end users here are hobbyists with limited budgets, not large corporations with enormously deep pockets. Uformia seem to have ignored the fact that the main reason that 3D printers have quickly gained such appeal is due to their rapid drop in prices. This also needs to be reflected in the software that they use. Larger pledge rewards were completely wasted, with backers willing to pony up $10,000 being promised all expense trips to Norway for ice caving in Svalbard. Come on guys, show us that you are confident in your product and your skills, and can offer us some relevant rewards. Offer me some personalised CAD work with your software that I can use in my new business, not some over-priced jollies to see Santa and the Northern Lights. http://uformia.com/

Cloud9

Despite failing to reach their Indiegogo funding goal, Anarkik 3D Design has an interesting sketch/modelling software known as Cloud9 that they describe as a modelling package for artists and designers, rather than a CAD package for engineers. Perhaps the most innovative aspect of this package is that they utilise a 3D virtual touch (haptic) device to replace the boring 2D mouse. It certainly makes sense that a 3D device would be a far more effective tool for designing 3D models but there are a number of disadvantages to be over come before this hits the mainstream. The largest of these is that a 3D mouse still costs in the region of $250.

Founders Ann Marie Shillito and Xiaoqing Cao unfortunately showed little understanding of how to successfully crowdfund a project, even though the idea itself is really fascinating. They presented themselves as a well-funded and established company that had originally been spun off from collaborative research at The University of Edinburgh. Their software is already a working package, which they are retailing on their website along with a wide range of rather pricey training courses. They then listed a funding goal of a massive $120,000, so that they would be able to fix bugs and add new features. Crowdfunding works best when you are starting a project from scratch, preferably a project that no financial investor would ever touch. What these guys needed was a Venture Capitalist, which is why they only ended up securing a measly $3,000 from the crowd. Even if supporters pledged $100, all they would have receieved was an abstract 3D model rather that the software that cost a minimum of $200.

Anarkik are excellent at coming up with catchy marketing terms but it remains to be seen if their software is genuinely useful, and if it can churn out practical designs that are suitable for 3D printers. Their introduction of the Novint Falcon haptic device is a genuine step forward though. They describe a haptic device as a 3D mouse that provides an interactive resistance known as force feedback, offering a sense of touch enabling the designer to explore the feel, the textures and even the elasticity of a virtual object. Certainly, I would like to try out both this device and the software, but like everybody else, I think I will be waiting for a printable version that I can download from Thingiverse. http://www.anarkik3d.co.uk/

As a short aside, a brief analysis of 3D printing Kickstarter projects revealed the following. Of the thirteen projects launched since October 2009, only six have successfully reached their funding goals, about 46 percent. The average funding goal of a successful project is $3,842 and the average funds raised is $11,039, or 287 percent. Based on this analysis, it is clear that unsuccessful projects are generally asking for too much money. For example, PotteryPrint was an iPad app concept to teach children about 3D printing. They raised only $6,000 of their $12,000 funding goal. Another example on IndieGoGo is Anarkik3D, which as described earlier raised less than $4,000 of its $120,000 funding goal. Both of these projects had good ideas and great production quality, but set targets way above the average successful funding level of $3,842. In doing so, it was difficult to find enough individual backers to support their idea. If you are thinking of launching a crowdfunded 3D printing project, these are important statistics to bear in mind.

CAD File Conversion

When looking to convert CAD files to .stl format, there are a number of options out there. The Irrlicht Engine is a liberally licensed, open source 3D graphics library, that is cross platform, written in C++, imports about twenty different mesh formats and can write them to .stl and .ply.

Meshlab has more than 100 mesh processing algorithms for cleaning, checking, converting, simplifying, filling, offsetting, remeshing, smoothing, etc. MeshLab, is an advanced 3D mesh processing software system which is well known in the more technical fields of 3D development and data handling. As free software, it is used both as a complete package, and also as libraries powering other software. http://meshlab.sourceforge.net/

Magics can automatically generate support geometry quite well. It is mainly used to generate supports for parts being made in SLA machines, but the options are highly customizable. Unfortunately it is not the cheapest software around. http://software.materialise.com/magics

3D design is one of the major bottlenecks that is stopping 3D printing from going mainstream. Until such a time that creating a digital representation of a physical object becomes as easy as ripping a CD or a DVD, we are unlikely to see the explosion in the availability of CAD files that will finally enable those of us with printers to create the wide range of items that we are looking for. Even so, the rapid pace of development described in this chapter is likely to change this situation in the very near future. Just think back to a time when websites had to be written in html code. Only the very motivated and technically competent were able to create an attractive looking homepage, and then go through the trouble of maintaining it. This is very similar to the situation with 3D digital designs. Creators need a certain level of expertise with complex and expensive software suites. 3D scanners and software like Sketch up and Tinkercad are quickly levelling the playing field. We only need to remember how the simplicity in creating Myspace pages led to an early explosion of personal websites. Now we have tools like Pinterest and Facebook that completely remove all the stress and hard work out of the process. Few people have actually bothered to become highly skilled website designers and yet Facebook is well beyond the one billion user mark, a fact that is even more astounding when we consider that the site is still blocked in the world's most populous nation, China. There was a time when songs, TV shows and movies were a rarity on the internet but now there are vast archives, with an almost innumerable selection of multimedia files. 3D resources such as Thingiverse and Grabcad are just a taster of what is yet to come when everybody and his dog can create a digital representation, and instantly share it with the rest of the world.

In the previous chapter we looked at how the Kinect is changing the field of computer scanning. It is interesting to note that another device is trying to change the way that we interact with 3D modelling software. The Leap is a small iPod-sized USB peripheral that creates a 3D interaction space of eight cubic feet to precisely interact with and control software on personal computer, enabling users to control their PCs in three dimensions with natural hand and finger movements. The developers were frustrated in traditional 3D modelling software, something that took ten seconds in real life would take thirty minutes with a computer. They felt that moulding virtual clay with a computer should be as easy as moulding clay in the real world, and that the mouse and keyboard were simply getting in the way. The Leap currently costs just $70 and yet can track individual fingers and their movements down to a 1/100th of a millimetre. It is able to distinguish thumbs from fingers, and even handheld items like pencils. The developer's code has already been released, and so it will probably not be long before we can mimic Tom Cruise swiping through Minority Report's 3D computer interface, and design our projects on holographic table top floating displays, in the same way that Tony Stark worked on his Iron Man prototypes.

5

Model and 3D Design Resources

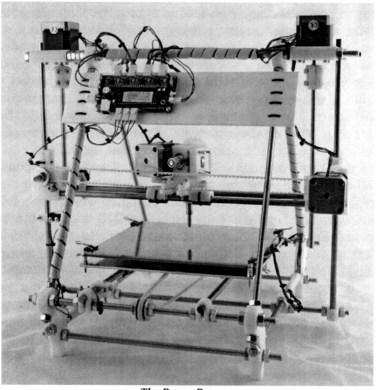

The Prusa Reprap

When physical products move from the analogue world to the digital realm, they usually acquire a new descriptive term. Songs that one generation ago were referred to as vinyl tracks are now known as MP3s, while photos have quickly become known as jpegs. These new words do not actually describe the original item, but a computer based digital representation. In 3D printing we are still at that fluid stage where the new term for these data objects has not yet been decided. It might be an .stl (short for stereolithographic file), perhaps a CAD file,

(which might be confusing when somebody eventually prints off a mediaeval detective) or perhaps the new term 'physible' will quickly catch on. Whatever we end up calling them, they are going to become immensely important in the very near future. Just as Gutenberg's printing press gave rise to bookshops and libraries, 3D printers will see the growth of enormous online resources full of 3D representations of all our real world objects. When the internet was first conceived, Google was but just a twinkle in a young coder's eye but has since become the dominant force in information indexing. Who can predict where we will eventually gravitate for our STLs and physibles? Here are a few of the first entrants onto the scene. http://www.Thingiverse.com

Thingiverse.com is a library of printable objects founded in 2008 by Brooklyn-based Makerbot, and currently the leading resource for individuals looking for objects to create something with their RepRap fabricators, CNC routers or laser cutters. To quote the CEO, "Up until now, you've been able to download books, you've been able to download movies, you can download music. Well, now you can download things. And, once you download the digital design, you can just crank up your MakerBot, fire it up, and print it out." At last count, there were more than twenty-five thousand designs that had been downloaded a total of 8.5 million times. Thingiverse is, by far, my favourite resource of this kind. Where else can you download designs for everything from a tape dispenser to a complete 18-hole miniature desktop golf course? http://physibleexchange.com/

The Pirate Bay has created a physibles category on its site, allowing users to search and locate torrents of 3D printer files. Despite the fact that the move generated massive media interest, there are still only a handful of pages of files, including such things as the famous Pirate Bay ship and a 1970 Chevy hot rod. What was much more interesting was the amount of self-proclaimed tech journalists making fools of themselves by claiming that TPB was hosting these files and describing it as a piracy site, even though TPB is simply a search engine akin to Google, that does not actually store anything except meta data on it servers. The one major impact that it did have was to bring the word 'physible' into common usage on blogs and website all over the net.

http://grabcad.com/library

GrabCAD is a website where CAD engineers display their work and make it available for download. The site currently hosts over 60,000 CAD models and has a very lively Q & A section.

The site includes a web-based 3D viewer that is not quite as full-featured as Sunglass.io but still allows panning and zooming from six predefined viewing angles, as well as an annotation function for user collaboration. Despite these interesting features, the site is already upsetting some sections of the slide rule set in that it is not effectively policing its uploads. While sites in other fields such as Tripadvisor and Megaupload have drawn criticisms for making vast profits off other peoples content, similar allegations are now being aimed at Grabcad. Controls and execution are required to ensure that those who are posting the models are the same as the people who actually created them. Fortunately, it is possible to tell who originally modelled a design by right clicking on a feature, and selecting Feature Properties.

Trimble 3D Warehouse
(http://sketchup.google.com/3dwarehouse/)

The Trimble 3D Warehouse (formerly Google 3D Warehouse) is an accompanying website for SketchUp where modellers can upload, download and share three-dimensional models. Because of the site's previous association with Google, there is much more of a leaning towards full scale architectural models, in fact there are detailed 3D virtual models of most major building structures of the world. Need a street in San Francisco? Here is a filmable virtual set. These models can then be loaded to Google Earth, after review for accuracy that checks if they are "Google Earth Ready." The warehouse is definitely worth watching to see if their recent acquisition by Trimble alters this focus, so that they realign themselves more with the 3D printer market.

As the technology progresses, look out for the development of a 3D object metacrawler, a search engine that will search all the free libraries and return an aggregate result for you to choose from, and who is to say that this new 3D metacrawler will not become the next Google.

While the sites mentioned above are more geared to the sharing of content, there are many more well-established 3D repositories where designers can sell their designs.

http://www.turbosquid.com/Search/Index.cfm?

The largest of these, TurboSquid, has more than two million members and well over two hundred thousand 3D models available for download, the most popular categories being weapons and vehicles. There are some free models here, and when comparing these different CAD sites, I searched for sword designs. Tubosquid came up tops with over three hundred free designs to choose from. Most of the graphics available here are the kind that are used in computer games, architecture, and interactive training rather than 3D printing. It does have a very useful CheckMate Certification program, which checks models against a unified 3D modelling standard developed by TurboSquid, and passing models are marked as certified in their catalogue. Downsides to the site include a poor reputation for customer service, and the fact that they only pay a measly 40 percent of sales to the actual artists. In comparison, The3dStudio.com pays 70 percent. Both sites offer affiliate programs for referrals of new buyers or sellers.

If you have an interest in these kinds of 3D repositories then I would recommend looking at the following page, which has comparison reviews of all the major players: http://3dprintingmodel.com/marketplace/indexMarketPlace.php

In the hunt for free files, many of the internal 3D models from modern computer games are easily exported to and printed out on your RepRap or Creator. My first experience with this was with the Halo Custom Edition game. Like many first person shooter games, there is a large behind the scenes community beavering away on new maps, characters and weapons. I looked at their weapons section at http://hce.halomaps.org/index.cfm?pg=1 and decided to work with my Singapore-based printer to see if we could improve on the 1.6 minigun that was produced by Hot Toys for their Terminator 2 figure.

The good news is that you can easily convert such models from most game formats, as long as you have a converter that is. New software called Mineways enables you to export your Minecraft creations into models and texture maps ready to send to a 3D printer. None of this is foolproof, and some models might need some tweaking to work properly, but the software is good at removing objects that are floating in space or are impossible to construct. It will also hollow out the interior of your designs, preventing overuse of the raw material and lowering the cost. Mineways is also the first to export with full colour. As a quick comparison, at the time of writing, the cost of using Mineways to print in 3D is about sixth-tenths of a cent per block vs. around 10 cents a block for LEGOs, a cost that is likely to fall even further as printers continue to improve in quality and resolution. I personally find that many of the 3D models found in these games are over simplistic in their design. For this reason, I will often go back to a site like fiverr.com and commission a SolidWorks designer to add some details, enhancements and authenticity to the piece.

Another source of inspiration might be the classic shoot'em-up game Quake. There is certainly software out there that will covert MD2 and MD3 files into an .stl format, so in theory you could immediately starting printing out ogres, grenade launchers and BFGs.

The digital age is bringing with it new ways to take the virtual world off of your hard drive and put it on the table in front of you. The possibilities are amazing! Imagine playing your own version of Call of Duty: Modern Warfare as a tabletop war-game, or creating an entire range of collectible miniatures based on Farmville? It might even be fun to dig back into the past, and model the star ships from classic games like Frontier: Elite II or Tachyon. There really is no shortage of possibilities, nor is there a shortage of skilled, and unskilled, technicians more than willing to help you achieve a new height of geekery. The only real limit here is the imagination.

6

Freelance Printing, Scanning and Designing

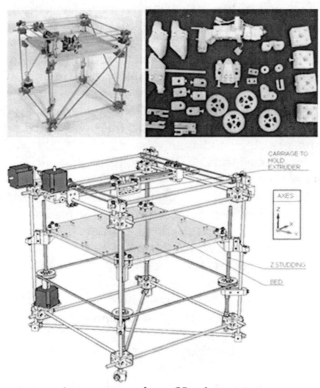

An open source home 3D printer set up

Out Sourcing

If you do not yet have your own 3D printer, I can recommend

that you start by using a 3D printing service. Even when using a commercial printing service, much of the personal fabrication experience remains, including the design, the modelling and the eager anticipation. There are a wide range of different services available, from home tinkerers on the various micro-tasking sites, all the way to large dedicated printer companies such as Shapeways and Sculpteo. They are affordable and will take care of much of the messy work for you.

Dedicated Printing Services
Ponoko (http://www.ponoko.com/)

Ponoko is one of the first manufacturers that uses distributed manufacturing and on-demand manufacturing, building on the success of the information age, and applying it to digital fabrication. Customers with digital designs can contract with Ponoko, and sell their objects either via the Ponoko site, or their own retail outlets. Ponoko gets paid based on the cost of the materials, plus a flat rate for every minute the fabrication machine is running, but designers who sell their products on the site set their own retail prices. The online manufacturing service now boasts over 1,600 material and color combinations available through their 2D and 3D services. Digital manufacturing, because it replicates objects exactly, and because it requires only that someone put the right material into the machine, can be done by anyone, anywhere. The manufacturers exist in a distributed network that is growing around the world, and often the manufacturer closest to the customer is sourced. So Instead of buying a mass-market table from Ikea, you can now have your own personal design, or a design that you pick out, manufactured by somebody in your own town, using locally sourced materials.

There are already more than 20,000 items on Ponoko's website—housewares, toys, and furniture—available for purchase. But Ponoko does not sell these products in the traditional sense. The items for sale are not held in inventory; they exist digitally as design files on the company's servers. What Ponoko really sells is access to rapid fabrication machines—laser cutters in New Zealand and Oakland, California, and soon, all sorts of machines all over the world—allowing people to make themselves stuff or to buy stuff that other people have designed.

To take one interesting example, Los Angeles designer Igor Knezevic sells his Bloom Lamp, a bedside lamp made up of eighteen precisely cut pieces that resemble a delicate flower for $160 on Ponoko. Unlike a store-bought lamp, this one costs Knezevic' nothing until someone pays for it. Igor stocks the lamps digitally and manufactures on demand. "Right now I'm making a couple hundred dollars here, a couple hundred there," he says. "But five years from now, people will still be paying a couple hundred bucks, and I won't have to do anything. That's revolutionary."

Ponoko and ShopBot recently announced a partnership where more than twenty thousand online creators meet over six thousand digital fabricators. The launch of http://www.100kgarages.com/ begins a new chapter in distributed manufacturing, mass customization, and mass individualization. As Bruce Sterling noted, "Everybody who knows anything about fabrication knows that scaling up fabbing has always been a big deal. A thousand fabricators are lot more than a thousand times one lonely fabricator." 100kGarages is an exciting new service for everyone who wants to have things made—by making it yourself or finding someone to make it for you. It's free for everyone to search and submit requests, and for fabricators to post profiles and bids.

i.materialise (http://i.materialise.com/)

i.materialise is the 3D printing service arm of Belgian additive manufacturing firm Materialise NV. With over twenty years of experience in the technology and more than seventy 3D printers, this interactive 3D print lab provides users with instant feedback on models as well as tutorials and an 'Easy Creation' page with gateways to browser-based 3D design applications such as Tinkercad and Google SketchUp. There is also a design gallery, where customers can buy and sell custom 3D designs which i.materialise will then print-to-order. i.Materialise is experimenting with a form of flat-rate pricing. Normally they employ the standard "how much material and what kind of material are you printing" approach, but perhaps this was seen as a barrier to expanding their business. For any object that fits completely within a volume of 125 cubic centimetres users pay a mere €12. Should they need a few more copies, prices are even better: add more for only €4 each.

Sculpteo (http://www.sculpteo.com/en/)

Sculpteo, a French firm, offers nine colour and material options, from resin to silvered-coated plastic. Prices range between $42.00 per 5cm of white plastic at the low end, up to $80.00/5cm for silver. Sculpteos service is currently available in Europe and North America. The method of pricing of 3D printed models is by volume of material used and not by the complexity of the model. A minor reduction in scale can change the price dramatically. For example, if a 100 cubic centimetre model is say $10, scale it down by 25 percent and the model will be approximately 60 percent cheaper to make. On the Sculpteo website there is a slider bar for sizing which dynamically shows this dramatic shift in pricing. The site also features a community page where users can find, upload, share or sell custom 3D designs.

Shapeways (http://www.shapeways.com/)

Shapeways 3D printing delivers designs free worldwide in a wide range of materials including plastics, stainless steel, ceramics, silver, and more. It is also an interesting marketplace where users can sell their designs and make ideas into reality. This is exciting because designers all around the world are earning money every day from this service. It does not matter if you are in Australia and your buyer is in the USA. Shapeways handles the financial transaction, fabrication and distribution. There is no need to invest in a large batch of products and have them sent from China, to be distributed then to individual retailers. Designs are produced on demand by Shapeways and sent directly to clients, while the designer receives a monthly passive income.

Shapeways has seen enormous growth in the number of community members, models uploaded, products 3D printed, shops opened and income earned by Shapeways shop owners over the last few years. In 2011, Shapeways 3D printed over 750,000 individual products and delivered them to people around the world, earning designers over $270,000 in revenue. Some 238,000 3D models were uploaded to the site by over 100,000 members. Over 2,500 shops opened in 2011 alone.

Shapeways recently cut the ribbon on a new factory space in Long Island City, New York (with a pair of 3D printed scissors obviously). When completed in 2013, it will be the largest 3D-printing facility in the world, housing up to fifty printers, and in useful proximity to their New York HQ, to which they relocated from the Netherlands back in 2010.

Kraftwurx (http://www.kraftwurx.com/)

Kraftwurx is yet another community and marketplace for 3D printing enabling engineers, product designers, industrial designers and 3D artists to buy, sell and 3D print customized products. Kraftwurx has many 3D printing veterans with many years of experience in turning ideas into reality. Products can be printed in more than forty types of materials including platinum, yellow and white gold, sterling silver, titanium, stainless steel, aluminum, nylon, ABS plastic, rubber, transparent plastics etc. Kraftwurx also offers over forty finishes for products including power coating, painting, polishing, plating, anodizing, brush effects and more.

These are just four of the many companies that are springing up at the moment. While it is slightly beyond the scope of this book to list and review all of them, there are many websites that already perform such a function.

My top recommendation at the moment is the work done by the 3D Printer Hub site.
http://3dprinterhub.com/3d-printer-services/#comparison

Micro-Tasking

All of the above companies are large organisations that specialise in additive manufacturing, and while they all offer reliable services, they are more akin to selling antiques and works of art at Sotheby's or Christies, rather than listing your personal belongings on an internet auction such as eBay. In this age of distributed networks, the increasingly attractive alternative is to look at the many micro-tasking sites that are springing up. These sites are platforms for freelancers of all kind, located all over the planet, who will perform a myriad of small tasks, including work that is particularly relevant to us, such as CAD design, object scanning and even 3D printing. The market is very much organised in the same way that early internet auction sites were when they began shaking themselves out. One major player looks as though it is going to dominate the western market, but there are some interesting smaller operations fulfilling important roles in specialist niches.

www.Fiverr.com

Fiverr is an Israeli based marketplace offering more than one million services range between $5 and $150. It hosts micro-entrepreneurs in more than 200 countries, lists over 120 categories and provides numerous tools for sellers to engage with, build and grow their customer base. These include systems for collecting payment, promoting services, managing orders, exchanging files and communicating with buyers. The website was launched February 2010, hosting over 500,000 different gigs the first year and has grown 600 percent since 2011, now being ranked among the top 100 most popular sites in the U.S. and top 200 in the world. The site adds about 1,000 new services—1,000 new gigs—per day.

The gigs, most fixed at $5, range from the ultra serious to the downright ridiculous. There is a good range of the more practical micro-tasks, everything from CSS micro-bugging and social marketing to resume revising and PowerPoint editing help. Of course this is the internet and so the amount of bizarre and oddball offers defies even the most active imagination. Members will Photoshop monsters into your family photos, pen Italian love poetry, write advertising messages on various parts of their anatomy and burn effigies of your enemies.

In January 2012, Fiverr launched Levels, a reputation-based promotion system. After sellers successfully complete at least ten transactions, they unlock advanced up-selling tools to offer Gig extras and charge more for their services. Fiverr's success is testament to an evolving economy, one where workers do not punch a clock from 9 to 5 and take home a steady salary.

With regard to the world of 3D printing, there are members that are skilled in a wide range of CAD software including SolidWorks, as well as a smaller number with home 3D printers that will fabricate your designs for you. Most sites also have request sections, so if you need tasks completed on Tinkercad, Sketchup etc., then this is the place to ask. Tucked away among the lunatics who will dress up as a dachshund and record a HD video of themselves doing a song and dance to promote your website, there are some very useful freelancers offering their services of Fiverr.com. The site itself it still a bit clunky, especially the communication pages between buyers and sellers, but this site being the first of its kind, it is bound to evolve over time. Bear in mind that few gigs actually cost only $5 and most will ask for multiples, but do not be afraid to negotiate to ensure that you receieving the very best deal.

Attack of the Clones

There are literally hundreds of Fiverr clones out there, including, quite predictably, a Fourerr, a Sixerr and a Sevenerr. Because the website script is widely available, more and more are springing up all the time, but precious few of them are lasting the course. I would like to recommend a small handful that have either managed to establish themselves over a similar time frame as Fiverr, or that have some small niche appeal which could make them quite successful in the near future. The first five that I have listed here are actual Fiverr competitors, sites that are aggressively trying to compete for a share of the market that Fiverr currently dominates.

http://zeerk.com/

Despite the strange name, Zeerk is experimenting with numerous innovative strategies to set themselves apart from Fiverr.com, rather than simply being yet another clone. In doing so, they have introduced a number of improvements to their site that are quickly becoming popular with the micro tasking community. These include customizable widgets so that sellers can embed their gigs on their own blogs and websites, four separate levels of upgrade (Bold, Featured, Highlight and Premium member), and payment options made available on a daily basis. In addition, there are no commissions on $2 or $5 jobs. The Zeerk team is also developing software with which users will be able to post their gigs on all Fiverr clones with just one click, something akin to the eBay Turbolister. With changes like this coming thick and fast, this is definitely a micro-tasking site well worth watching.

http://gigbucks.com/

GigBucks is a very popular alternative to Fiverr, and probably the second most successful micro-tasking site in terms of traffic. Although it hosts gigs for all the categories found on Fiverr, the smaller community means there is also far less competition for workers. On Gigbucks the jobs often outweigh the community, making it easier for newcomers to find work. Gigbucks is a great jumping off point for those looking to explore the world of micro-jobs, allowing people to work how, when and where they would like. Gigbucks offers a limited registration process; while Fiverr and Fiverr clone sites require a much lengthier registration process.

Gigbucks also appears to have much quicker customer service turnarounds. Questions can take two to three days to be answered on Fiverr compared to within twenty-four hours on Gigbucks. Once again, this might have something to do with the smaller community size.

www.tenbux.com

Tenbux is one of the oldest Fiverr clones and so their much copied design does not really stand out from the rest of the market. Even so, they are one of the most active competitors. Obviously the tasks here are twice the price of those at Fiverr.com and there are plenty of net entrepreneurs out there making a good living from Fiverr arbitrage. Even on Fiverr.com, users will often end up paying for extra services anyway, and so Tenbux can often streamline that process in advance.

www.fivesquids.co.uk

This is a very active UK site that often contains significantly different content from its US counterparts. This in itself can make up for the slightly higher price of tasks at five pounds sterling. Even in the twenty-first century the UK market can still be somewhat insular but this site provides a useful doorway into services and customers that may not be accessible from other points of entry.

www.justafiver.com

There is little to set this site apart from the hundreds of other clones out there except that it has already gained a fair amount of traction, and is now receiving a good deal of promising traffic. The only thing I do not like about this site is their insistence on using such poor grammar, when they insist on beginning every sellers offer with the words "I'm gunna..." Still, no site is perfect and with so many choice out there, it is very difficult to pick winners and losers. Imagine trying to back a winning horse when there are maybe 250 runners in the field. Still, this is my wild card choice, at least until the next generation of micro-tasking sites begins to show up.

Beyond the Clones

The five sites that follow are niche sites of which you should be aware as they may fulfil important roles in the future.

www.forbitcoin.com

While all the other micro-tasking sites use traditional currencies, this venture uses the Bitcoin digital alternative. Apart from this, it is similar to many other Fiverr clones. What I really like is that next to the Bitcoin rate is the equivalent to US dollars in parentheses, which is very useful for those who are relative newcomers to both the site and the world of Bitcoin. Buyers pay in Bitcoin, and sellers have Bitcoin paid into their account, minus a 10 percent listing fee. This is an interesting option for those who are worried by the fact that we have already lost trillions of dollars to greedy bankers by placing value in rectangular paper cut-outs with pictures of dead people on them.

www.xFiverr.com

xFiverr offers a free and easy to use micro-job platform for freelancers involved in the various adult businesses, to offer their services priced from $5 to $75 per trade. Most micro tasking sites specify no erotica or adult related material, so this is an interesting niche with plenty of potential

www.lisili.com

While Fiverr dominates the English language internet, it remains almost completely unknown is Asia. The development of the Chinese internet has shown that goliaths in the West can be quickly felled by local upstarts who understand the importance of local language. Google is dwarfed by Baidu, eBay was forced to leave with its tails between its legs by Taobao, and Twitter is a faint squeak compared to the roar of Weibo. Unknown to most Westerners, China has its own enormously successful versions of sites such as Groupon, Paypal and Youtube. At the moment it looks as though lisili.com is going to be the front runner in the micro-tasking market place, but these are still early days and the Chinese internet can be very unpredictable. Google's handling of Klingon is still quite a few steps ahead of its Mandarin translation service, and so many of the descriptions might seem a litlle strange when read in English, but the one thing that does jump out here, is the vast number of services available on this site that do not exist on any of the other Fiverr clones. If your Chinese is not yet up to scratch, then it might be worthwhile hiring a native speaker on Fiverr.com to help you out with research, listing and querying. Even if it takes a little investment to start, the fee on lisili.com is only 15 RMB, which is significantly less than any of the Western clone sites.

www.rupees4gigs.com

With almost as many internet users as China, India is also fertile ground the micro tasking trend. Rupees4gigs is still in its formative stages but is locally owned and run, and is in a good position to leverage the wealth of English speaking talent that makes up the Indian subcontinent. Prices begin at five hundred rupees and while the site is merely a blip on the radar compared to Fiverr.com, it is worth watching for the long term.

www.1kjobsonline.com

I personally like to hedge my bets by backing a relative outsider. In this case, it would have to the Nigerian micro tasking site 1kjobsonline. Nigeria is the most populous country in Africa, the seventh most populous country in the world and an amazing one out of four every four Africans is Nigerian. A population of this size and influence simply cannot be ignored. In addition, anybody that has spent any time travelling will know that there are successful Nigerian communities all over the globe. This particular site lists services that are available for 1,000 Naira, and might be a useful connection to some of the hungriest and most creative entrepreneurs on the planet. Again this site's traffic is almost nothing when compared to Fiverr.com but I always like to have a wild card ready just in case.

The world of micro-tasking is still very fluid, with new sites opening and closing all the time. Therefore, if you are interested in following developments in this area, I would like to recommend a couple of sites that do a good job in bringing up-to-date news on this particular niche.

http://www.warriorforum.com/warriors-hire/

The War Room is one of the most active entrepreneur websites on the internet. The site has more than half a million members and there are at least ten thousand people on line at any give time. This creates a huge pool of collected information and with micro-tasking being such a hot topic at the moment, this becomes a very good place to keep abreast of the latest developments. In addition, it is also a good place to advertise your services as well as search for freelancers. Most people here are SEO orientated, but that does not mean that they do not know of CAD designers and 3D printers that they can recommend. I have always found the site to be filled with an amazingly wide variety of individuals that make it their business to keep up with the very latest mega trends.

www.gigblab.com

Gigblab is a blog-type website that reviews and critiques Fiverr clone sites. The site owner is an active micro-tasker herself, and so she is keen to pass on her knowledge in the field in order to draw in new customers to her own gigs.

Another area worth investigation for you to market your 3D printing services is that of online auctions. Start with the bigger operations such as eBay, Etsy and Taobao, offering to scan, model and print, (depending on your capabilities), whatever the customer desires. Simply set a flat rate per gram of ABS and let the crowd come up with tasks for you. Not everybody is willing to fork over a grand for a 3D printer, but they might have a secret project for which they might need such a service. Also, do not neglect one of the oldest ways of drumming up business. Whilst less targeted and probably not reliable for regular work, your local classifieds can also be a useful resource, and many towns have their own classified sites or a Craigslist website that can be used to promote your work locally
.

PART II

Financial Implications and Opportunities

7

Designing New Products

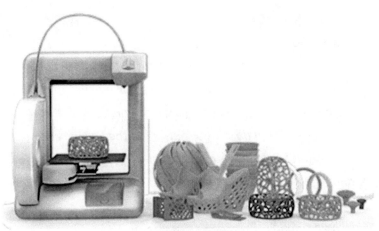

The Cube by 3D Systems

Designing New Products

Just as computers were once seen as little more than overgrown calculators before some of the more innovative applications came along, 3D printers are going to stay in the same hobbyist category until users start printing genuinely creative, worthwhile products. This is where we need to exercise our collective imaginations. This section is an attempt to start the ball rolling by suggesting ways in which we can turn 3D printer outputs in financial profits.

In a recent online question and answer session on the popular tech site Slashdot, Steve Wozniak, the inventor of the Apple Macintosh, clearly demonstrated that being a visionary is much like riding a bicycle, a skill that remains with you your entire life. Notice how his response significantly widens a rather narrow question, and shows that there is always a much bigger picture to consider:

> by medcalf (68293) on Monday October 01, @12:37PM
> (#41514561)
>
> *Do you think 3D printers can rejuvenate the electronics hobbyist market, or that the increasing sophistication and miniaturization of electronics makes that a forlorn goal?*

> by SteveWoz (152247) on Monday October 01, @02:54PM
> (#41516505)
>
> *I think 3D printers may be a big factor in the future hobby market. But sometimes such products have application outside of the hobby market, applications which you can't pin down at first. The Apple] [could do a lot of things but the unseen killer app Visicalc really changed things. Maybe for 3D printers it's low cost and high resolution that will lead to something we can't imagine now. When we started Apple we didn't imagine enough memory to hold a song.*

The main obstacle to the adoption of 3D printers and people using them to build what they want is a lack of awareness of what can be accomplished. The first section of this book concentrated on introducing the technology of additive manufacturing, and investigating its current capabilities. Now it is time to begin thinking about how we can put these capabilities to good use. Early computer pioneers created spreadsheets, AutoCAD and word-processing. They took the existing technology, and came up with excellent uses for all the computing power that they had harnessed. 3D printers are about to go mainstream and history has now come around full circle; we now have this fantastic technology in our hands, but what are we going to do with it?

According to a 2011 *Economist* article, "More than 20% of the output of 3D printers is now final products rather than prototypes, according to Terry Wohlers, who runs a research firm specializing in the field. He predicts that this will rise to 50% by 2020."

Try to think in the right direction when deciding what to print. Current generation technology still has plenty of limitations. Be familiar with your machine's strengths and weaknesses. Ensure that you leverage the strengths and minimize the weaknesses.

For a start, 3D printers are still very slow compared to their high-end 2D laser counterparts; anything that you print should therefore be as small and as lightweight as possible.

The same Economist article continues:

Aircraft-makers have already replaced a lot of the metal in the structure of planes with lightweight carbon-fibre composites. But even a small airliner still contains several tons of costly aerospace-grade titanium. These parts have usually been machined from solid billets, which can result in 90% of the material being cut away. This swarf is no longer of any use for making aircraft.

To make the same part with additive manufacturing starts with a titanium powder. The 3D printer spreads a layer about 20-30 microns (0.02-0.03mm) thick onto a tray where it is fused by lasers or an electron beam. Any surplus powder is reused. Some objects may need a little machining to finish, but they still require only 10 percent of the raw material that would otherwise be needed. Moreover, the process uses less energy than a conventional factory. It is sometimes faster, too.

There are other important benefits. Most metal and plastic parts are designed to be manufactured using traditional methods, which means they can be clunky and contain material not necessary to the part's function but necessary for machining it. This is not true of 3D printing; "You only put material where you need to have material," says Andy Hawkins, lead engineer on the EADS (European Aeronautic Defence and Space Company, parent company of Airbus) project. The parts his team is making are svelte and even elegant. This is because without manufacturing constraints they can be better optimized for their purpose. Compared with a machined part, the printed one is some 60 percent lighter but still as sturdy.

If aerospace engineers can do this, then this should also be our inspiration. What products can we manufacture with designs so elegant that they could reduce as much as 60 percent (or maybe even more) of total volume?

To prove their point, the engineers at EADS have created a fully functioning bicycle, showing how the technology can revolutionize the production of everything, from aircraft and satellites, to much more down to earth forms of transportation. British engineers printed the bike using a powder composed of nylon and metal, which results in a frame that has the strength of steel, while also being 65 percent lighter than aluminium, and yet has only six individual parts.

These fantastic products are a little out of the realm of the beginning 3D printer, requiring DMLS (Direct Metal Laser Sintering) systems, but the principles hold true for many of the products that can be manufactured using the standard range of polymers available for more basic model.

3D Printed Amplifiers

Kickstarter and other crowd-funding sites can be very useful for inspiration when looking for new products to print. For example, one such innovative product line is that of iPhone and iPad amplifiers, simple plastic shells that can boost sound outputs by up to 400 percent. At first, these were very simple designs, but now a company called Simply Amplified has launched a beautifully sculpted range of 3D printed amplifiers known as Symphony Shells. Not only are these designs great to look at, the Urchin, the Murex and the Nautilus are all selling for $35 each. Because of the large number of loyal Apple customers, this has the potential to be a huge market and is something that could do quite well in a rapidly growing market like China.

8

Niche Markets

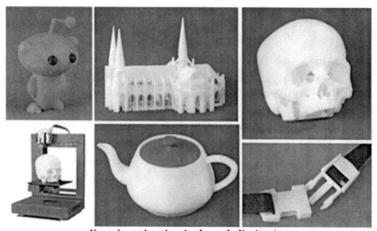

Your imagination is the only limitation

When Apple first released the iPad, few outside the Sci-Fi community knew what a tablet was, let alone what it could be used for. The first tablets may not have been very impressive in terms of features but they were extremely easy to use. They made it so intuitive that anybody could find a use for them in their everyday lives. The 3D printing industry is currently going through this same stage; the market is quickly filling up with simplified, user-friendly versions of highly complex industrial machines, and people are looking for ways to make the technology relevant to their lives. We hope that this section of the book helps somewhat in finding some important breakthroughs.

Begin by looking for small niches rather than huge global markets. Remember that a 3D printer can print just one or a few customized items at a time. Without needing huge investments in retooling and production line changes, the market with the best potential is the small run, quick turn, custom fabrication market where you might only print a hundred, or a dozen, or perhaps even just a single piece. These products generally have such a high margin that the size of the market is far less important. Try not to dream of economies of scale, and instead seek to fill the voids that economies of scale create.

Look for markets that match your capabilities. Currently, if you have a basic printer, you can print small items with a relatively high degree of detail, but not in multiple materials or with very complex internals. This is not to say that these drawbacks will not quickly be overcome, it is simply re-stating the abilities of the current generation of machines. Smaller items are generally better. More detail means a longer print time, but that level of detail could actually be a selling point with some items. Spare parts are often small and limited in availability, which presents a perfect opportunity that is covered in more detail in a later chapter. As the pet market continues to grow, it is obvious that smaller animals need smaller items. We might not be able to print high-end equestrian supplies just yet, but we can still cater to household pets of various miniature descriptions. Highly customized short print runs could be very desirable in the right circumstances, as are additions and extensions to existing products. Here is a detailed look at some of these possibilities.

9

Untapped Markets

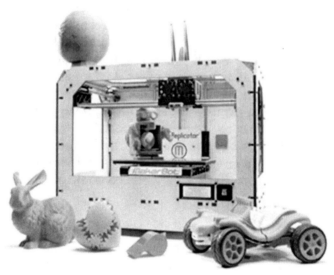

We are the makers

Last year the excellent 'printthat (http://printthat.wordpress.com/)' WordPress blog featured an article entitled "Practical Payback Period" where the author discussed the typical return on investment of a typical $500 3D printer. Although he began with a statement that could be considered contentious, he does go on to show quite clearly that just about anybody can have a 3D printer pay for itself:

> *I doubt that the proliferation of 3D printers will turn a lot of people into "makers." Most people probably aren't going to ever*

design a single printable object. Does that mean they'd never get their money's worth out of a 3D printer? Well, I'd like to argue that the average person absolutely WOULD get their money's worth out of investing in a 3D printer.

While the list of printable objects that he analyzed is interesting, it is hardly a definitive guide for the 3D printing entrepreneur, although it does give some useful information about various price points.

Here are a few of the most enlightening examples:

Project: Tripod mount
Estimated savings - $20.00
Link: http://www.thingiverse.com/thing:8679

Project: Lens gear for follow focus
Estimated savings - $50.00
Link: http://www.thingiverse.com/thing:8658

Project: Peristaltic pump
Estimated savings - $124.00
Link: http://www.thingiverse.com/thing:8652

Project: Solder fume fan mount
Estimated savings - $40.00
Link: http://www.thingiverse.com/thing:8642

Project: Ukulele bridge
Estimated savings - $7.00
Link: http://www.thingiverse.com/thing:8492

Project: Third hand PCB vice
Estimated savings - $20.00
Link: http://www.thingiverse.com/thing:8194

Project: Orange juice squeezer
Estimated savings - $30.00
Link: http://www.thingiverse.com/thing:7924

Project: Collapsible traffic cone
Estimated savings - $12.00

Link: http://www.thingiverse.com/thing:7788

Project: Bird feeder
Estimated savings - $10.00
Link: http://www.thingiverse.com/thing:4847

While many of the other items he examined, such as picture frames, door stops and bag clips, are simply too ubiquitous to be serious money makers, this pared down list does highlight some higher end items that may be a useful guide to future profitability.

If driven by curiosity, then you probably had to jump straight to Wikipedia to find out the function of a peristaltic pump. Unlike the dialysis machine pumps that that are, relatively speaking, better known, Thingiverse.com has a number of pump designs that are intended to be used inside 3D printers, as part of the extrusion process. Even so, this does prove that higher priced items can be produced with these machines. Not that it is likely that kidney failure patients will be buying replacement parts from 3D home printers any time soon, but longer-term trends may surprise us.

While some items, such as the orange squeezer, are more likely to be a 99 cents item down at the dollar store, others do suggest patterns and potential. Bird feeders will be covered later in the Upcycling section, but the commonality of practical, useful tools does otherwise stand out. These items seem complex in concept, and yet simple in terms of production. At the beginning, not everybody will have the design capabilities to come up with new tools; perhaps due to lack of familiarity with the CAD software, but that should not stop us from pursuing simpler concepts. What follows is a look at some of the products that can conceivably be printed almost immediately. Farm out the CAD work if necessary, but it should not be so expensive that you cannot still make large profits on the finished items.

10

Three Pioneering Printers

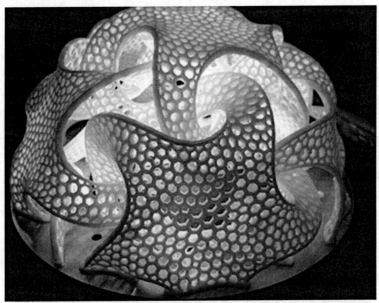

Dodecahedron lamp made by California artist Bathsheba Grossman

Many users are already using their 3D printers to turn a profit, albeit on a slightly smaller scale than some of us would like. Here are three of my favourite current examples, showing good use of ingenuity and practicality.

http://www.bathsheba.com/

One notable member of this first batch of entrepreneurial printers is Bathsheba Grossman. She creates sculptures using computer-aided design and three-dimensional modelling, utilizing

3D printers to physically manifest her ideas. Many of her sculptures are primarily mathematical in nature, often depicting intricate patterns or mathematical oddities. In fact, rather enigmatically she describes her work as being "about life in three dimensions: working with symmetry and balance, getting from the origin to infinity, and always finding beauty in geometry." Even more interesting is the following extract from her website.

> I have a grass-roots business model. I don't limit editions, I price as low as costs permit, and most of my selling is direct to you, by way of this site. My plan is to make these designs available, rather than restrict the supply. It's more like publishing than like gallery-based art marketing: we don't feel that a book has lost anything because many people have read it. In fact it becomes more valuable as it gains readership and currency. With the advent of 3D printing, this is the first moment in art history when sculpture can be, in this sense, published. I think it's the wave of the future.

There are already a dozen or so designs that are downloadable from her website, and we look forward to seeing a lot more.

Interestingly, she does not use any of the big name auction sites, instead using her own website as a sales platform. Her designs start at around $40, for what she calls the smaller 'pony-sized' renditions, and in my opinion, they are worth every penny.

Sean Charlesworth is a toy collector from New York with a degree in 3D modelling and animation, and a fascination for rapid prototyping. When considering his student assignment options, he decided that an octopus vehicle with articulated arms would be visually striking. With inspiration from the Nautilus in Disney's *20,000 Leagues Under the Sea*, and having a distinct steampunk feel, the model was built over the course of two semesters. Jules Verne would be proud of this 'full metal octopus', entitled The OctoPod Underwater Salvage Vehicle, or O.P.U.S. V for short. He documents the entire design and build process on his blog at http://opus5.complex88.com/. The model was printed on an Objet Connex500™ Multi-Material 3D Printing System which has the ability to print with 107 different materials, and his final model certainly shows it.

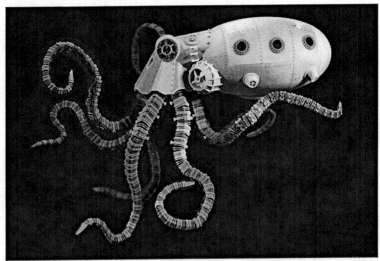

The O.P.U.S. V

Sean's background is in modelling for the entertainment industry and so he used Cinema 4D and Maya, even though they were probably not the best choice when designing something so mechanical. The most complex parts were the tentacles, so he rejected traditional joints and instead printed a flexible core with Objet Tango material and fused Objet Vero knuckles to it for added detail. With a small shaft down the centre and inserted brass armature wires, the tentacles can be posed very dramatically, even though it took four versions to perfect this technique.

The level of detail is truly amazing. All of the arms are fully articulated, and the suckers cupped so that they actually stick. The insides are just as detailed as the exterior. For example, LEDs mark internal hatches and an operational hoist raises and lowers a hook through an iris doorway. The cockpit is filled with buttons and switches, as well as a captain's chair, and lit sonar displays, with portholes lining each side of the cabin.

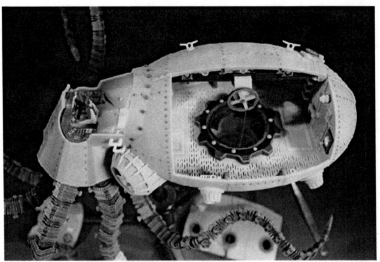

The O.P.U.S. V Interior View

The O.P.U.S. V certainly sets the standard for the rest of us, and must have designers in large companies such as Hasbro seriously worried about their futures. I wonder how long we will have to wait for a full-scale version? This innovative model, as a whole, is a major accomplishment for one person, but many of the clever aspects of it could be transferred to other products. The suction cups, for example, offer possibilities for everything from toys to Halloween pranks, and even devices for more serious uses.

Polymath and material scientist Neri Oxman is best known for her work in environmental design and digital morphogenesis. She currently teaches at the Massachusetts Institute of Technology Media Lab, where she founded the Material Ecology design lab.

http://web.media.mit.edu/~neri/site/projects/projects.html

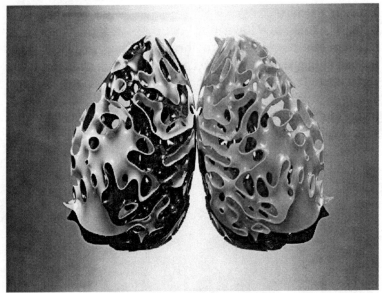

The 3D Printed Art of Neri Oxman

Her latest exhibition at the Centre Pompidou in Paris, entitled "Imaginary Beings: Mythologies of the Not Yet" is a collection of eighteen prototypes for the human body, inspired by Jorge Luis Borges' *Book of Imaginary Beings*, a bestiary and zoological collection of 120 mythical beasts from folklore and literature.

The eighteen nature-inspired, human augmentations are amplifications of mythical human functions such as the ability to fly, or the secret of becoming invisible. "Each 'being' in the series encapsulates what was once considered magic and becomes actuality, as design and its material technologies offer more than meets the skin: spider suits, wing contraptions, and ultra-light helmets; these are all what she considers mythologies of the 'Not Yet'."

Oxman has created a thought provoking selection of futuristic designs inspired by technological advancements, but based on fantasy and popular myth: from the Golem of Prague to robotic exoskeletons, from Daphne's wings to flying machines, from Talos' armor to protective skins. All of the pieces were created using an Objet Connex 500 3D printer, combining a library of algorithms inspired by nature, and the very latest multi-material 3D fabrication techniques. She worked very closely with Objet to customise their technology and take advantage of the latest innovations to project the future in modern design.

Oxman explains: "Revealing nature's design language, this collection of objects represents a library of design principles inspired by nature suggesting that the ancient myth and its futuristic counterpart unite where design fabrication recapitulates fantasy."

She is pushing the boundaries of 3D printing, and for that she deserves our attention. If the next Steve Jobs turns out to be a woman, then it might well be Ms. Neri Oxman.

11

Miniatures

The Multi-Talented Ultimaker

At this stage in the evolution of 3D printers, it makes sense that smaller versions of regular objects are going to be some of the most profitable products. Miniatures have always been popular as luxury items and despite the economic downturn, they still command a captive audience today. If you are unfamiliar with the miniatures market, I would suggest that you start your research in a much earlier period, which has since set the bar for the centuries that have followed.

Hidden away in the Grünes Gewölbe (Green Vaults) of Dresden, is a huge collection of crown jewels and precious objects belonging to

Augustus the Strong, Elector of Saxony. This extravagant megalomaniac was famed for being able to snap horseshoes in two with his bare hands. He was also a hunting fanatic, specialising in fox tossing, where he would hurl live animals high into the air and onto to their deaths, all for his personal pleasure. Despite such cruelties, he was also a great art collector and employed Johann Melchior Dinglinger as his court goldsmith. Dinglinger was one of Europe's greatest goldsmiths, working in the grand rococo style of Cellini and Jamnitzer.

The Birthday of the Grand Moghul Aurangzeb

The most impressive of the three thousand pieces that are on display in the specially commissioned complex of strong rooms, is Dinglinger's vision of the royal court of Aurangzeb, a seventeenth-century Moghul Emperor. Augustus was fascinated by his Indian contemporary, who was believed to be the richest man on Earth. Dinglinger spent nearly eight years working on 'The Birthday of the Grand Moghul Aurangzeb.' The work depicts 137 figures modelled in pure gold, each one ornately enamelled and jewel-encrusted. The Emperor is seated on his ornate throne, giving audience to noblemen, princes, and rajahs, who have all arrived to pay him tribute on his fiftieth birthday. The court is an open-air doll's playhouse, complete with toy soldiers, tiny elephants, horses, and even camels. Richly dressed crowds fill the audience chamber, which is a fantastical rather than entirely accurate representation of a distant land, its charm increasing further because of Dinglinger's wonderfully playful imagination. Instead of Indian motifs, Dinglinger decorated the walls of this playhouse with dragons and pagodas, as if Aurangzeb were not the Moghul Emperor but the Emperor of China. Several groups of envoys arrive from different parts of Asia to honour the wealthy but notoriously cruel ruler. A delegation of Chinese plenipotentiaries that have travelled from the Manchu capital of Shenyang, features one member carrying a tiny fan which even has Chinese characters painted on its reverse. This level of attention to detail is absolutely exquisite. Other figures carry colourful parasols and unusual gifts. The walls of the court are mirrored, cleverly reflecting the proceedings and the glittering enamel, jewels, gold and silver.

Rajahs Paying Tribute

Dinglinger was paid some 55,485 Thalers for what is essentially a Fabergé-style set of toy soldiers. This proves that miniatures have always been a very lucrative market when done well. I therefore urge you to leave the low budget plastic army men to the injection moulders in China, and focus instead on richly imagined, highly detailed pieces that collectors will admire and covet. Here is a selection of practical ideas that you can begin researching and utilizing straight away.

12

Doll's Houses

The world of doll's house furniture is one of those very profitable market niches that does not garner much public attention. This market goes a long way beyond Barbie and Ken, and well into craftsman-made, artisan products, which create a passion and sometimes even an addiction among their adherents.

While there are plenty of brands out there with which you should familiarize yourself, the two that are examined here are Re-ment from Japan, and Bespaq, who seem to use mainly Chinese work. http://www.re-ment.co.jp/

According to the Re-ment's Wikipedia entry "The company's name is derived from a combination of the phrase 're entertainment', alluding to their desire for innovation in the toy market. Established in 1998, Re-ment currently sells a line of highly-detailed miniature food, furniture and animal figures as well as mobile phone charms, doll fashions and magnets." A quick check on eBay will show you that some of the larger sets often fetch $400 or $500 per piece. Again from Wikipedia, many of the Re-ment products "resemble the plastic sample food found in the windows and display cases of restaurants throughout Japan. Targeted at the adult collecting community, these 1/6 scale toys are typically displayed in dioramas and doll houses or used with action figures and fashion doll's such as Blythe or Barbie."

This obviously has the potential to become a bread-and-butter product line for 3D printing manufacturers. What Re-ment basically does is take an ordinary, everyday product, and then scales it down until it is 1/6 or even 1/12 of the original size. With the right .stl file, a 3D printer can do this with almost any object.

http://www.bespaqcorp.com/#link1

Bespaq is a western retailer that prefers to remain more mysterious about its background. They do have a website, but it is still little more than a bare template at the time of publication. Perhaps this goes to show that you really do not need thousands of dollars of flashy internet presence, as long as your product meets market expectations. This about.com page tells much more about the company than the company website.

http://miniatures.about.com/od/dollshousefurniture/p/Be spaq-Dolls-House-Furniture.ht

Despite all the commentary from around the web about 'museum quality' and 'Platinum Editions', much of Bespaqs' stock is manufactured in industrial Anhui, one of the poorest provinces in China, and is widely available in the wholesale markets of Guangzhou, Yiwu and Shenzhen.

While Bespaq seem to have cornered the market in 'classical' furniture, there are still plenty of opportunities for other, smaller producers. For suitable inspiration, look to the eBay seller kenneth9134.2007: (http://myworld.ebay.com/kenneth9134.2007?_trksid=p2047675.l2 559) who, as well as selling Chinese made products, also custom builds his own pieces, including room boxes designed to appeal to an even smaller niche markets. His recent 'Gothic Moon' and 'Chinoiserie' pieces both sold in the region of $500 each.

There are some truly beautiful pieces, with levels of details of which, for the moment, 3D printers can only dream, but this situation will not last long. The day will come soon when items like the classic dollhouse room stand can be printed on inexpensive machines. This is a complete room in miniature, boxed to fit into an existing dollhouse. This means that a room within a room, within a room is completed at an amazing scale of 1/144.

Most 3D fabbers are unlikely to begin at this advanced level, but it is wise to start becoming familiar with eBay's doll's house miniature listings, analyse the market and see where the likely gaps are to be found. One suggestion is to lean towards the more exotic end of the spectrum. There are plenty of factories making miniature Chippendales, but far fewer cater to more minority needs. With my personal experience, an interesting choice would be to choose Buddhist or Tibetan themes and aim at the wealthy West coast market, but you may have an equally interesting background to provide you with suitable inspiration.

A relatively easy starting point when creating doll's house miniatures is to focus on something small but essential, such as curtain poles for example. This part of the market is very buoyant and, even amongst the specialist sellers, there is not currently a great deal of competition. Clare-Bell Brass Works of Maine has been manufacturing the finest quality, handcrafted solid brass miniatures in Colonial, Williamsburg, Americana, Georgian, and Contemporary styles since 1975. One of their sets of three five-inch drapery rods (product no.1785) in their original box recently attracted seventeen bids to finish at $29.76. Of course, there is no reason why miniature brass curtain poles should actually be made of brass; a 3D printer is quite capable of producing telescopic rails, complete with tiny curtain rings in ABS, PLA or even cured resin.

Clare-Bell is an excellent source of inspiration for those new to the doll's house miniatures market. Especially impressive is their range of LED light fixtures, which include intricately detailed chandeliers, floor lamps, wall sconces, table lamps, and candelabra. As LED technology continues to improve and prices drop even further, this will rapidly become a technology and market sector that will be well worth further investigation.

Another important factor in Clare-Bell's success is their focus on the antique market. Period pieces generally fetch higher prices than their contemporary counterparts. A good example of this is Re-ment's Japanese Samurai era vintage food set. Six assorted sushi rolls, a traditional teapot and tea set is far more popular that a similar twentieth-century sushi set, and this factor should be taken into consideration when deciding which items you are going to print.

Of course, this is just a suggestion rather than a hard and fast rule. So before you begin printing a full range of furniture from the classic French comedies, at least investigate a few up dated pieces that are still popular. A great contemporary example is the 'Lights, Camera, Action Photo Studio Set' that was produced exclusively for the 2008 Barbie Convention.

Better yet, rather than recreate existing items why not plunge straight into the OOAK sector of the market. The abbreviation OOAK stands for the expression, "one of a kind." The term originates in yachting to describe a regatta race in which ship builders were allowed to enter as many different models of yachts as they manufactured, but no more than one of each model. Since then, the term has found a different and expanded use as an Internet acronym, especially with regard to the sale of handmade merchandise, which is "one of a kind" with respect to actual production. The term has widespread use in the cottage industry of doll making, but is also used in any manufacturing sector in which the one-of-a-kind nature of a product signifies its value and importance.

Here are two sites to help you familiarise yourself with this market.

http://www.ooakartistemporium.com/
http://ooakguild.com/index.php

The website http://weburbanist.com/ is an extremely useful source for modern interior design inspiration, with the added advantage that post-modern furniture has far less in the way of curlicues and flourishes that your first 3D printer might find difficult to handle. Rococo chaise lounges and high back velvet studded thrones suitable for a Louis XIV revival, might provide a great deal of challenges in term of detail and finish for a basic Reprap. Far easier would be some of the modern classics. How about the Thompson inflatable chair, a 1966 Eero Aarnio Ball, or aluminum Batoidea? How about a classic tube chair or one of those sofas that resembles the front end of a sports car, or maybe even a classic Gaetano Pesce UP5?

If you do not know much about the evolution of chair design, then a good place to start might the BBC documentary, *Are You Sitting Comfortably*, where Alan Yentob, previously Director Geneal and now Creative director of the BBC, explores the history of the chair in all its many forms and functions:

http://docuwiki.net/index.php?title=Are_You_Sitting_Comfortabl y

Of course, larger items are going to require a lot more work in terms of creating suitable .stl files, so perhaps it would be better to start with much smaller items. Maybe some miniature coat hangers as mentioned before, or perhaps some simple S&M gear for the dollhouse dungeon?

13

Action Figures

Most people have imagined themselves as a superhero. Now a company called Firebox can help you out with that by providing a superhero action figure with your own head on it. All you need to do is send them your picture and some cash. Currently, Firebox sells five models: Superman, Batman, Batgirl, Wonder Woman, and the Joker. Unfortunately, the heads do not include the relevant masks and the hair is limited to a thin layer of thermoplastic, which does not look very realistic. Perhaps most disappointing is the price, a whopping $130. Still, this is just an initial experiment and before long, any Comicon attendee or Cosplay conventioneer will be able to sit down in their favourite figurine manufacturer's booth, have their head scanned and the image reproduced onto whatever exclusive line is being offered at the event.

It is not surprising that there is already a shop in the Tokyo electronics district of Akihabara that does exactly this. The main studio of the Clone Factory features a chair in the middle of the room that is surrounded by digital SLRs. Printing is done with a ZPrinter 650 and the final product is known as 'jibun-san', which roughly translates to "myself." It takes a few days to prepare a clone, so if you are visiting Tokyo and want to take it home as a souvenir, make sure you book in advance. The cost is still a whopping 138,000 yen and the surface objects are a bit rough due to the limitations of the printer, but the final product is covered in a top coat to protect the surface.

The website also ran a poll to see which other characters were most popular among consumers. Some of these results might be useful in deciding what kind of products might be successful if you are planning to use your 3D printer for business. Moe girls received a massive 32.47 percent of the vote but other options included, Rei Ayanami, AKB48, Gundams, mini poplars, Gunpla runners, Shinki Renge minions, Gunpla parts, Bishonens, Ecchi Girls, Gackt, Sho Jo Ji Dai, HoN Characters and Vocaloid.

When readers were asked about what kind of body they would prefer, then the following responses proved to be equally revealing. Stormtrooper 6.47 percent, Iron Man 9.37 percent, Master Chief 4.18 percent, Maid Outfit 8.09 percent, Solid Snake 5.86 percent, Perfect Grade Gundam 3.1 percent, Mirai 1.42 percent, Super Sentai 1.55 percent, Gantz 3.91 percent, My own body 17.65 percent and Commander Shepard 1.62 percent.

Other suggestions included Hideyoshi Kinoshita, Char Aznable, Custom Dollfie Heads, Otonashis, Ultimate Hentai Kamen battle outfit, Ryo Hazuki, Akiyama Mio, Black Rock Shooter, Volks or Obitsu bodies, Lolita, Gendo Ikari, Super Tengen Toppa Gurren Lagann, Oppai, Tactical Dreadnaught Armour, Starcraft 2 Marine, Sieg Kaiser Reinhard von Lohengramm, Lady Gaga, SNSD Girls Generation, Mokujin, Kamen Rider, Kenshiro, Cloud Strife, Evangelion and Akatsuki. Unless you are already a hardcore Cosplayer, then you might not have heard of half of these characters, so this could be a good place to start your research: http://www.dannychoo.com/post/en/26119/Human+Cloning+in+Japan.html

A second 3D printing photobooth is now open in Japan, and, those who wish to buy themselves a mini-me can go to the Eye of Gyre exhibition space in Harajuku for the procedure. The miniatures come in three sizes, roughly 4, 6, and 8 inches, and cost the equivalent of $265, $400, and $530 respectively, with modest discounts for groups. This is not a casual, walk-in affair; if you want one of these miniatures, you will need to make reservations ahead of time. Despite the price tag and the need to schedule an appointment, this is some remarkably detailed 3D printing, the likes of which is not often available for public use.

Well positioned on the leading edge of miniature figures is the Moddler Company, located in San Francisco. Started by vfx veteran and Emmy winner John Vegher, Moddler specializes in turning digital models into incredibly detailed physical models with a resolution of only 16 microns (.0006" or .016mm): that is about 1/5th the thickness of a human hair. For comparison, Cubify resolution appears to be 250 microns, (1/4 millimetre, or 1/100 inch), Shapeways frosted ultra-detail (FUD) has a resolution of 0.1 mm (50 microns.).

They also offer 3D scanning services with scanning resolution down to .1mm. Founder John Vegher, has over fourteen years of visual effects experience on such feature films as "The Matrix Reloaded," "The Matrix Revolutions," 'Terminator 3" and "Fantastic Four." Models can be printed in light blue, black and grey and can be primed and painted. Moddler uses an Objet Eden printer and costs around $25 for a single humanoid figure or $80 for something dreadnaught-sized.

> *Like visual effects in the mid 90s, when I began my career working on Judge Dredd, the technology that enables 3D printing has progressed by leaps and bounds in recent years, and possesses incredible creative potential which is just beginning to be realized. Few people outside the industrial world (where it has been used by automotive, aerospace and OEM companies in one form or another for some time) are using it. I am able to utilize my visual effects technical know-how and experience to bring this digital technology to bear in the entertainment industry to help digital designers, directors and producers achieve their creative vision.*

http://moddler.com/

Ease of use is a huge selling point for this new technology, and I already know of one fabricator whose twelve-year-old daughter prints doll house furniture on his MakerBot. By comparison, in a CNC machine shop, the full-time machinist that already has ten years experience is still "the new guy," as there is so much to learn when it comes to machining. The other big drawback is that when you are driving cutting tool through steel stock there are enormous side forces. Vegher describes 3D printers as being small, light, and office friendly, while CNC mills remain huge, nasty machines that weigh thousands of pounds, and will rip off your arm, given half a chance.

One simple example of a typical 3D printed product might be the Cosmic Cube, better known as the Tesseract, one of the most powerful artefacts in the comic book universe of Marvel characters. According to agent Nick Fury, it holds great power that is almost unlimited. Black Widow states that it has enough power to destroy the entire planet. In fact, the Tesseract has the capability to open rifts through space and time. Which is how the Red Skull met his end and how Loki transported himself and later, the Chitauri, to Earth through a portal. More importantly to us, plastic 1:1 replicas of the cube (essentially a small box with a couple of LEDs to make it glow) regularly sell on eBay for around $70. Amazingly the 1/6 version, (ideal for a Reprap) goes for around $20. There are no .stl files on Thingiverse for a cosmic cube, but there are designs for many other kinds of cube, ranging from a selection of Rubik's variations, to at least half a dozen versions of the Companion Cube, an artefact from the first person shooter, Portal.

I grew up near the Palitoy factory in Coalville, Leicestershire, the facility that used to produce the Action Man/GI Joe lines that were so popular with children in the seventies and eighties. The company experienced a huge spike in production when the first Star Wars movies were released, and the facilities struggled to keep up with demand for Snow Walkers and Millennium Falcons. Shortly after that last hurrah, Hasbro took over and the Coalville plant was shut down, with most of the work being outsourced to Southern China. Despite the appalling environmental conditions, I am quite lucky to spend a lot of time in Dongguan and Guangzhou where most of the global 1/6 scale figures production has been relocated. These days the Action Man brand has been replaced by brands like Hot Toys and Soldier Story, and these items have evolved from playthings for boys, to highly desirable collectibles for men with large disposable incomes. It is common for some of the more sought after figures to sell for $1,000 a piece on eBay, and collectors will pay premium prices for accessories with which to customise their acquisitions.

While many lament the relocation of industries like these to Mainland China, the improvements in detail of the figures, their clothing and equipment has been very impressive. The production of 1/6 related items is quickly becoming (if it is not already so) a modern day Chinese art form, equivalent to the porcelain production that came out of Jingdezhen, or the pottery that emerged from Yixing. If you still think that these figures are just plastic dolls, then have a look at the intricately detailed equipment of the Navy Seal UDT Halo Jumper.

Navy Seal UDT Halo Jumper

The amount of equipment included with this figure and the level of detail of all that tiny gear is quite impressive.

Another good example is the Deluxe Suit Up Gantry from the movie Iron Man. This one sixth-scale replica sports an impressive eighty plus articulation points and even has a light up feature. The rear hydraulic arm features a total of nine individual articulated joints, and fifteen individual joints on the mechanical claw that attaches the helmet alone. The accessories and accoutrements of these twelve-inch figures are light years ahead of the cheap toy soldiers of yesteryear in terms of skill and production. It is quite clear that the action figure collectors of Hong Kong and the West have developed some discerning, and demanding, tastes.

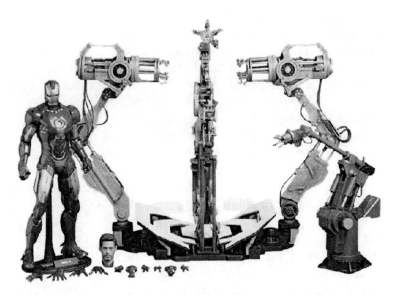

Deluxe Suit Up Gantry

With the advent of 3D printers, it is foreseeable that the 1/6 scale area will improve faster than ever before. While current ranges are dominated by military figures and blockbuster movie characters, there is the possibility for a much broader scope of action figures that will appeal to a much wider base of collectors. One only has to look at the Japanese market to see where this is heading, with lines such as Ashley Wood and Cygirls, moving increasingly away from battlefield replicas and combat figures. Before 3D printers, producers were limited by relatively large production runs that were required to make to make a new line profitable, for example; the Pearl River Delta factories in Guangdong require a minimum order of five thousand pieces. With a 3D printer, it is now possible to do just a handful of figures or accessories, and at the same time add cachet to your product by its inherent rareness.

I urge you to study this fascinating niche market see the opportunities that await. Of all the lines that are exported back to the West, these are definitely some of the most fascinating. Additionally, the market is sizeable enough for me to share here with you some of my trade secrets, new projects and product developments that are currently already under way, without any fear for my own business. The only issue is where to start on this vast subject.

Firstly, some of the key rules that apply to 3D printers: keep your products as small as possible, respect the limits of the current generation of open source machines. Focus on uniqueness to ensure that you are taking full advantage of the machines one-off capabilities. Keep all of this in mind when you decide which 1/6 scale items you are going to print, and you will soon be producing highly profitable items for this growing niche market.

Perhaps the easiest way to explain this is to simply provide some examples of the lines upon which my designers and printers are currently working. I have always felt uncomfortable selling products that were directly linked to the military or that actively promoted violence. This first occurred to me when I bought a knuckleduster in China for less than a dollar and resold it on eBay in the UK for nearly fifty UK pounds, a profit of almost a hundred fold. Initially I was ecstatic at discovering such a high margin item, and was soon fantasising about all the money that I would be making if I could send home a dozen of these a week. It slowly dawned on me what I was actually selling, when a friend from the East End of London explained to me why the police come down so hard on anybody carrying brass knuckles. Unlike a knife, which can be used for many purposes, brass knuckles have no legitimate purpose except to cause physical injury. Even a flick knife can be used to cut up fruit or carve a stick, whereas a set of knuckledusters has only one purpose. This revelation made me look very carefully at all the products that I was exporting, and made me quite uncomfortable with more than a few of them. I was doing very well with police patches and military insignia at the time, but felt very disquieted with the so-called morale patches commissioned by Blackwater, with their expressions of racial hatred, despite the fact that they were really good sellers. It was at that time that I started commissioning my own non-military designs, and enjoyed surprisingly good sales, as well as much improved peace of mind.

The same has been true for 1/6 scale figures, and I now try not to resell items that are overly militaristic or that needlessly glorify violence. I personally am much happier with lines that celebrate the historical, or encourage educational aspects. While I was familiarising myself with 12" scale products, I was experimenting with all kinds of sniper rifles, rocket launchers and field artillery. Nowadays, I still buy a few of these pieces, but I have my designers customise them into victoriental steampunk blunderbusses or intergalactic plasma repeaters. I am not trying to give you a lesson in morality here, but this will help to explain why I am focussing on some of the more obscure items of the genre.

Of course, not everybody has these concerns. I have one friend that is using his 3D printer to create 1/6 scale weapons from the *Game of Thrones* series, a gratuitously violent show if ever there was one. 1/1 scale replicas of swords such as Arya Stark's Needle, Jon Snow's Longclaw and Eddard Stark's Ice regularly fetch thousands of dollars on eBay, and so it makes perfect sense that 1/6 scale versions will sell like hot cakes to collectors and customizers. I have already seen the sample prints that he has completed of Robert's Warhammer, and they are most impressive in terms of quality and detail, and will look even better when fully painted.

Actually, this raises an important point about being located in the production zone where all of these items are manufactured. It allows us to see what is being made and where there are important gaps in the market. Game of Thrones for example has been a massive hit all year, and still there are hardly any examples of related merchandise in the wholesale markets, making it clear that a nimble 3D printer has a good opportunity to jump in long before the big boys begin to dominate. Another advantage is that a product can be developed and produced in a fraction of the time that it takes a goliath like Hasbro to set up tooling, negotiate production and arrange marketing. A home-based 3D printer, even if they are using a freelance SolidWorks designer based halfway around the world, can still have a saleable product online in just a couple of weeks.

I personally try to stay away from movie and TV tie-ins, in order to avoid the unwanted attention of copyright lawyers and other corporate mercenaries. Early in 2012, there was a great deal of hype surrounding the release of the *Prometheus* movie, Ridley Scott's first science fiction movie in years, and the resurrection of the *Aliens* saga. I was very tempted to jump on this bandwagon and work on some 1/6 scale replicas, and maybe even some 28mm models. As it turned out, the film proved to rather disappointing in terms of costume design and special effects. I was similarly tempted to print a few items based on the hugely successful *Hunger Games* movie, but there again, the props and the equipment were basic to say the least.

These days, I tend to focus more on genres and old classics rather than the latest released films and recent TV hits. Not only does this keep me away from potential legal issues, it gives my creativity much more freedom in terms of what I can imagine or design. As a concrete example, why would I copy items straight from a show like *Buffy* or *Twilight*, when I can pick and choose from the entire *Dracula* mythology, and print out entirely unique vampire hunting equipment and suitably Gothic paraphernalia? Why would I want to copy wholesale from films such as *Judge Dee* and *Tai Chi Zero*, when I can develop my own range of completely individual oriental steampunk gizmos? Why should I go to the trouble of licensing tired old *Star Wars* clichés, when there is an entire galaxy of pacifist space opera and galactic exploration literature out there with which I can experiment?

Of course, I am not the only one thinking in this way. One of the larger twelve inch figure factories in Guangzhou is moving away from the traditional battle field soldiers, and developing the domestic Chinese market with representations of Bruce Lee, Ip Man and Jayden Yuan. Others are exploring the growth of anime, manga and cosplay, with many taking a distinctly hentai direction. I myself am looking very closely at the UK cybergoth sub culture, and small diorama pieces for the customisation crowd.

Of course, just because I do not want to deal in arms, whatever the scale, you may not have the same sentiments. Companies like Zytoys are already producing a selection of the latest semi-automatic sniper rifles such as the Cheytac M200 Intervention and the USMC M4A05, incorporating incredible detail, that most current open source 3D printers would to struggle to replicate. Rather that compete directly with these guys, I would prefer to push the boundaries of my machine into other areas. Uniqueness sells well in this market, so I personally would look at some of the stranger rifle manifestations in the arms markets. Items such as the 'round-the-corner' rifle or the Kriss Super V sub-machine gun would both be interesting contenders. The internet movie firearms database (http://www.imfdb.org/wiki/Main_Page) would certainly be a very useful resource if you do decide to go in this direction.

It is not surprising to learn that there is already an entire subculture devoted to exotic weaponry.

The 'SINZA—Exotic Automatic' (http://sinza.forumotion.com/) for example, is a discussion forum for exotic weapon design and construction with nearly twenty five thousand members. Fans, builders and collectors share their experiences with a wide range of automatic bladed weapons, including switch-blades and xiphoids (a type of retractable forearm dagger). There are schematics for projects as exotic as assassin railblades and even a machete shooting slingshot crossbow. More traditional firearms crafts can be observed at a range of other sites including:

homegunsmith.com
weaponsguild.net
weaponeer.net

One aspect that is very popular with collectors is increased functionality. If you can use your design skills and your 3D printer to add some kind of working mechanism to your model, then you will be well ahead of the crowd. As examples here, I am talking about crossbows that can load and launch miniature bolts, or grappling hook launchers that can actually fire their missiles a reasonable distance. Collectors will pay a premium for these kinds of innovations.

Look carefully at the performance of 1/6 accessories sales on eBay and you will soon notice how even the smallest accessories can fetch $10 or $20. Learn as much as you can about this market and try to put yourself in the shoes of collectors who are willing to pay these premium prices, so that in the future, you too can meet their particular needs. Guangdong might be ground central in terms of production, but it is the retail outlets of places like Richmond House in Mong Kok, Hong Kong that are where some of the most avid collectors congregate. Take a look at their Facebook pages to see what is currently hot, pages like Figures Station (http://www.facebook.com/station23987654) where the pre-order announcements will give you a good idea of what is popular, and what is currently in the works.

Another resource that I find especially useful is the One Sixth Warriors website (http://www.onesixthwarriors.com/forum/front-page-news/).

Despite the growing number of collectors, there are very few documentaries on the subject of 1/6 action figures, compared to say, railway modelling for example. There is however one film that I would highly recommend entitled 'Marwencol,' that shows action figure artwork taken to a totally different level, as well as focussing on the valuable therapeutic aspects of the hobby. Here is the Internet Movie Database Review of the film.

On April 8, 2000, Mark Hogancamp was brutally attacked by five men in his hometown of Kingston, New York. The assault left the ex-navyman, carpenter, and showroom designer in a coma for nine days; he emerged with brain damage that initially made it impossible for him to walk, eat, or speak. Physical and occupational therapy helped him regain basic motor skills, but after less than a year he discovered that without insurance, he could no longer afford it. Determined "not to let those five guys win," Hogancamp turned to art as a therapeutic tool. He revisited his childhood hobbies of collecting toy soldiers and building and painting models. Commandeering a pile of scrap wood left behind by a contractor, he constructed "Marwencol," a fictional Belgian town built to one-sixth scale in his backyard. He populated it with military figurines and Barbie dolls representing World War II personages like Patton and Hitler as well as stand-ins for himself, his friends, and his family. Finally, he dusted off an old camera and used it to capture staged events ranging from pitched battles between occupying German and American forces to catfights in the town bar.

http://www.imdb.com/title/tt1391092/

14

Gaming Miniatures

Most entrepreneurs could be forgiven for thinking that gaming miniatures are an insignificant sector of the market. On the contrary, Reaper Miniatures launched their Bones Kickstarter campaign (http://www.kickstarter.com/projects/1513061270/reaper-miniatures-bones-an-evolution-of-gaming-min) on July 23, 2012 asking for $30,000. By the time that their campaign ended, just over a month later on August 25, 2012, nearly 18,000 people had pledged more than three and a half million dollars. If you still think that miniatures are a minority niche market not worth your attention, then you might want to think again. These miniatures are not mere tokens, like the Monopoly 'old boot', but are highly collectible and mostly intended to be assembled and painted by the purchaser. There are even derivative markets for professionally painted miniatures on eBay and specialist hobby forums.

According to Wikipedia, the 25/28 mm models (≈1:73.2) are "the most common size of miniatures, as...used by Games Workshop. While original 25 mm figures matched 1/76 models (4 mm scale or 00 gauge), there developed wide upwards variation in figure height. True 28 mm figures are close to 1/64 models (S scale), but may appear larger due to bulky sculpting and thick bases."

There are already a handful of 3D printers beginning to serve the gaming community with some smaller items, but the rest of the market is wide open, and there are excellent opportunities in producing high quality diorama items in the $100 to $200 range. I am experimenting extensively in this area, but I am keen to share my experiences so that others can also take up the baton.

While Games Workshop is one of the largest players in this niche, this has not always been the case. Many readers who have enjoyed this hobby might have fond memories of painting up busty Barsoomian slave girls from Ral Partha or Grenadier produced dragon riders. High quality hand painted figures still sell well, but for beginning 3D printers, smaller accessories might be a better starting point. Simple spears currently fetch a couple of dollars, but that is just the beginning as the range of medieval weapons is huge. A good point of reference to begin with would be some of John Mollo's arms and uniforms books. Mollo was the costume designer responsible for the first Alien movie, as well as the first Star Wars movie, and so his credits are impeccable. Once you have produced your fill of halberds and morning stars, you can move on to the classic *Palladium Book of Exotic Weapons*, by Matthew Balent. Here you will find all kinds of bizarre killingry from lantern shields to bohemian fighting spears, each one a fine challenge for your 3D printer.

If you would prefer something a little less violent, then perhaps a better place to start would be scenery. Giant mushrooms and monster ferns sell well, depending on their quality and aesthetic value. I am currently trying some simpler organic models such as gnarly tree stumps and that D&D favourite, the Beholder. This is a demonic floating eyeball, loaded with extraneous eye stalks. Looking at some of the old TSR representations, (the original publisher of the Dungeons and Dragons rulebooks) this particular beast is desperately due for a visual makeover. If you are a fan of the swords and sorcery genre, there are all kinds of equipment and accessories that you can print for other eager gamers. A few people are already covering the bases with items such as sacks, barrels and chests, but I am trying to outdo these guys with heavily bound treasure caskets filled with tiny precious gems, and barrows of tempting loot that will make any player character drool. Topside, I am experimenting with gallows, gibbets and guillotines, but it is underground where I am going to have real fun. Thingiverse has long had some basic files for coffins and gargoyles, but I already have my designers working on some highly customised editions that Vincent Price would be proud of. Down in the crypts and the oubliettes, you will find all kinds of skeletal remains surrounding evil altars and monstrous effigies. Cauldrons, chopping blocks and dimension portals will undoubtedly prove popular additions in this area. Evil Priests and demonic monks in long robes and dark cowls are always popular with gamers, and ideal for beginning printers, as the details are mainly cloth folds rather than complicated weapons and extremities.

Make your products really shine by adding in lots of detail and perhaps even some electronics. Many readers will have already seen Tony Stark's high-yield arc reactor power source, that has been recreated on Thingiverse, but think how well that kind of LED technology would do in dungeon fixtures, ranging from simple cressets to eerily glowing high altars. Of course, there will always be a demand for suitably Gothic pillars and arches, as well as a full gamut of heavy doors and portcullis gateways. In addition, my own fascination with secret passageways is bound to have a strong influence on the models that I will be producing in the future.

There are many specialist sellers making a good living out of 28mm gaming on eBay, and some of the best in terms of inspiration, include **dzur2003** (myworld.ebay.com/dzur2003?_trksid= p2047675.l2559),

monkeydogworkshop
(http://myworld.ebay.com/monkeydogworkshop?_trksid=p204767 5.l2559) (who does a nice line of flames and ruins) and enjar (myworld.ebay.com/enjar?_trksid=p2047675.l2559) (with some great DIY terrain models.)

Dutchmogul
(http://myworld.ebay.com/dutchmogul?_trksid=p2047675.l2559) is one seller who is really breaking ground in 3D printing by offering models that have been downloaded directly from the Thingiverse repository. As an avid science fiction fan, I am keen to replicate his success.

The following items of scenery already exist, but there is always room for improvement and customization: consoles, comms stations and computer banks. Everything from power generator, regulators and holographic projection units to satellite dishes and jack in the box alien egg chambers. My chief SolidWorks designer is currently splicing together a teleporter pad and the lid of an iris box, to create a command deck portal that will be the envy of every star ship captain in the Federation.

It does not really matter whether you work in the realm of star ships or silver dragons, the real key to this market is contextualised setting; collectors will pay a lot more for an entire scene than they will for individual pieces. Therefore, a fully equipped dungeon is worth much more than the sum of its parts. The most lucrative opportunity lies in complete haunted graveyards and fully equipped torture pits, or fully furnished command decks and loading bays. Some of the traditional manufactures that have excelled in this field are companies such as Armorcast, Micro Art, War Torn Worlds and

Itar's Workshop. By combining quality design and imaginative construction, sets from these producers very often push the hundred-dollar boundary. Often times they will be simple trenches or walls, ponds or temples. Occasionally there are complex catwalks or bunkers, but the market is as large as the imaginations of designers and collectors alike.

While Games Workshop might be the Goliath in terms of production, it is other, smaller companies that are leading the way in this hobby. One example of the cutting edge of modern miniature design is Hitech Miniatures (http://hitechminiatures.com/), whose products sell very well on eBay. Most of the figurines are so highly complex and detailed that they are probably best left to the professional artists, but there are a few reliable areas where the newcomer can break into this market. Rather than look at producing actual figures, focus instead on accessories, bases and plinths, items like those that Hitech and others already produces, and items that are always popular with customisers and painters. Accessories in the Hitech range include helmets, shields and halberd blades, but that is just a starting point, as discussed extensively above.

Bases and plinths offer up a great opportunity to produce high margin items. Small, undecorated bases are so common that they go for mere pennies. Specialised bases on the other hand command a premium. For example, the Bone Field Bases offered by Secret Weapon Miniatures (http://secretweaponminiatures.com/), which are a little bit larger than usual at 60mm and one eBay seller described them as being "of a shallow depression design and are meant to be filled with a blood recipe to give the impression of being ankle deep in gore." These gruesome bases sell for $5 to $10 each at time of writing. Secret Weapon already produces nearly twenty-five different styles of base ranging from lava flows to broken flagstones, but there is still room to experiment here. I am working on some rune mosaics and Himalayan village cobblestones but I am sure that you can think of many others.

For the more advanced fabber, a step beyond accessories and bases might be simple war machines, such as bunkers and gun turrets, both of which sell well. The manufacturer Flames of War does some very attractive, but relatively simple reinforced concrete machine gun nests, which most 3D printers should be able to embellish and improve upon. Think about rocket launcher emplacements, anti-aircraft guns and a selection of tank traps, all easy to produce, but always popular.

Large pieces like these need not be one hundred percent printed. Sometimes the bulkier parts of the assembly can be upcycled from ordinary household products. The set of pictures below demonstrates how this works, showing the various stages in constructing a model radioactive waste silo. On a piece like this, the most sensible parts to print are the more complicated details. These include the piping, the riveting and the valve handles, all time consuming to make by hand, sometimes impossible to mould, but a cinch for a 3D printer.

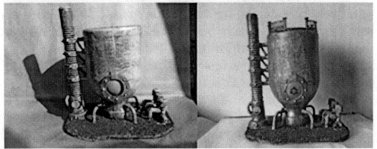

Radioactive Waste Silos

For those seeking more inspiration an excellent recommendation would be the website http://www.coolminiornot.com/. Here the best artists in the field come together to share their latest creations and it is a fantastic place to see how and where the hobby is pushing its boundaries. Another professional modeller website worthy of note is Industria Mechanika (http://industriamechanika.com/blog/gallery/), who produce some really imaginative steampunk-styled models.

For those still in need of convincing that toy soldiers can be a very profitable line, some fine examples can be found within the ranges produced by King and Country. Founded in 1984 in Hong

Kong by two expatriate Scots, Andy Neilson and Laura McAllister, this company represents the top end of the market. Andy is a former Royal Marine Commando and has been interested in toy soldiers since a very young age. They produce a number of ranges of all-metal, hand-painted 1/30 scale military and civilian miniatures.

In addition, Andy's brother Gordon oversees an impressive range of scale model buildings, fighting vehicles, tanks, ships and aircraft, all made of polyresin. Production is centred just across the border in Mainland China, while the models themselves are sold at premium locations on Hong Kong Island. I think it is particularly telling that the King and Country store I visit most frequently is in Pacific Place, Admiralty, one of the territories most upmarket shopping complexes. Up on the second floor, King and Country's neighbours include an Aquascutum and a Bang and Olufson. Clearly, these are not your common or garden toy soldiers.

Among their best-selling ranges are the "Streets of Old Hong Kong"—a colourful series of Chinese figures and buildings depicting street life in-turn-of-the century Colonial Hong Kong. Despite the high prices, these are some of the more outstanding miniatures in the market, mainly because they are non-militaristic, something that is comparatively rare among figures at this scale. Other ranges stretch across a very wide spectrum, from "The Life of Jesus" all the way up to "The Leibstandarte Adolf Hitler Regimental Band".

King and Country figurines are 1/30 scale or 60mm, slightly larger than the average 1/32 scale or 54mm toy soldiers, giving more room for adding lifelike detail to the faces of their exquisite miniatures. This is clearly reflected in the prices that these figures command. Expect to pay almost a $100 for a single figure, tanks at maybe twice that price, and a whole lot more for their spectacular dioramas. Recent postings on a collector's forum indicate that their Arnhem Bridge setting now commands a whopping $10,000.

Part of the skill in producing and selling products for wargamers and roleplayers is setting the right price point. To illustrate this, here are two recent examples of larger science fiction assault weapons that would make interesting 3D printer projects. By comparing both models side by side, one can glean a number of insights into why one sold very quickly and the other simply languished in the idea-only stages.

The first is an eBay listing from earlier in the year, pasted here in its entirety:

OOP Armorcast Mad Cat/Timber Wolf.

Mad Cat

Out-of-print heavy stalker tank from Mark Mondragon's DreamForge-Games, famous for the Gabriel and large-scale Leviathan models. This is the big puppy. It comes with all the parts and, for those parts already put together, put together cleanly and well. It also comes with an additional PPC arm. This is one of the iconic Mechs of the Battletech/Mechwarrior universe, but you already know that, don't you. This beautiful model was produced years ago and is now out of print and exceedingly rare. It is a perfect scale to be a Warhammer 40K super-heavy walker for Apocalypse games. Before it became a collectible, some have used this model as a Tau titan as well. Made from polyurethane and created for 25-28mm tabletop war games, it stands 5½" tall 10" long and 6¾" wide when completed. It has customizable hard points (weapon mounts) and your choice of two different types of main guns and four varieties of secondary weapons. The main hull, solid cast in one piece, is 7" long, and with the gun barrel attached, stretches out to nearly 11"! This would be great for any 28mm wargame and would be a sweet Imperial Guard titan in games of Apocalypse. A review of this model was done in 2005, at the following website:

http://www.starshipmodeler.com/rv/vh_bwidow.htm

This very thorough description helped the auction garner a dozen bids and eventually sold for $366

Now let us look at a more recent Kickstarter campaign for a similar heavy assault vehicle that launched on December 16, 2011.

Ghost In The Shell T08A2 Tank

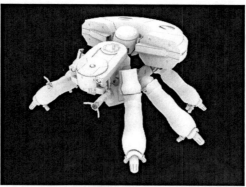

T08A2 Tank

A 1/6 scale T08A2 Tank will be given life right here on Kickstarter.

The Ghost in the Shell is an iconic anime film envisioned by legendary Japanese director Mamoru Oshii. The 1996 feature animation deals with the exploits of the cyborg Major Motoko Kusanagi, a member of a covert operations division known as Section 9. The division specializes in fighting technology-related crimes and hi-tech enemies. One of these such enemies is the T08A2 Heavy Assault Tank.

This six-legged, spider-like tank comes complete with machine guns and cannons attached to its imposing frame. We wanted to create a toy that was well designed, engineered and manufactured from premium materials. A product that your friends would stop In surprise and ask you where the hell you got it from?? There will be two releases of the figure; a regular pose-able figure of 5000 (1/12th scale (12in x 19in), and a deluxe limited edition of 1000 (1/6th scale 22 in x 24in). The limited edition will have battle damage, a diorama of the battle scene from the movie, and a battle torn Motoko Kusanagi (We are working on the figure having camouflage that is similar to the movies effects).

The tanks head as well as appendages can rotate and lock into position. The legs of the tank are pose-able and allow the figure to be placed in a number of very cool poses.

This figure measures at 12" in height and 24" in diameter.

So here is where you come in. Like most designers our dream is to eventually bring our ideas to life but funding, manufacturing and distributing a new product is a different story. Kickstarter is a great way to obtain our vision without sacrificing the integrity of the project. We love creating awesome works without the big company politics. By pledging at least $50 you are being put on the pre-order list for the T08A2 tank and helping make what we believe is a very cool project a reality.

We hope that you are inspired and excited by the idea and choose to support the project. Please spread the word and share with all your friends. Everyone knows at least one person that loves anime.

THE TANK. One limited Batou 1/6th scale Action figure (ghost in the shell movie version) Estimated delivery: Apr 2012 Pledge $1,000 or more—1 backer

The most obvious difference between these two items is the price, and that is clearly why the Ghost In The Shell T08A2 Tank did not succeed in attracting enough backers to go into production. Perhaps the biggest mistake in the second description is that this project was openly described as a toy. If you want to charge very high prices, then you would be well advised not to describe your products as toys. Ferrari and Lamborghini do not describe their sports cars as toys and neither should you.

A closer look at the two descriptions reveals a number of other telling factors. Both are filled with rich detail about the construction and dimensions of the model involved, but the main difference is that the first seller showed clearly that the model have a very specific purpose for wargamers. He even recommends games for which it would be most suitable. The second description clearly fails to do this, and is trying to sell the piece simply as a decorative item. Impressive though the construction may be, this particular niche market is simply too small for items that are only to be used as ornaments or memorabilia. While the Batou tank might do well in Hong Kong or Japan, the designer may have over estimated the popularity of anime in the west, and might have been more successful if he had chosen to build something that was more widely known by western Science Fiction fans. One other thing to consider is the scale. The Mad Cat was designed on the 28mm scale, while the Batou was supposed to be built at the 1/6 scale which is much, much larger and on a par with GI Joe or Action Man figures. While there is a considerable market for 1/6 figures as I have already discussed, it is very different from the 28mm market, and holds a number of pitfalls that must be avoided by the 3D printer.

To summarize, pick your price points carefully, ensure that your customers have a good practical use for your items and make sure that you produce them at the right scale.

Kickstarter has at least a dozen very well funded projects involving 28mm miniature figures, from which you can learn how the market responds. Here is one of the more bizarre examples:

Low Life Miniatures by Andy Hopp
A highly detailed line of miniatures based on the weird and whimsical Low Life game by Andy Hopp (but usable anywhere). Launched: August 24, 2012 Funding ended: September 23, 2012 http://www.kickstarter.com/projects/1359565526/low-life-miniatures. 309 Backers pledged $52,966 of $4,000 goal.

Low Life is a roleplaying game setting produced by Andy Hopp and published by Pinnacle Entertainment Group and Mutha Oith Creations. It has been critically and publicly acclaimed for its uniqueness, originality, and artwork. The most recent book, *The Whole Hole*, will be in stores soon, as will Dementalism, the first Low Life card game.

> *GAZILLIONS of years in the future...*
> *Every possible calamity, cataclysm, apocalypse, and cosmic hangnail has befallen our beloved Mutha Oith during a bygone era known as The Time of The Flush. Now, After the Wipe, the ancient Hoomanrace is extinct and the wobbly orb is wrecked. Oith's current denizens evolved from the lowliest of the low: the resilient roach, the indomitable worm, the everlasting snack cake - the dregs that survived.*

The initial set included nine figures, all produced in 30mm scale. This project just goes to show that even the most outrageous figures can become a profitable line of miniature figures, and in this case the project garnered more that ten times its original request in cash pledges. Reaper, King and Country and even Low Life all go to show that the miniatures market is a bustling, active one that is ideal for home 3D printers.

Apart from terrain and scenery for wargamers, there are plenty of other options out there to produce items for role players. One of my favourites is the dice tower. There are dozens of basic acrylic versions of these but a well-designed, custom piece should appeal to a discerning enthusiast with deep pockets. This will mean an attractive design, an imaginative drop sequence and a large landing area. If you are looking for inspiration, a recent eBay auction for a "Handcrafted Tigerstripe Maple" Dice Tower Boot Chamber Board Games with tray ended at $67.95.

Another key item for role players is a good selection of dice. There are some intriguing designs for steampunk dice showcased on the Tinkercad site, a repository similar to Thingiverse. There are designs for four-, six-, eight- and twelve-sided models. There are also skeleton dice, cage dice and you might even want to think about creating a set of loaded dice as a novelty item.

15

Radio-Controlled Scale Models

Paparazzi Drone

Thanks to some rather dubious military decisions, drone has become a very dirty word in the twenty-first century. Though likely to conjure images of covert military operations, it is not a connotation that the term, or the technology, necessarily implies. Fundamentally, a UAV or drone is merely an unpiloted flying machine, and that is a potentially useful thing to have for all sorts of civilian applications. According to a recent *Wired* magazine article (which is well worth a look), the US army owns and operates a grand total of 7,494 of these high tech aerial assassins, but, interestingly, this number is easily eclipsed by the number of ordinary folks that own simpler home versions of the technology. One company alone, DIY Drones www.diydrones.com/), claims to have shipped more than

1,000 units in the last couple of years, and eBay lists around two thousand drone items at any one time.

The truth is that drones are much more than the unmanned missiles that people might perceive them to be. The toy industry and the hobbyist community have already caught up and taken over the military industrial complex in terms of price and availability, just as the home-brew computer club knocked corporate computing off its lofty perch back in the seventies. This is especially interesting as many people are now claiming that 3D printing may do the same to big manufacturing quite soon.

In the meantime, the civil drone market is flourishing. Just a quick scan of eBay will show you that all kinds of fantastic machines exist in this market, from small 'parrot' drones controlled with an iPad or iPhone to completely assembled octocopters capable of carrying full-sized digital SLR cameras. In between, you will find hexacopters, quadrocopters, microcopters and multicopters. All have autopilots but no guided missiles, and are usually limited to a few hundred feet, but evolution in this field is moving at an incredibly advanced pace. Just as smart phones have made some incredible leaps over the last few years, drones or UAVs (Unmanned Aerial Vehicles) are making parallel strides based on exactly the same technology.

Fortunately, for 3D printers, the technology is not quite perfect just yet; trial and error calibration means that there is a big market in replacing broken struts and blades. Motor mounts, frames and landing gear are all possible with even the most basic of printers. The Carboncore Multicopter listed on Thingiverse is a mean looking machine that looks as though it has come right out of some dystopian cyberpunk nightmare, yet all of the components can be made on a home 3D printer. (http://www.thingiverse.com/thing:23570).

The whole drone market is still at a very early stage of development. While the military have found special uses for these machines, they have now escaped into the public sphere, where future developments are a tantalising market possibility. Just as the internet morphed and transformed itself into a very different beast once it was freed from the shackles of DARPA, who knows what uses drones will be put to once the price drops down to that of other everyday appliances. I personally am looking forward to my ultra-sensitive metal detector drone, autonomously covering half a dozen fields and creating a highly detailed treasure map of hidden goodies, while I sit having my lunch under a nearby oak tree. Just think of all the monotonous metal detector swinging saved by not have to cover the entire area by hand!

Of course, not every drone listed on eBay is the kind described above. Drones are integral part of the science fiction scene and there is a multitude of types on the market that are popular with modellers and gamers alike. Tiny 28mm Tau Empire gun drones are common and inexpensive, but there are other possibilities for creative 3D printers. Miniatures designer Forgeworld (www.forgeworld.co.uk/) does a nice line of Tau Drone Sentry Turrets, which retail around $80 a pair, but there is plenty of scope for other sci-fi drones. I was especially impressed by the very nicely done 'Dr. Who custom Dalek Aerial Targeting Drone' which recently fetched 40 UK pounds with six separate bidders on eBay. (As an aside, while Dr Who is still a very collectible show, there is also a massive amount of competition in related items. That other Classic BBC sci-fi series, Blake's 7, has equally ardent fans and a market that is far less saturated. Rather than printing Daleks and Tardis replicas, why not try Liberator communicator bracelets, and Scorpio clip guns. These kinds of items have a much higher scarcity and the potential for much better sales.)

Science fiction drones come in all shapes and sizes, from Giger-inspired aliens to cute little guys like Duey from Silent Running. Readers might be surprised at the size of some UAVs. Weifang Tianxiang Aerospace Industry Co. Ltd. Of Shandong manufactures an unmanned helicopter capable of flying as high as 3,000 meters at a top speed of 161 km per hour, with a payload of 80 kg, and can be controlled from a maximum distance of 150 km or programmed to fly automatically. The helicopter is used to conduct geological surveys as well as aid in emergency rescue operations, aerial photography and forest fire prevention.

Drones of all types are definitely an up and coming segment of the market and must be researched in detail in order to find long-term profitable niches. The intention of the aforementioned information is to provide some useful inspiration to do just that.

Further reading:
Here come the drones! By Chris Anderson
http://www.wired.co.uk/magazine/archive/2012/08/features/here-come-the-drones

http://diydrones.com/
This is the home for everything about amateur Unmanned Aerial

Vehicles (UAVs). This community created the Arduino-compatible ArduPilot, the world's first universal autopilot (planes, copters of all sorts, ground rovers). The APM 2 autopilot hardware runs a variety of powerful free Arduino-based UAV software systems.

There is also the business end of the community at

http://store.diydrones.com/

To come right up to date with this exciting technology, look to some of the Youtube videos posted by the The Perching Project of the Biomimetics and Dexterous Manipulation Lab at Stanford University. (https://www.youtube.com/user/bdmlstanford) Their experimental footage of fixed wing models that can perch and observe are eye opening to say the least. Demonstrations of 'precise aggressive manoeuvres' with autonomous quadrotor swarms at the GRASP Lab, University of Pennsylvania, including flips and flight through very small windows, are acrobatically impressive enough to make a humming bird envious, and will impress even the most well informed of anti-drone activists. For a balanced and broader perspective there is also a three part 2012 documentary by Alternate Focus entitled *Drone Wars*. The film covers the history of unmanned aerial vehicles and their trial uses in wars since the early part of the twentieth century. It features commentary by the designers of such vehicles, as well as congressional representatives who defend their use. The film also interviews critics such as Tom Hayden, along with historians and business owners who explain the down side of targeted killing from a safe distance by armchair "video game warriors."

Even more relevant for readers interested in the business opportunities associated with UAVs is an episode of the Australian current affairs show *Foreign Correspondent*. Series 20 Episode 21, called 'Rise of the Machines', focuses much more of the positive commercial aspects of this technology than other programs.

16

'Green' Products

Hermit crab shellters by Elizabeth Dema

Just because a 3D printer extrudes fossil fuel based plastic, does not mean that the products cannot be a huge benefit to the environment.

Rocket Pot containers, developed by Peter Lawton of Australia, root-prune trees by guiding root tips to open air. Plants can be held safely for much longer than in other pots. The roots do not spiral and plants look healthy. When the Rocket Pot is removed and the tree is planted, the abundance of active roots grow outwards and downwards to colonize the new site. The tree grows like a rocket, hence the name. Best of all the pots are easily reproduced for home use on a 3D printer.

http://www.rocketpot.com.au/

I really like the Maddigan's Milker as a potential 3D printing project.

http://maggidans.com/milker.htm
http://www.youtube.com/paulwheaton12#p/u/0/GsDyp9gf17s

Currently priced at $45 each, these would go down very well in the emerging Urban Farming market on eBay or Taobao.

Most home aquaponics owners struggle when they come to fabricating the bell valve. Despite the fact that there is a great set of instructions on the web:
http://www.doityourself.com/stry/aquaponics-how-a-bell-valve-works

This is a difficult and sometimes frustrating part to manufacture. Unless of course you have a 3D printer. Again these would sell well on eBay and Etsy at around the $20 mark.

Did you know that the American hermit crab population is currently facing a massive housing shortage and that there are simply not enough shells left on beaches for hermit crabs to inhabit? Many have been trying to shelter themselves in glass jars, plastic containers and pieces of human refuse. Thus far, scientists are not sure whether this problem is due to pollution, or global warming or maybe over-collecting of seashells by humans. In an attempt to remedy this environmental problem, scientist and artist Elizabeth Demaray has decided to help out by researching hermit crabs' tastes and preferences, and designing tiny plastic houses that can be printed on 3D printers.

The new designs have a number of advantages. They are much lighter than the calcium carbonate of seashells, so do not take as much energy to carry. Plastic is non-biodegradable, and so these new houses are expected to outlast the crabs themselves. In her laboratory beta tests, 25% of hermit crabs opted to dump their old seashell house and upgrade to a new plastic house. Demaray believes that her designs will be even more popular in the wild, where hermit crabs grow much faster and the housing shortage is more pronounced. Although Demaray is currently looking for corporate sponsorship for this project, the thought of logo-ed hermit crabs wandering the beaches seems rather implausible. Fortunately, Thingiverse already hosts fifteen different shellter designs, ranging from conches to turritellas, and from nautili to golden rectangles.

None of these are currently available on eBay or Etsy, even though they are striking, attractive designs. www.tinyhousedesign.com/2008/07/14/one-square-inch-house-the-hand-up-project/

In 2007, hunters shot an Alaskan bald eagle in the face and left her for dead, but she was then found by Jane Fink Cantwell, a bird conservationist. The bird's entire upper beak had been shot off, the equivalent of losing a limb for birds that use their beaks for feeding and preening feathers, and clearly a death sentence for this majestic creature. Janie and her small volunteer staff at the Raptor Chapter kept the bird alive through liquid tube-feeding until mechanical engineer Nate Calvin was able create a prosthetic beak using a 3D printed nylon-based polymer. This magnificent bird of prey has since recovered to full health and has been named Beauty, and most deservedly so.

This work was much more of an effort to increase the quality of the bird's captive life, rather than facilitate a release back into the wild with a new beak, but that should not restrict future projects. Contrary to initial thoughts, the beak actually needs to be 'weaker' not 'stronger' since the limitation is the connection points and the purchase available at those attachments. A new design is in the planning stages which will have 'give points' designed to allow the beak to flex before damage can be done at the connection points.

Beauty the Eagle

The success of this project has led to the consideration of how 3D printing can be applied to the rehabilitation of other animals afflicted with similar damage. With the financial rise of the Chinese has also come a growth in the black market trafficking of endangered species body parts. These most famously include shark fins and tiger penis, sometimes for consumption, sometimes for pseudo-scientific medicine. One of the most horrific trends is the growth in illegal poaching of rhinos for their highly prized horns. A single specimen can now command up to $500,000 from Chinese buyers. In the most recent cases, well-funded poachers with high powered rifles and night vision goggles have been flying night raids into nature reserves by private helicopter. Upon immobilising these magnificent creatures, they proceed to hack off the horns, either with machetes or chainsaws. Unsurprisingly, few of the rhinos survive, situations quite similar to enormous sharks killed simply for a single fin.

Printing a replacement horn for a rhino is obviously many magnitudes more difficult that printing a beak for an eagle, but this is a project that is being pursued. Designing a replacement is feasible from a mechanical standpoint, but has some incredible challenges from a practical viewpoint (controlling the animal during and after the procedure, limiting/assessing a 'typical' use/load scenario after attachment).

Chainsaw Attack Survivor

Alex English of ProtoParadigm (www.protoparadigm.com/), offers many free designs for garden accessories. Here are four to be starting with:

1. The seed spacer sows seeds at different widths in a

hexagonal pattern. This way the leaves of plants will shade the soil, help control weeds, and produce more per square foot from your garden. .stl files with 1.5", 2", 3", and 4" widths are available.

2. Slug traps have a small reservoir about half full with beer. Greedy slugs are caught and make tasty treats for the ducks.

3. The garden trellis-netting hook, designed for hanging a garden trellis net for peas and green beans.

4. A watering spout that turns any standard two-litre soft drinks bottle into a watering can.

Shaan Hurley of Salt Lake City has used his 3D printer to produce cabbage moth (plutella xylostella) and cabbage butterfly (pieris rapae) decoys to save his back yard vegetables.
http://www.instructables.com/id/3D-Printing-a-Cabbage-Moth-Butterfly-Decoy-to-Sa/

Having seen the tiny white eggs all over his cabbages, which went on to hatch into caterpillars that voraciously devoured all his greens, he decided to work with the territorial nature of these insects. This is a brilliant alternative to spraying pounds of toxic chemicals all over your home-grown vegetables, and begs the question of what other decoys could be printed. A small hanging kestrel or similarly sized bird of prey will keep the sparrows off that freshly sown lawn seed, a pole-mounted owl with a swivel head to keep the starlings on their toes, or a long-legged heron to keep competitors away from your precious Koi carp? The warty snout of a 'gator or the half-submerged fin of a great white might have a similar effect on human trespassers.

Decoys for attraction are mostly used by hunters but might also be utilised by permaculturists and other enlightened gardeners to attract beneficial species to their projects. Pigeons and doves provide valuable nitrogen fertilizer to orchards and pasture for example. Perhaps another innovative and practical use of your printer might be to produce some miniature representations of the produce to use as markers for freshly planted seeds.

Evil Face Planter

The 'Evil Face Planter (www.thingiverse.com/thing:21191)' has been downloaded more than seven hundred times in the last year, making it one of the most popular stl files on Thingiverse. The 'splinter effect' seen on the planter was apparently unintentional, the result of a misaligned platform. The overhangs and cracks absolutely make this print, giving it a fantastic weathered wood look. These layer gaps are an excellent example of how mistakes can transform good designs into masterpieces. In fact, that is what design evolution is all about. This just shows the positive effects of being able to copy freely, and how such freedom brings about unexpected improvements. One downloader printed the first 12mm with clear PLA, so that he can still see the roots of the plant growing, and the rest with glow-in-the-dark Glowbug Yellow. A true work of art and something only possible with this kind of distributed production and open-source styled collaboration.

17

Upcycling

The work of Samuel Bernier, upcycler extraordinaire

According to Wikipedia, "Upcycling is the process of converting waste materials or useless products into new materials or products of better quality or a higher environmental value." Recycling in fact has two halves: Downcycling means smashing things up into their component parts, before purifying and reconstituting them. Upcycling on the other hand, takes the original form, and improves upon it, sometimes aesthetically, more often it terms of practicality. Wikipedia ends the article with this insightful statement:

> *"Upcycling" has shown significant growth across the United States. For example, the number of products on Etsy with the*

word "upcycled" increased from about 7,900 in January 2010 to nearly 30,000 a year later—an increase of 275 percent. As of October 2011, that number stood at nearly 167,000, an additional increase of 450%.

This is a clear indication of a rapidly growing market, and one good source of inspiration, also pointed out by Wikipedia, is the Inhabitat.com site. Here, for example, there are sections for Landscape, Interiors, Furniture, Products, Gadgets, Fashion, Graphics, Transportation, and Energy, with many reproducible ideas suitable for 3D printers.

Hobbyist Samuel Bernier has some fantastic ideas on his site, including caps that will turn an old tin can into a birdhouse, or those same used beans tins into a set of dumbbells. His Instructables.com page is home to some very interesting finished products.

Dirk Vander Kooij has produced a number of items made from ground-up recycled CD cases, which are extruded by his industrial robot's arm in a continuous thread, layer by layer. Rather than downcycling the jewel cases, why not follow the Bernier concept and simply upcycle them for completely new purposes? A 3D printer can easily knock out plastic inserts that transform the use of a CD case. One insert might be to hold coins, another to hold a treasured piece of jewellery such as a necklace or a bracelet. Thingiverse already has some good models of chess sets. If scaled down these could fit snugly inside an old jewel case. The same is possible for a travel version of backgammon, draughts, or a wide range of other board games. 100 Amazing Upcycling Ideas Anyone Can Do (http://toponline engineeringdegree.com/?page_id=116) is an inspirational web page that hosts, well, one hundred ideas for upcycling of course!

18

Spares

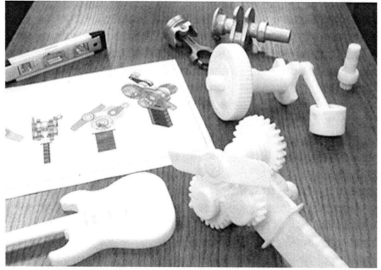

Even complex working parts are capable of being produced with the latest generation of home printers

3D printers could utterly change the concept of the hardware store, as we know it. Craft and DIY stores could, in the near future "stock" all manner of screws, bolts, nuts and washers without needing the space for miles and miles of cupboards and shelving. All they would need is a library of 3D models and everything that a customer requires is made to order. Adding a 3D scanner to the equipment list would also allow for custom replacement parts. Imagine your local garage storing designs instead of parts, and printing that new water pump on demand, complete with all the latest upgrades and tweaks. The workshop could print up small trim parts rather than having to maintain a full inventory, or have them shipped in. It is doubtful that Gutenberg foresaw his printing press evolving into anything like Kinkos, but this might be one direction in which 3D printing is heading. These shops would certainly need a good selection of equipment, not only to provide the right specs and textures, but also the correct tensile properties. Portable 3D printers could also change the repair industry as we know it too, allowing a repair technician to produce parts as and where needed.

The beginning of this trend is apparent when looking at eBay sellers such as natspaul123 (http://myworld.ebay.com/natspaul 123/). For $100, he is currently selling (among other 3D printer parts) a full kit of Mendel Max 1.5 printed parts. The complete set includes many upgrades, including a Wades accessible tilt screw extruder with herringbone gears, lm8uu Y carriage, Lm8uu X carriage, and upgraded feet. Of course, these are ABS plastic parts and do not include any of the 'vitamins' or electronics, but this is certainly the beginning of a new trend. Anybody with a 3D printer can now start printing sets of parts so that their machine can be replicated. In fact, because of the continuous nature of upgrades for these machines, you could even print an entirely upgraded version of your current machine. The desktop machines such as RepRap and Makerbot are quickly proving to be popular all over the world. This has meant that some of the components are hard to find in Europe because supply is not meeting demand. As sales continue to grow, this is definitely an area worthy of further investigation.

So, what else in the way of spares can you be producing to ensure that your 3D printer is paying for itself? Here are a few suggestions to give you a head start.

K'nex may not be as famous as Lego or Meccano, but it could be a good place to start for 3D printers. Many of the parts are relatively small pieces of simply designed plastic, such as connectors and pulley wheels, and therefore should be quite manageable, even on some of the earlier versions of the first generation DIY printers. A quick look at the K'nex section of eBay should provide plenty of inspiration, as many spares are still in high demand. Simple blue spacer rings are only about a quarter of an inch in diameter, and yet lots of twenty still sell well, representing the lower end of the market. Gears, pulleys and rods are all popular, and so it would be worth analyzing sales over a period to see which parts are the most in-demand.

Meccano and Lego are much more mainstream than K'nex, but

are still worth market research. Meccano collectors tend to look at the age and the collectability of the piece more than anything else, so assume that replicated pieces will not be as desirable as vintage parts. Even so, there will be some spares that will always be in demand and, with tools like eBay, it has become a simple analytical process to determine which parts are most sought after. Determining the demand for various Lego parts is a more difficult process due to the vast array of parts available and the size of the market, but is a worthy endeavor given the longevity of the product line and the seemingly never-ending demand. The other problem is quality control; The Lego Company notoriously makes their bricks with very tight tolerances, far smaller than most homebrew machines can achieve just yet. If your machine can achieve these high standards, bear in mind that avid collectors tend to go for large, complete sets. The original Millennium Falcon, for example, still sells for around $1,000, but the amount of time necessary to produce such a large set, with almost 1,000 pieces, would be prohibitive. Perhaps instead, focus on spare parts for similar in-demand sets. After all, if it is so popular, parts are bound to be lost, broken and misplaced along the way.

One more area worth investigation might be that of adaptors and universal joints. For example, US-based F.A.T Lab and Sy-Lab have recently created the Free Universal Construction Kit, a set of three hundred 3D printed "adapter" blocks. This allows different types of brick toys to be assembled together. Users can build with a multitude of bricks like LEGO, Lincoln Logs, K'NEX, Zome and Tinkerbots. If you already have a 3D printer of your own, the templates are freely downloadable in .stl format.

Another potentially profitable area for the budding 3D entrepreneur is Radio Controlled Racing Cars. Some of the higher end models such as the Savage X Super Truck or the HPI Baja 5T sell for thousands of dollars. There are some important brand names to look for in this arena as always, and these include names like Kyosho, Traxxas and Losi. While engines and chassis are still mainly made of metal, there are plenty of opportunities for 3D printers to fill a demand for plastic accessories such as wheels, fins, bumpers etc. Classic models have had recent revivals, Tamiya has occasionally re-issued popular classics such as the Midnight Pumpkin, the Frog and the Lunchbox, and there is an ever-present community dedicated to modifying and racing the Clodbuster model. Tamiya also manufactures more realistic radio controlled models, such as the

Subaru Brat (tamiyausa.com/product /item.php?product-id=84237) and the ever-popular Bruiser (tamiyausa.com /product /item.php?product-id=58519). Spare parts, accessories and upgrades for these radio controlled models make for a lively market.

If you are a fan of all things radio controlled, then another market to explore is micro-heli parts. A surprisingly large number of spare parts are fashioned from plastic and reproducible by a 3D printer. For example, the 'MicroHeli Blade SR CNC Delrin Main Gear W/Hub' for use with Honey Bee FP helicopters has a MicroHeli list price of $22.99 and weighs only 10.4 grams. The Tail Push Rod Guide (MH-MCPX005T2), designed to replace stock plastic tail servo guides for Align T-REX 450 PRO helicopters. It is CNC cut with lightweight delrin, and has screws to be able to adjust and secure the position of the push rod guide on the T-REX 450 PRO tail boom. It weighs just 0.7g but retails for $14.99. CNC Blue tail bevel gears are an upgrade described as improving tail control performance on the WALKERA 35 helicopters, and are described as being favoured by many expert model chopper pilots. At just 1.6 grams these lightweight parts are a good choice for potential marketing, but material suitability should be checked when planning to produce spares for flying objects.

Many different toys and collectibles require spares and replacement parts. Obviously some are going to be easier to print, and it would take a long time to develop expert knowledge of the many different parts that go to make up Transformers, for example, and you would need to have considerable expertise and experience in this very specialized area. Do you for example know what a 'Machinder Chogokin Popy Popinika Japanese Mazinger 7' looks like? If not, then it might be a better idea to find a niche with which you are more familiar. There again, a six inch Transformers Masterpiece Optimus Prime "MEGATRON GUN" still goes for $50 a pop, so the market potential could justify an investment of time to expand your knowledge.

One of the easiest forms of market research is browsing eBay's completed sales with search terms like parts and replacements. Anyone with an eBay account can do this and it can help to build a good picture of what products sell well. Also, start sifting through the attic and look for those small parts and accessories that are often lost over time. Action Man and GI Joe sets are often missing some missiles or other small extras. Successfully replicating these parts not only will make many collectors very happy, but should also be provide a good profit at the same time.

Think about all the toy brands of which you are aware, and then think carefully about what your printer can handle. You might want to try plastic shell bodies for slot cars. Others might prefer custom-made dinosaurs as additions (or replacements) for the popular Aurora prehistoric range. Another opportunity is accessories for the WWF wrestling toy range. Small parts ranging from briefcases and folding chairs to benches and folding stepladders are easily accomplished with a 3D printer. A table, chair, ladder combo can see prices of up to $25 from collectors, which leaves a good margin for the printer.

In the appendix, there is a complete guide to miniature scales for reference. A strong understanding of these scales and their common uses is crucial to knowing where to focus your manufacturing efforts. NASCAR fans prefer 1:18 accessories for their workshop and pit stop dioramas. Other auto enthusiasts lean more towards 1:64 or even 1:87 scales, however these scales require a higher resolution and therefore a more expensive machine. Inspiration for accessories and parts for auto-racing dioramas and custom model builders are easily found in real life, your own garage may even end up being a source of ideas!

Just as modelers need spares, so do gamers. Twenty sided dice for D&D players and other role-players start at a few dollars each, and are an ideal product for a well-calibrated printer. One seller is already doing a good trade in spare parts for the classic board game 'Operation'. How about replacement parts for Cluedo, Mousetrap or Sorry? Everybody inevitably loses at least one of these tiny pieces during a toy's lifetime. Studying the parts section in toys and games on eBay can provide all the data needed to make decisions about what to print. How about some replacement or even some newly designed Spirograph rings and gears, or maybe some custom parts for Mr. Potato Head?

Game tokens of all kinds are always in demand and an easy place to start is with the 30mm replacement red and yellow checkers for the Connect Four game. This old favourite sometimes often also requires replacement legs and side sliders. Battleships is another candidate, having lots of parts that end up down the back of the sofa or in the dog. Both ships and pegs are very feasible for even the most basic 3D printer. Hungry Hippo had plastic marbles that always went missing after a few sessions, as did many of the plastic Ker-Plunk straws. Fortunately, for those seeking opportunity, the same is often true for Cranium, Happy Trails, Crazy Forts, Game of life, Trouble and

Boggle. There are a great many fantasy board games that will also need spare pieces including Dark Tower, Dragon Strike, Green Ghost, Witch and Heroquest. More serious strategy games are perhaps the worst option for 3D printers; games such as Stratego and Conquest have large numbers of intricate parts, as do Axis & Allies and Risk, both of which are well represented on eBay. Lesser-known games, due to scarcity, are a better choice of niche market for the newcomer.

Battling Tops is the most famous of a number of games where players launch spinning tops into an arena. They game was introduced by Ideal in 1968, and their simple construction makes them ideal for a 3D printer project. The object of the game is to have the last standing spinning top. The game takes place on a circular concave arena with four spinning top launch positions. Players wind a string (attached to a pull-tab) around their tops, place them in the launch positions, then pull the tab vigorously to release the top. The concave surface forces the tops together to battle.

A newer incarnation of the game was released under the name Beyblades, by Japanese toy manufacturer Takara Tomy, in 2000. The game includes spinning tops, an arena and a 'launcher'—a device for bringing the spinning top up to speed, with an integral ripcord. As in the original game, the last top still spinning wins. The first generation of Beyblade tops are made entirely of plastic, with the exception of weight disks, and consist of four basic parts: Bit Chip, Attack Ring, Weight Disk, and Blade Base. In official competitions, players are allowed to repaint the Beys but not modify or create their own parts. Even so, that does not mean that attack rings that give added advantage over other blades would not be popular amongst home aficionados.

For more information, visit the Beyblade wiki site (beyblade.wikia.com /wiki /Main_Page) or the World Beyblade (www.worldbeyblade.org/) website

One market already being exploited by 3D printers is that of parts for Nerf guns. Thingiverse already has a number of .stl files for such parts and the market on eBay is quite buoyant. If you are not familiar with this brand, then I suggest, these recent wired articles are great introductions to the subject:

How Nerf Became the World's Best Purveyor of Big Guns for Kids (http://www.wired.com/design/2012/09/how-nerf-became-worlds-best-purveyor-of-big-guns-for-kids/)

A History of Nerf and the Pursuit of the Perfect Blaster (www.wired.co.uk/news/ archive/2012-09-10/nerf?page=all)

This popular toy, originally licensed by Parker Brothers, was dubbed "Nerf" after a kind of foam bumper used to push drag racing cars to the starting line, which is in turn an acronym that stands for "Non-Expanding Recreational Foam." Nerf blasters have a very well developed modding community devoted to customising and upgrading these toy guns. Many prefer the available disc projectiles to the darts. The discs are more slender and they easily slip into small crevices, meaning that a great deal quickly go missing, allowing a good opportunity for 3D printers to provide replacements, for a fee.

Spares and replacements are definitely going to become the bread and butter of some printers. This is an advantageous arrangement given parts no longer have to be stored in warehouses or distribution centers, incurring vast overheads. You simply have an archive of 3D designs on your computer, a photo of the finished product, and then you print on demand. Over time, vast libraries of parts will build up both in the public and private domain. In fact, this has already been going on for hundreds of years. The British Royal Naval Dockyards in Plymouth already has for centuries maintained a large storage area containing wooden templates of nearly every part imaginable needed to build a warship.

The following story of an antique sewing machine collector recounts how 3D printers are already starting to make impacts in this area.

On the subway ride home I thought I'd peed myself, and discovered why the seller had been so eager to get rid of the machine. Cradled in my lap was a fairly rare 1965 overlock machine, Singer 460/13, and somewhere between 72nd and 14th Street it produced a large, oily wet spot spreading from crotch to mid-thigh on my jeans. It was leaking oil like crazy, a detail the Craigslist seller had neglected to mention while taking my money.

Back at home I took the machine apart, put it back together and spent a week getting it running again. I also found the source of the leak: A ruined gasket whose online price is $1.50. It's an irregularly-shaped 2-ounce piece of rubber and no one in the *world seems to stock it any more. This isn't the first time one of my projects has stalled for want of a sub-10-dollar, no-longer-available part. And this is why I want a magic 3D printer that can make things out of metal, plastic, and rubber.*

I might be screwed, but I was heartened to read MakerBot's story of Malcolm Messiter, a guy who fixes old machines like me. Messiter's machines, however, play music. His 1970 Robert Goble self-playing harpsichord was out of commission with bad "jacks," the little plastic bits that hold the thingies that pluck the strings in place.

To replace all the jacks on this instrument with custom wood pieces (there are 183 of them), Malcolm would have had to shell out something like $3000. And having custom plastic pieces made for the job? Forget about it.

But Malcolm has The Replicator, which can make anything, including 183 harpsichord jacks, and then 183 more. And now he has a functioning harpsichord. As far as we know, and as far as Malcolm knows, he is the first to perform this life-saving operation on a harpsichord. Like so many people on Thingiverse and others in the MakerBot world, he's a total pioneer.

Malcolm tells me that, all told, these pieces average 3.62 grams when he makes them at 75% infill and one shell. MakerBot sells Natural ABS for $43 per kilogram. This means the entire repair set costs about $28.48 in materials.

Of course, this is not just about making useful spares, combining accessible spare part designs with the process of upcycling opens up possibilities for new designs and enhancements for our favorite items. This is just what Ponoko user 'ZoeF (www.ponoko.com /showroom /ZoeF/profile)' has created for his Ponoko showroom, in the form of a circular border frame for the popular strategy board-game, Settlers of Catan. The design is for an interlocking border to be made on a 3D printer out of just about any 3mm material available. The designer has claimed a Non Commercial No Derivatives license, and is asking US$5.00 for the files, but nobody doubted it would be long before similar designs were being sold on eBay. There are already two separate sellers selling very nice borders:

1. mccheyne_beeman
(http://myworld.ebay.com/mccheyne_beeman/)
2. cfarrkc
(http://myworld.ebay.com/cfarrkc/?_trksid=p4340.l2559)

eBay has a relatively few sellers doing business in modern spares and expansion parts, although a few games like Wedgits and Hive are supported. Suggestions with potential include 'Peg Perego' and Thomas the Tank Engine track expansions, which command relatively high prices, although something of that scale will require a substantial amount of ABS, so a recycler is an advisable investment as well.

Another interesting example of this kind of innovation is the printable straw connector. Now you can create all kinds of wildly imaginative geodesic spheres, tensegrity towers and abstract sculptures, just with a packet or two of straws. For full details of how to print out these connectors, consult this 'instructables (http://www.instructables.com/id/3D-Printed-Straw-Sculptures/)' page.

There are too many different potential niches to list all of them here, but these starting points are all fine examples of printing inspiration. How about specializing in parts for model rocketry? This is one of the most active 'toy' sections on eBay, and there is definitely room in the market for nose cones, baffles and mounts.

Did you know that immediately prior to setting up Microsoft, Bill Gates was working for a company called Micro Instrumentation and Telemetry Systems (MITS) in Albuquerque, New Mexico, developing the programming language BASIC? Much of their work was to produce miniaturized telemetry modules for model rockets. Soon after this, they developed the first commercially successful home computer, the Altair 8800. Everybody knows that Bill Gates dropped out of Harvard when he saw the potential of the personal computer, thereby becoming the world's first software multi-billionaire. If it worked for him, could it not work for you?

It is said that history does not repeat itself, but there really does seem to be a strong connection between rocket hobbyists and computer whizzes. Father-and-son backyard experiments are already sending smart phones up on weather balloons to snap pictures at the edge of the earth's atmosphere.

Lunar Robotics is working on an open source Kickstarter project that will enable anybody to launch a 4-to-6-foot rocket to the moon carrying any three pound payload for just $5,000. Launching the rocket into space from a balloon is expected to be as easy as "fire and forget," and a simple ham radio aboard the rocket could beam telemetry data back to the human user on the ground. True to the DIY spirit, the team also plans to use mostly commercially available parts for building the rocket.

And here is the interesting part:

> *"Ideally, the goal is for everything to be off-the-shelf or as close to off-the-shelf as possible," Pierce explained. "Anything that's not could be manufactured with a 3D printer or CNC machine."*

If the evolution of personal computers was anything to go by, we can expect the cost of this overall project to drop dramatically as designers and 3D printers constantly improve the basic parts set.

Teenage Engineering, the Swedish manufacturer of the popular synthesizer, the OP-1 has responded to criticism about the high costs of buying and shipping its collection of accessories by letting customers 'print' their own parts. While perhaps like me, you have never heard of the $849 OP-1 synthesizer, among musicians it has long boasted cult status. Resembling a children's toy, it is all-in-one compact sampler, four-track recorder and mixer, sequencer, MIDI controller and synth, not to mention a growing variety of accessories that extend its capabilities even further.

For users outside of Scandinavia, the shipping cost of the OP-1 accessories all the way from Stockholm is very high, and so as an alternative, the company has decided to put CAD files of the parts onto an online library in both .step and .stl format for free download. This is the first company that I have seen to offer printable parts, and is an incredibly smart move, as it takes away the need to warehouse and distribute replacements. Knobs and dials are the perfect static, detachable objects with which to begin this new paradigm. Technical manuals are already distributed digitally, and anyone that wants a hard copy can print one, so why not do the same with accessories?

More exciting yet, this also means that their fans have an opportunity to modify and customize aspects of their synthesizers. The company has already stated, "It will be exciting to see what people will be doing with the 3D models, how many will print them, and if anyone even will go ahead and do custom modifications." How long will it be before tinkerers are adding gears and pulleys to the tops of wheel and crank caps to create amazing new sound effects for example?

It will be fascinating to see how this develops in the future. If the company decides to make all replacement parts and add-ons downloadable and 3D printable, they might not need to manufacture parts at all in the future; they can simply release the file and the synthesizer owners can print it at home. This immediately does away with the need to mass-produce, hold inventory or distribute. All they need to do is design and release. Will it improve customer loyalty in the longer term? Will customers prefer to buy machines which they know they can obtain spare parts, rather than those which later become obsolete and fall into obscurity?

The development has already caused quite a stir in the various synthesizer discussion forums, with many users pledging to open up their precision calipers and throw up models for parts that they already own. There is excited talk of printing obsolete parts and 'hot rodding' existing gear. There are even requests for specific parts such as Moog knobs, sliders for DX synths and Casio SK8 battery covers. Owners constantly complain that these small parts seem to 'grow legs', and would probably order two or three for just this reason. How long will it be before a whole website for synth parts from classic lost knobs, to cases for popular DIY projects springs up? If you have an interest in music, then this is an opportunity that you cannot afford to ignore.

It is clear that the vast market in spare parts will create many opportunities for those looking to monetize the 3D printer investment. Although it might seem rather counter intuitive, this wide open playing field might in fact turn out to be one of the first manufacturing battle grounds. At a recent conference on rapid prototyping a delegate from the appliance manufacturer Whirlpool was asked if they were not thrilled and delighted at the prospect of not having to supply simple parts in the future. He dryly replied that spares are one of their most profitable lines of business.

19

Metaphysical

Pyramids for health

Despite the fact that eBay has recently banned the sale of all spells and items with purported 'magic' qualities, there is still a big market for 'new age' items, so it is time to drop all those preconceptions and put your imagination into overdrive.

We have already talked extensively about miniatures for doll's houses, and a range of Victorian séance items would certainly be popular items. From simple Ouija boards and phrenology busts to complex ether collecting electrical devices, you could really let your imagination run riot here.

Perhaps an easier place to start might be with Pyramid connectors. Many people believe that pyramids have ancient powers beyond the understanding of modern science. Back in 1959 for example, Karl Drbal, a radio engineer from Czechoslovakia was awarded a patent (No. 91304) indicating that that the cavity of a little cardboard model of the Great Pyramid of Cheops can affect the steel edge of a razor blade.

Apart from sharpening razors, other experiments have shown that pyramids really do have some strange and inexplicable properties. These include purification, dehydration, and preservation. For a longer list, consult this page (www.iempowerself. com/84_pyramid _power.html) on the web.

A range of connector kits for various sized pyramids is a good way to start into the metaphysics market. Start with a five-piece set, utilizing the same 51 degree 51 minutes angle as was used at the Great Pyramid of Giza. This makes an ideal kit for making large pyramids for meditation or smaller pyramids for healing. In fact, sizes of 1 foot to 12 feet pyramids are possible using these connecting corners.

In China and South East Asia, it is becoming more and more common to see solar powered Tibetan prayer wheels adorning the dashboards of both public and private vehicles. Just like nodding dogs and fluffy dice before them, these are quickly becoming hot items in the West. The number of different designs is growing each year. What started with simple spinning temple bells has quickly progressed to highly detailed representations of the goddess Shiva with a hundred windmilling arms. The solar rotating displays used on the base structures for these prayer wheels are available on eBay for just a few dollars. While these designs are popular in religious locations such as Thailand and Yunnan, there is certainly room for original 3D printed designs, as well as adapting the technology to other religions and perhaps even other areas of interest. While Tibetan prayer wheels might be preferred in pious locations such as Lhasa, Chiang Mai and Shangri-La, Westerners might prefer to have a revolving sports hero adorning their dashboards. Hello Kitties might be popular in Japan and perhaps windmills in Holland. How about a small orrery for science geeks amongst us and maybe even a section of Babbage's Difference Engine for the computer nerds? The way that 3D printers are developing, putting together a complex gear system that moves in multiple planes would not be out of the question. The only limit here is your imagination.

While some people might laugh at the claims made for 3D metaforms, the prices these items command justify serious consideration. 3D metaforms are ideal for additive manufacturing processes. They are comparatively easy to model in current software but are very difficult to sculpt, model or fabricate with traditional methods. Believers claim that the 3D Star is an empowering tool for experiencing higher consciousness and the prices paid for such items reflect the level of commitment people have to this belief.

Some simple market research in the New Age arena will yield many possibilities for an innovative fabber and their 3D printer. The 5D Star Tetrahedron is one of the most basic shapes found in the three dimensional universe, and yet is believed by some to take the ubiquitous, chaotic EMF radiation surrounding us and move it into coherent life enhancing rhythms. Other shapes with more impressive names boast an even wider range of claimed abilities. Star icosahedrons are often associated with emotional healing properties, while the metatron cube is a powerful form for manifestation and personal integration, allowing mortal users to experience the divine power of creation. At least that is what is says in the sales pitch.

Golden Mean Dividers are a tool for measuring artistic balance, using the Golden Mean. This mathematical proportion (also known as Phi, The Golden Ratio and The Divine Proportion) is a simple ratio (1 to 1.618) that is considered aesthetically beautiful, and has been used in art and architecture for thousands of years. It repeatedly shows up in nature and in the human body, particularly the human facial structure. Working the same way as a drawing compass or callipers, the dividers maintain the ratio of the distance from a to b as the Golden Mean, as well the ratio between a, and whole width (a+b) as the same proportion.

An open source set of plans have been made available at ponoko.com, by Kiwi designer, Nick Taylor of Weird Sky Designs, who has been manufacturing some of the very best examples on the market or more than three years. His versions come in three sizes, and include smart leather or wooden cases. His customers come from a very wide range of professions; musicians, furniture-makers, specialist artisans (potters, pipe-makers and woodworkers), architects, and product-designers. Perhaps most interestingly, the largest and fastest growing demographic of his customers are cosmetic surgeons.

All of these products, functional or not, offer opportunities to someone looking to capitalize on their machine. As always, it is recommended that you pursue markets that hold a genuine interest; your customers can tell the difference!

While some people might laugh at the claims made for 3D metaforms, they might be laughing on the other side of their faces if they were selling such items on a regular basis. I personally reserve judgement on this kind of product and go with the philosophy of Japanese stem cell researcher and recent Nobel prize winner Shinya Yamamato. In an NHK documentary, he described modern science as the tip of an iceberg, with the vast majority of human knowledge remaining submerged deep in the waters that surround us. If this kind of viewpoint can bring about such important medical breakthroughs, then I am quite happy to give all kinds of psychics, new agers and sacred geometrists the benefit of the doubt. Just remember that the best selling book in history, the Bible is believed by many to have mystical powers. If Gutenberg and his contemporaries had demanded scientific proof of God, the afterlife and the angelic host before printing copies of the Old Testament, then it is highly unlikely that printing would have taken off the way that it did, and modern society might be a very different place indeed.

20

Skulls and Bones

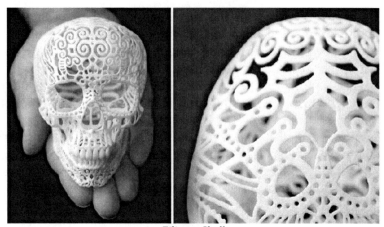

Filigree Skull

Back in 2011, Chicago artist Joshua Harker raised more than $77,000 for his Kickstarter project entitled, "Crania Anatomica Filigre: Me to You." The exquisitely detailed 3D printed skull was featured in Forbes magazine. You can find out the full details of the project over at the Kickstarter site (www.kickstarter.com /projects /joshharker/crania-anatomica-filigre-me-to-you), but suffice it to say that these small 2.6" x 3.5" x 3.5" inch skulls are now selling for $495 per piece on Etsy and $100 on eBay. This should be a clear indication that the skull is a popular motif and will sell well in many different areas.

Because this is 3D printing, the focus here is on miniature skulls and their markets first. Looking at the 1/6 action figure scale it is clear that skulls are a popular item. A closer look at eBay completed sales shows that this is indeed the case. A 1/6 scale action figure dealer from Guangzhou in China sells gold and silver plastic skulls in this scale for $3.99 on a regular basis. Another Chinese seller has sold a massive 524 sets of twenty 28mm scale skulls in the last few months. Neither of these products have been customised or redesigned in any way. They are just basic human skulls, but in miniature plastic form. An American seller recently disposed of a pair of stunning, 1/6 scale set of male and female vampire skulls, based on the horror comic book miniseries, *30 Days of Night*. These miniature reproductions were fashioned after real human skulls; shown with jaws agape baring their sharp, flesh-tearing teeth. They measured approximately 2.5" high and came with separate display bases, measuring about 1.7" wide. Best of all they sold for $69.99 for the pair. The design was much better, and I admit that they were produced by Hot Toys in a factory in China rather than on a 3D printer, but whatever they can do, we can now replicate. A collector in Houston recently sold a pair of 1/6 scale skull trophies, part of the accessories for the Chopper Predator, a figure based on the Predator movies, again by Hot Toys. They look like a couple of ritualistic voodoo staves, two rope-tied skulls on short poles, but they sold for a whopping $114. The original Predator figure comes with a number of skull trophy accessories, which regularly sell for $20 a piece.

An even more impressive newcomer to the market is anatoys-kr (http://myworld.ebay.com/anatoys-kr/) on eBay. His current best seller is a three piece, 1/6 scale handmade custom damaged skull set. The skulls are designed cracked, corroded and bullet damaged, but they are high quality pieces with great detail, and very popular with customizers and collectors building their own diorama sets. In addition, this very creative seller is selling an interesting selection of other 1/6 scale items including skeleton parts and UAV drones. It looks like he is making $100 to $200 per week at the moment, and this is quite impressive considering that he still has less than half a dozen product lines.

Skulls and bones are surprisingly popular ornaments. Even at 1/6 scale, the predator figures have a scaled down trophy necklace that commands a good price despite its minuscule size. Skull necklaces and bracelets are consistently good sellers among the Goth community, and skulls can decorate a great deal more than that. Think about custom hood ornaments for cars and costume embellishments for Cosplayers. You might be surprised to learn that skulls are even popular with doll's house collectors. Regular scaled down examples sell well but more imaginative creations will really excite potential bidders.

Because of this, one of my upcoming 3D printer projects is definitely going to be 1/6 and 28mm custom printed skulls. Not the regular example from Hot Toys that are all over eBay, but my SolidWorks designer is creating a batch of demonic, alien and horned skulls that I can print off cheaply and easily. It turns out that skulls are a very easy item to customise; tattoo artists have been doing it for years. There are just so many configurations. Skulls with helmets, skulls with crowns, and skulls with fangs. Skulls with tusks, skulls with arcane symbols and skulls with candles. Dragon skulls, cleft skulls and shattered skulls, the list of possible permutations just goes on and on. Look at companies like Alchemy for more information and think creepy, dark and Gothic. Soon you will have some of the hottest selling 1/6 and 28mm diorama accessories on the market.

21

Pets

Plastic parts for pet play areas

While it might not yet be profitable to print out an extra-large kennel for an enormous Tibetan Mastiff, the pet market still has many opportunities for 3D printers, as long the guidelines of volume and scale are followed. If you think about smaller pets such as hamsters, gerbils, chinchillas and maybe even ferrets, then there is plenty of scope for small printed accessories. To begin your research, try finding out what twister hay holders are, and then look for resting mats. If this area of the market appeals to you, begin by looking at small animal housing. There are numerous brands on the market, including Crittertrail, Habitrail and Hartz, and the possibilities for accessories, add-ons and custom tubes are equally numerous.

Another interesting area to investigate is aquarium accessories. All kinds of artefacts could be placed at the bottom of a fish tank, rather than the very limited range of accessories that just a handful of manufacturers retail. It is very easy to imagine crazy cultural anachronisms to half bury in the gravel, from Corinthian columns to Easter Island Moai. Here is a chance to extend that range as far as your imagination can stretch. Rather than mass produced Statues of Liberty, you can now put almost any statue from just about any period in history that you can think of, at the bottom of a fish tank. It does not matter whether you have a couple of fun fair Guppies, or thousands of dollars worth of expensive Aruwana, they can now swim around completely personalized underwater environments. Bear in mind that smaller residents especially like small holes to weave in and out of, so when you print out your new *Escape from New York* underwater diorama, make sure that it is suitable for the fish as well as being dystopian and apocalyptic.

Collectors of small animals not well-served by mass production industry. Consider all the rare and exotic small creatures that people take care of as pets: African pygmy hedgehogs, sugar gliders, pygmy marmosets, degus, iguanas, frogs, toads, box/aqua turtles, sea horses and even pet spiders. These are all small niche markets to which big factories just cannot cater, but are almost perfect for a 3D printer. You might also be surprised to learn that there is a very sizeable market for crickets in China. Traditionally, katydids were kept in tiny holders fashioned from gourds and bamboo, while tiny gilded cages were the height of domestic luxury for these creatures. A 3D printer could replicate these easily, and produce some fascinating new designs for this niche hobby that is currently undergoing a revival among the growing middle classes of twenty-first century China.

For smaller animals, how about some scaled down agility training devices. Hoops, weaving poles, teeter-totters and any obstacle that you can think of, are a chance to print some interesting miniature designs. These are all popular for dogs, and you could certainly produce some items for miniature breeds, but what about other species such as hamsters and gerbils. In fact, any of the pets that we have referred to so far might appreciate their own custom training sets.

Just as 3D printing will create many boons for the human health industry (see below), these advances could also be applied to the species that we enjoy keeping as pets. A simple starting point might be a pair of simple tick removal tweezers, but might go all the way up to canine mobility units for those loyal companions, who, through injury or old age have lost the use of their back legs.

Do not just think about biological pets. Technology based pets such as Hexbugs and zhu zhus need accessories and habitats too (Hexbugs even have zip lines and battle bridges.) If 3D printed parts are suitable for small pets then why not micro pets?

Resolution: 4 Architecture have already designed and printed a number of birdhouses inspired by the classic urban tennis-shoes-over-the-telephone-wire trick. Sarah Rich of Inhabitat.com wrote about the birdhouses: "The geometry and fabrication process create a continuous surface printable in one volume. The holes both texture the shell and allow nests to peek through. They are also scalable according to the size of the bird they are built for. The birdhouses can be clustered in various sized groups and slung over a tree branches, creating a (utopian) bird community...The birdhouse proves that nothing is too small to test grand ideas." Of course, birdhouses come in all kinds of wild shapes and sizes, and this is a field where the imagination is the only limiting factor.

Without a doubt, a leading innovator in the pet field of 3D printing is Shane Graber, or sgraber (www.thingiverse.com/sgraber) on Thingiverse. Shane has kept saltwater tanks for the last twelve years, is a research scientist, lives in northern Indiana, and is a proud Advanced Aquarist (http://www.advancedaquarist.com/) staffer.

"Picture this: It's late Saturday night and you hear a noise coming from your fish room. Upon investigation, you find your return pump is buzzing loudly and not pumping water. "Huh? What's going on here?!" You disassemble the pump and discover that an impeller blade has sheared off, and you don't have a replacement on hand. ... However, you are no ordinary hobbyist because you have a 3D printer at your disposal. You fire up your favorite modeling program and quickly model a replacement impeller then hit the [Print] button. The printer begins spitting out molten plastic. Fifteen minutes later you are fitting your replacement impeller in place and have saved yourself a lot of heartache and worry—and possibly the lives of many critters in your tank."

Amazingly he uses his 3D printer for making seahorses feeders, protein skimmers, brine shrimp hatcheries, nori seaweed clips, sponge filters, and custom power head nozzles. All of these are essential items for the advanced aquarist and it is these niche areas that 3D printers are really starting to blossom.

Retail, brine shrimp hatcheries cost anywhere from $10 to $15 per piece. While that is not expensive, 3D printing them costs just $2.00 for the plastic. That is a cost saving of $8.00-$13.00 per hatchery. Sponge filters retail for $10 to $15 per filter. Again, they are not expensive but the cost will add up as more larval tanks are setup. This part also costs about $2.00 in printing plastic. Your savings: $8.00-$13.00 per filter.

22

Custom Items and Works of Art

The Nylon Airbike

It is always artists that first push the limits of a new media. A growing number of individuals are already taking up the challenge and experimenting with this new technology. Geoffrey Mann from London's Royal College of Art for example, has been creating lamps by capturing the flight of a moth trapped inside a traditional light fixture, and printing out its path using plastic. His entire show was apparently bought out within hours. The artist who has a fascination with "transposing the ephemeral nature of time and motion" has created a studio practice that "challenges the existing divides between art, craftand design."

Rachel Harding's '3D lace' takes traditional textiles and transforms them into three-dimensional objects. Fabrics including laces, tweeds and damasks are extruded to create stalagmite structures, and while each retains a certain sense of decorative grandeur when viewed from above, in profile they become something both beautiful and terrifying.

Traditional mould manufacturing and machining techniques have been quite limiting and cannot come close to the levels of meticulous detail and part-within-part structures offered through 3D printing. Design rules have prohibited the creation of products with hollowed sections, intricate centres, organic curves and movable, interactive pieces. The introduction of 3D printing means that we can defy some of the rules of traditional manufacturing. The world has already been dazzled by Escherian prints, such as the ball-within-a-ball, collapsible prints, foldable prints, and all kinds of kinetic puzzles. Rather than simply list off some of these extraordinary prints, here is a list of the ten most influential print artists (fabbaloo.com /blog/2012/7/19/a-showcase-of-influential-3d-print-artists.html).

Somewhat unsurprisingly, the fabulous works of M.C. Escher have already been realized as actual physical objects using a 3D printer. For examples of the three-dimensional models that were designed and built using geometric modelling and computer graphics tools Gershon Elber's site (www.cs.technion.ac.il/~gershon /Escher ForReal/) is a 'must see'.

For more fascinating examples of pushing the design boundaries using a 3D printer, here are a few leads that are definitely worth following up.

3D designer, Virtox has created a unique piece known as "Gyro The Cube". It consists of three cube-like pieces, interlocked together and when used properly, this model will actually spin in the palm of your hand. This is one of the most impressive kinetic models to date, and really needs to be seen on video to be properly appreciated.

The Shakuhachi is an intricately designed flute that was fabricated in a single print. While the piece is undoubtedly beautiful, it really begs the question, what is next? There are already custom designed and 3D printed guitars, flutes, and ocarinas, but what else can we expect?

Perhaps my favourite art piece at the moment is the iris box. This is a tube or box container with five blade-like pieces that form the circular top, and are twisted open, very much like an automatic portal in a science fiction movie. Receptacles like this would be great for housing miniatures or other small products that you are fabricating, and this leads into a whole new area that I simply do not have space to cover here; the concept of custom packaging.

23

Cosplay

Cosplay conventions and festivals are already big business in the developed world. The San Diego Comicon, the Tokyo Comiket and the Paris Japan Expo are all major annual events, but none of these are growing at the same phenomenal speed as their Chinese counterparts. Although the USA alone has more than one hundred similar events annually, the largest of these drew only 130,000 this year. I attended the Kunming Cosplay Convention in the summer of 2012, an event that has grown to exceed this number in just five years, whereas it took the San Diego Comicon nearly forty years to reach the same levels of attendance. The irony is that most people have never even heard of the city of Kunming. Now that momentum is gathering, changes are happening very quickly, the *Economist* reported nearly eight hundred thousand at Hong Kong's latest Cosplay convention, and I personally saw even greater numbers at last year's Guangzhou event. Next year, every provincial capital in China will has its own major annual event, and we can expect major tourist locations such as Lijiang and Guilin to use their beautiful natural surroundings to draw even larger crowds of fans and collectors. Any Westerners looking for an opportunity to make a dent in the massive trade deficit with China should sit up and take a good long look at the possibilities for Cosplay.

In 2012, the best selling items at the mainland Chinese shows were cheap plastic samurai swords, furry kitten ears, and bright pink dayglo wigs. Most of the booths were carrying identical stock, and so there is still plenty of room for new comers. Just seeing all the browsing teenagers with their Androids, iPads and high end EOS digital SLRs made it obvious that they have sizable disposable incomes to burn. Only one vendor was offering 1/6 scale collectible figures from manufacturers such as Hot Toys, Sideshow or Soldier Story, and nobody was selling high end costumes. An August 2011 article in the *Economist*, described the meteoric growth of the Hong Kong Ani-Com and Games Convention. With over 800,000 attendees, and 170 exhibitors, it was reported that one small exhibitor alone took in over 5 million Hong Kong dollars, selling figurines based on popular Hollywood films. Gatherings on the mainland are often even larger, hardly surprising when you consider that China has hundreds of cities with populations exceeding a million people, and dozens more with a staggering ten million plus.

Cecil Harvey's Dark Knight Armour

The subject of Cosplay provides an opportunity to introduce the work of Neal Bockhaut, namely his recreation of Cecil Harvey's Dark Knight armour (nealbombad.deviantart.com /gallery/29118155), the main protagonist in Final Fantasy IV. Harvey is captain of the Red Wings and the hero of this classic Nintendo console game. The level of detail is mind-boggling, but best of all, it was made with a 3D printer. The level of work that went into this costume is prohibitive for people trying to make a living, though one interesting aspect of the project was the use of a free software program called Make Human to create a mock human form closely resembling his measurements that was used as a virtual mannequin when designing the armour. Using the best reference images he could find, he then modelled each piece of armour in 3DS Max starting with low poly proxies, slowly adding more and more levels of detail.

Most people know that Tony Stark 3D prints his Iron Man suits, both on-screen in his personal sci-fi fab-lab, and also off screen in the special effects studios, where the film production company uses that latest high end printers to make those fantastic costumes. This is perhaps the first time that a fan working outside of Hollywood has used similar techniques to achieve such impressive results. While Neal is a truly a pioneer in the field, Cosplay is growing so fast that I predict that there will be hundreds, if not thousands of equally impressive outfits being printed out this time next year. Personal armour is an enormously fertile field for inspiration, and Neal has only touched on the very beginnings of what will be possible in the very near future. Back in the Tudor golden age of plate armour, suits were seen as items of high fashion, and we are quite likely to see a resurgence in this trend. The 'Almain Armourer's Album' was the catalogue of master armourer Jacob Halder, who worked in England during the reign of Elizabeth I. The 'Album' contains design drawings for some of Queen Elizabeth I's leading courtiers, advisors and military leaders including Robert Dudley, Earl of Leicester, Sir Henry Lee and Sir Christopher Hatton. Some of these examples were outrageously expensive and were the equivalent of owning a private jet in today's terms. The BBC documentary 'Metalworks' provides a fantastic insight into the world of Tudor armour, especially the second show in the series which looks specifically at the Greenwich armouries of Henry VIII.

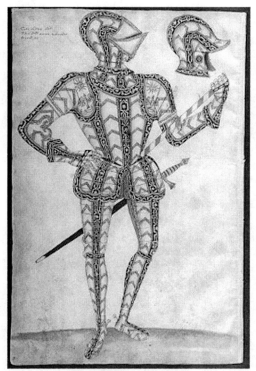

Tudor Armour Design

Armour remains a staple of fantasy genres, from Japanese manga to science fiction of the far distant future. Hollywood representations of body armour have often been substantially scaled down due to budget limitations, a good example being the costumes in the Starship Troopers movies, which bore little resemblance to the original Heinlein novel. As fans gain the freedom to experiment at home, we can expect to see more and more extremely complex set ups. I personally like the classic lines of the Greenwich style, but I am also excitedly anticipating the visually arresting examples of Daedric armour from the Skyrim video games. At the last Chinese Cosplay convention I attended, I was amazed by all the katanas, halberds and giant broadswords that I saw being carried quite openly on the city subway. Surely it will not be long before the same trains will be ferrying fully armoured fantasy knights from the university campuses to the downtown convention centres.

Daedric Armour

Returning our gaze to China for a moment, to look at the serious business implications of these Cosplay events; conventions in the PRC are growing at a spectacular speed. But, as previously mentioned, there is a still lack of really good products for the attendees to buy. Chinese fans have large disposable incomes, but little to spend it on in this particular market. Screen quality Imperial Stormtroopers, impressive Iron Man Mark IV suits and hulking, heavily armed Space Marines have the potential to quickly become very profitable items in China, especially if western designers can buy a 3D printer on site, and print everything locally, and the legal issues can be addressed productively. China is no longer the backward rurality that many Westerners imagine. The economy has grown at an amazing speed. It was not so long ago when Mercedes Benz and Porsche and BMW were practically unknown in China, and now they can be seen in even the most remote parts of the country.

China has some three hundred billionaires, and over a million millionaires, most with very spoiled offspring that are able to buy whatever the hell they like. China does not have Halloween or Mardi Gras, but the long traditions and brightly coloured costumes of minority cultures are desperately seeking a voice. Here is a hobby where the younger generation can really express themselves and their ideas, rather than just being big brand sheep. Below is a list of Cosplay conventions scheduled for Southern China in 2013, just in case you are feeling adventurous.

The three largest events are as follows:

1. Hong Kong Fifteenth Ani-Com and Games Convention 31st July-04th August
2. The 2013 Guangzhou International Comic and Animation Festival 1st-5th October
3. Chinajoy aka the Tenth Annual Shanghai China International Animation Game Expo Shanghai International Expo Centre 26th-28th July

In addition to these, there will be Cosplay conventions at each of the following southern provincial capitals.

- Guangxi: 04/24/13 at Nanning
- Hainan: 04/13/13-04/15/13 at Haikou
- Fujian: 05/20/13 at Fuzhou
- Hunan: 04/29/13-05/1/13 at Changsha
- Jiangxi: 06/22/13-06/24/13 at Nanchang
- Guizhou: 06/09/13-06/10/13 at Guiyang
- Jiangsu: 04/25/13 at Nanjing

24

Health

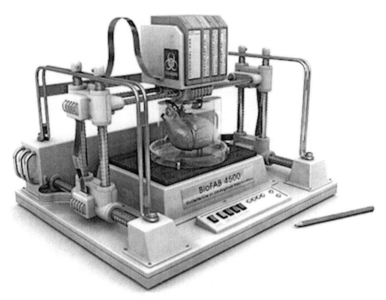

Printing parts for humans

While many seem to be waiting for chemical compound scale 3D printers that can produce MDMA and DMT on demand, there are already plenty of ongoing developments that are breaking boundaries in human health care.

Here are a few examples to inspire you.

Two-year-old Emma LaVelle was diagnosed with arthrogryposis, a condition that limited the use of her arms due to underdeveloped muscles, and prevents her from playing with other children. Now, with the aid of 3D printing, Emma can lift toys and draw pictures with her friends. Stratasys has worked with staff at the Alfred I.

DuPont Hospital for Children to create a custom plastic robotic exoskeleton, allowing Emma a freedom that she had previously never known. Emma calls her exoskeleton her "magic arms" and the printed jacket can be easily adjusted as Emma grows, just as easily as printing replacement parts—breakages are an inevitability in the rough and tumble world of toddlers.

At the other end of the longevity scale, doctors at the University of Hasselt BIOMED Research Institute in Belgium successfully implanted a 3D printed titanium mandible into an eighty-three-year-old woman patient in Belgium. The jaw replacement made from titanium powder weighs almost the same as an actual jaw, and will allow the patient to eat and speak as normal once she's healed. With this innovative procedure, a world of bone-replacements will be opened up, and it will be very interesting to see what titanium replacement the researchers at Hasselt take on next. "Computer technology will cause a veritable revolution in the medical world. We just need to learn to work with it," said Professor Jules Poukens after the surgery. "Doctors and engineers work together around the design computer and the operation table: that's what we call being truly innovative."

In a separate and equally important medical advance, Mark Frame, a trainee surgeon in the UK has developed a program that can print 3D bones. Traditionally, bone models cost thousands of dollars and took many weeks to complete. The new 3D printed models run around $150, and take just a week to complete and ship. Frame has been working with a Netherlands-based company that has the capability of turning CT scans into real-to-life bone models. Renowned surgeon, Dr. Aman Khan recently told the BBC, "A model used to cost more or less the same as the surgery itself and therefore it often wasn't an option. We couldn't justify that kind of cost for a procedure which is already very expensive."

Teeth are a logical next product, and in fact are already on the market. A number of companies use SLM technologies to make caps and crowns as well as other devices. Even so, technology is right on the precipice of being able to grow a new set of teeth from scratch. With bones, it will more than likely be some manipulation of osteoblast production rather than outright replacement. This is a far superior option in that it avoids surgery and simply means taking another set of pills. 3D printing will have a lot to contribute as far as building the supportive matrix and perhaps laying down the initial seed cells, but optimal tissues and organs, particularly load-bearing ones, will need to be grown. Imagine a 3D printed tree in a hurricane, the designer would have had no way of knowing where exactly to apply extra material for strength, and would end up overcompensating in the wrong places. A tree needs to feel and be moved by the environment to know where and how to grow. The same process may be important for teeth and bone.

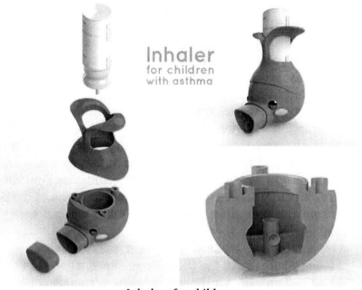

Inhalers for children

Luis Daniel Ibarra, an industrial design student in Mexico has created an ergonomic inhaler designed focused on toddlers with asthma. Toddlers often have problems using common inhalers. Their tiny hands have neither the size nor strength to reach or push down on the cannister. With this new model, they can use both thumbs and both forefingers to push down firmly and not have to struggle. In addition it is an attractive curvy design with a smiley face, which is so much more amenable to children than the sterile looking dispensers with which most of us are familiar. This could be a great starting point for new design ideas. The traditional inhaler is often used in the media to represent nerdiness, and is regularly featured at the beginning of bullying scenes in Hollywood movies. Why shouldn't geeks have inhalers with cool designs, in the same vein as cool phone covers and modded PC cases? I will be keeping a careful eye on Grabcad and other design repositories to see what creative solutions spring up in this area. I can definitely see some imaginative, cool looking inhalers finding a solid niche in the open market.

Beyond the realm of bones and prosthetics, 3D printing has been used to print chemical reaction vessels, print reagents as "chemical inks" in them, and create new chemical compounds. The developers say that "people in far-flung regions could make their own headache pills or detergent. More importantly the technique might also allow people to print and share recipes for niche substances that chemical or pharmaceutical companies do not make—because there are not enough customers, or they simply have not yet dreamed up those ideas." This has huge implications for remote areas and third world countries.

The technology is already here, but how long until it is widely used? How long will it be before any patient can go into a suitably equipped clinic for a full scan, and come out with a USB drive full of data that maps their own skeleton completely? This information could be carried like a donor card, so that if you do have a bad traffic accident, surgeons can immediately print out replacements while you are still on the operating table. Take this a step beyond healthcare; this kind of data can be used to collect measurements for personal shopping. When a sales assistant asks for your shoe size, or glove size or an inside leg measurement, just hand over your CT info on the USB, and your purchases are immediately customized to your own specific size. You can already take a scan of your feet to fashion design students Naim Josefi and Souzan Youssouf, who worked with Materialise will make a made-to-fit Melonia shoe. They can turn your scan into custom-printed shoes. In spite of their skeletal, almost fragile look, they are strong enough to walk on, as demonstrated by models on the fashion runway.

These products themselves have health implications. The economy of scale of shoe production has to optimize itself in order to suit as many people as possible. This leaves most shoes fitting only the statistical majority of people. Custom fitting orthotic shoes for those with musculo-skeletal issues and for diabetics can cost in excess of $400. 3D printing has the potential to reduce these costs and shorten the wait time, as well as making custom-fit shoes, a better product for everybody's foot health, an affordable choice.

25

Crafts

Crafting is one the largest untapped markets on eBay of which many people are still completely unaware. All kinds of hobbyists are busy beavering away making all sorts of handicrafts in the comfort of their own homes. Tatting (a form of needlework) for example, has a surprisingly large and voracious audience in these circles, even though the practice is relatively unknown. The men and women who are really into scrapbooking, card making, and such will jump at the opportunity to make their own napkin holders, salt and pepper shakers, and other doodads. I expect to see Etsy filled with 3D printed items in a few years. Spend some time, familiarize yourself with the craft market and you will find many opportunities to monetize the output of a 3D printer. Here are a few suggestions with which to begin:

Rubber-stamping is a surprisingly large niche market. The number of products for this activity that a 3D printer can produce is enormous, including mounts, handles, or even the stamps themselves. Then there are stamping wheels, easy grip handles, and paper shapers.

Highly customized buttons are also an interesting possibility in the crafts field. I recently saw a set of three identical vintage Toshikane porcelain buttons depicting the face of Hanya, a vengeful female ghost spirit from traditional Japanese masked Nô theatre sell for $50. The image had orange-red-coloured skin, gilded teeth, eyes and horns, and black hair. The reverse was flat black, with a small loop for thread. The Toshikane Company was located in Arita City, Saga-Prefecture, and Southern Japan; for many years, between the period 1930s to 1960s, they produced some of the world's finest porcelain, and were particularly famous for porcelain buttons. Nowadays, so many of the original vintage pieces have chips or other damage, but there is still a big marketplace for similarly stylized buttons. Think about different themes, such as western, steam punk, Goth or designer suit buttons.

Molds are surprising profitable in this market. Rubber molds for concrete garden ornaments fetch up to $500 dollars each, depending on their quality. Have a look at the eBay seller known as rivers-edge-hunter (http://myworld.ebay.com/rivers-edge-hunter/) for some inspiration in this area.

A recent competition on instructables.com (these contests are a a fantastic source of inspiration) involved a small 3D puzzle with just two plastic pieces. Even though the competition is long finished, the puzzle design is still very useful. It consists of two very simple pieces shaped exactly alike, that can be assembled to form a pyramid and includes an stl file for six sets. The pieces are small, fit into your pocket and like the competition organiser, will allow you to take them with you to give away to friends and strangers alike. In his own words "Trust me, you'll want a lot of them. They make great hand-outs." The puzzle itself is deceptively simple, just keep both pieces face to face, and rotate one of the pieces by ninety degrees and the puzzle is solved. I can still remember when I used to to go out clubbing, always carrying a couple of small puzzles with me as a little icebreaker and they always did the trick, so I am especially keen on these kinds of products.

26

Miscellaneous Ideas

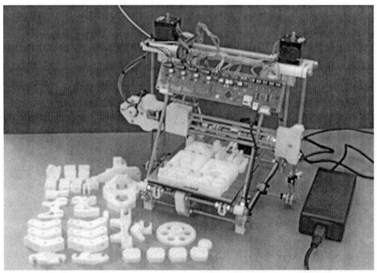

The Reprap demonstrating its self-replication capabilities

Crafting is just one of many markets worth investigating. A good search of the sports section can throw up some fascinating possibilities. Have you ever thought about designing and printing your own frisbee? You might be surprised at how much vintage discs can command in the online auction market. How about custom fishing lures? Small, low density and easy to produce, these are a great specialist line for beginning printers. How about custom grips for bicycles? Plastic has revolutionized many areas of sports, and 3D printing may do the very same.

One area that I personally am keen to pursue is that of reproduction electrical switches for homes that still have that vintage look. On a recent trip to Yunnan, China, I was lucky enough to stay at the Linden Centre, a fully restored courtyard complex that was voted the best hotel in all of China for 2011. Despite the beautiful surroundings, (the owner is an American oriental antiques dealer) I was a tad disappointed by the modern white plastic light switches that looked completely out of place in an otherwise beautiful renovation. I am therefore keen to produce some very tasteful Georgian or Victorian reproduction light switches for the many similar renovations that are now taking place all over China. I am confident that they will also go down well in the American and European steam punk and Goth subcultures. I have already seen some rather tasteless light pulls in the shape of hanged men (the 'Hanged Harry' range) and inverted satanic crucifixes, and I know that I do far better than these.

Artist Jeff Lipton has customized his own personal fabricator into a gorgeous steampunk style. Steampunk is an artistic image that developed in the late twentieth century as homage to the look and feel of Victorian era technology. Steampunk usually features classical materials like wood, iron, and polished brass, and this custom job boasts all the necessary hard wood and gilded metal finish.

While there are certainly myriad uses for this technology, one line of items that will hopefully become a commonplace 3D printed product are Halloween costumes. Holidays and festivals are going to become a huge pool of innovation for 3D designers. Soon consumers will be able to have a string of custom Christmas lights to your very own specification. There are already a dozen or so designs available at Thingiverse and we can expect to see a whole lot more as the festive season draws closer.

Having lived in Asia for such a long time, chopsticks are obviously very close to my heart and to me having at least a couple of stylish pairs says much more to me about their owner, than the latest model Benz or BMW. For both health and environmental reasons, I always carry my own pair. In Japan, some 26 billion pairs of disposable chopsticks are thrown away each year, which equates to approximately two hundred pairs for every man woman and child. In China the number is more than double this figure and rising at a much faster rate.

In Korea, one injection moulding manufacturer already uses ABS and PLA to produce a range of these utensils, including some very cute Hello Kitty training chopsticks. Another producer markets pairs of ABS chopsticks modelled on katanas, the swords wielded by

Japanese samurai warriors. These give a whole new meaning to the phrase "food fight", and are must haves for fans of Japanese culture, or those who delight in surprising their dinner guests. Hong Kongers might be more impressed with a Bruce Lee inspired set of Nunchuk chopsticks, complete with a small silver chain connecting the two lengths.

The Japanese toy manufacturer Kotobukiya recently released a fantastic range of Star Wars Light Saber Chopsticks including both Darth Vader and Luke Skywalker versions, both of which light up in their respective colours. The Darth Maul Version even connects together to create his signature double bladed staff of mayhem. In the USA, Arthur Court Designs produces a very collectible set of Dragon/Griffin chopsticks that were probably inspired by his extensive naval service in the Pacific and Far East during World War Two.

I have seen some really crazy designs in my travels, from a pair that looked just like creepy millipedes to a Japanese commemorative set that were in the same shape as the Shinkansen Bullet Train. I personally would like to have a travel set, with the severed bowl of a miso soup spoon, that I could use as both a container for dipping sauces such as soy sauce, but also as a stick rest. I once saw a pair of wonderfully creative eyeglasses with telescopic chopsticks built into the temple legs (the parts that go back over your ears).

Chopstick cases are just as important as the sticks themselves and so why not design and print out a ninja-type dagger sheath, or a beautifully decorated faux cloisonné holder that would be fit for the empress dowager herself?

Of course, this is just scratching the surface of the chopstick market, which is growing enormously even as I write this. I will not go anywhere without my own collapsible pair, and not only are they stylish, they are great conversation pieces.

I am predicting that there is going to be a considerable market in custom printed USB covers. This is the ultimate twenty-first century tchotchke and with a 3D printer, there is a unique design possible for absolutely everybody. Global Sources (www.globalsources.com /NEWS/20- unique-USB-flash-drives.html?WT.mc_id=4009043), a Chinese Alibaba-type website, has a list of twenty interesting styles that are already available all over Yiwu, but this should be good inspiration for someone creating stylish designs of their own.

As you can see there are already guns, bombs and assorted 'bling', but having seen the R&D departments of most Chinese factories, I know that every single one of you can do better.

I recently met up with an old friend who has long had a business in Hangzhou that makes figures and toys, primarily for gaming companies, as well as large quantities of decorative wax candles. With the advent of 3D printers, he can obtain 3D models from the client, print out the model the same day, with accurate dimensions, colours and precision, make changes, and then send it off to the factory to produce the moulds for production. Previously, each mould would cost around $5,000 to make, with each change costing hundreds of dollars—significant changes resulting in another $5,000 to restart the mould.

Cost savings aside, he also saves about six months in development time. The clients love it, because they can see a physical version of their model almost instantly; the boss loves it because he can work easily with the client to make changes, and the factories love it because they have a final product and order without months of delays.

Of course, as a home printer, you may not have access to your own factory with full injection moulding facilities, but that does not mean that you should not consider moulds as profitable finished items in themselves. There are many kinds of small moulds that you can produce, many of which already have open source 3D models available on the internet.

Let us start with sushi moulds. These are very cute items, mainly from Japan but quickly growing in popularity in the West. Some of my favourite designs include pandas, Pikachu and the inevitable Hello Kitty. Often they come with seaweed cutters so that you can decorate your little kitty with nori faces and sliced sausage hair bows. These moulds need not be limited to Japanese icons, but you can use your imagination and come up with sushi designs from the entire treasure trove that is our collective cultural legacy.

Whatever ideas you imagine, there is a pretty good chance that there is already an ice cube tray in that particular design. There have in fact been so many great designs introduced to this market over the last few years, many of these could be used as inspiration for sushi moulds. Star wars fans are well catered to with trays that produce ice cubes in the form of R2D2, Darth Vader, X Wing Fighters and even Han Solo encased in carbonite. Some of my favourites include miniature Titanics (sold under the ultra corny brand name of 'gin and titonic'), scaled down brains (marketed as brain freezes) and some very cool B52 bombs. I absolutely love the weighted ice cubes that float on top of your drink in the shape of penguins, polar bears and even shark's fins. I also really like those that are in the shape of diamonds, Lego bricks and ice space invaders, but I think there is still plenty of room for innovation here. And not only in ice cube trays but for lollipop moulds too. Just think of swords, dolphins and gargoyles. Famous skyscrapers and Saturn rocket ships, basically anything long and thin will do the job.

Do not forget about related items like ravioli and other baking moulds. These are used extensively in China for making dumplings, but also come in very nice apple-shaped designs for making fruit pastries. While all of this might be obvious if you already blessed with an entrepreneurial nature, one innovation that you may not have heard of is the fruit mould. These moulds are attached to fruit while they are still on the tree. It is possible that the idea evolved from the French Poire de Prisionnierre, where medieval vintners would insert young fruits into brandy bottles while they were still forming on the branches, and then later detach the bottle and fill it with Eau de Vie. These have evolved into plastic moulds that seem to work well with everything from pears to pumpkins. Up in the orchards of the Tibetan foothills, I have seen pears grown into the shape of the mini Buddhas, and in Japan, where speciality fruit sells at high prices, there are square, pyramid and even heart shaped watermelons. It probably will not surprise you to learn that someone has already grown enormous phallic cucumbers and honeydews, but even so, the moulds themselves are still quite difficult to find and therefore a good product for a 3D printer.

On a final food note, there is also a large market potential for cookie cutters. Again, the bounds of this market are limited only by the imagination. Actually, cookie cutters have come a long way since those basic metal stencil shapes that we all remember from our childhood. Modern plastic cookie cutters are designed specifically for quarter inch cookie dough, and have a number of added features that the home 3D printer can easily incorporate. These include three dimensional imprint lines that create a very clear design on the finished cookies. These make very useful design lines for when it comes to adding icing, M&Ms and sprinkles. On the edges, you can incorporate air holes to prevent the dough from sticking and you might even want to include a hanger hole so that your cutter can double as an ornament. This is a good idea for Christmas cookie cutters. Functional handles will also make a cutter more desirable because of its ease of use.

Before you ask, yes, there are already dozens of Star Wars and Star Trek cookie cutters on the market, but with your own 3D printer you can do small runs of much more obscure images from classics of the past. How about a Ray Harryhausen tribute set of harpies, cyclops and hydras? Maybe a Rocky Horror set of transsexuals, groupies and balding butlers? Perhaps even a Merry Men set featuring friars, maids, archers and other assorted denizens of Sherwood?

Golf tees fit all the requirements as a potential 3D printed product. They are small, uncomplicated and easy to customise. It might seem that a simple small piece of plastic would not have much to offer in terms of customisation but most of the bulk production is very standardised. Novelty and custom pieces are quite hard to find and sell very well in the gifts market. There are a few examples around such as the naked lady tees, and tees that look like nuts and bolts. I have even seen one in the form of a cheeky gopher. A couple of flat top tees might make a nice gift for the practical joking golfer out there. There is plenty of scope for experimentation in this area. My favourites so far are the hand carved tees of Don Mertz, that look to me like Ents from the *Lord of the Rings*.
http://woodbeecarver.com/whittle-tee-noggins/whittle-tee-noggins

If Don can be this creative then we should be able to come up with plenty of interesting designs. I am looking forward to trying miniature Corinthian columns and maybe a tiny Bathsheba type vortex, but I am especially looking forward to seeing the original designs of the growing 3D printer community.

To close this section, here are some interesting miscellaneous ideas of my own that might also spark an entrepreneurial fire in a few readers:

One of the most interesting designs that I have found on instructables.com is the Helical Shelf System by Edrawle. "This furniture explores how 3D printing can unlock new possibilities in form, mechanisms and personal fabrication. The shelf system is comprised of triangular helices, cogs, belts and wooden shelves. The helices move together and cause the shelves to move up and down. The helices and feet are great examples of the complex forms easily achievable with a cheap 3D printer."

The creativity of this design spurred me onto to thinking what other complex forms are now practicable with additive manufacturing and how we can redesign everyday objects with improvements in terms of both efficiency and aesthetics. There is something about helices that are innately fascinating, from the beautiful design of London's St Mary's Axe building all the way down to the DNA spiral, proteins and even helical virii. We have all seen Da Vinci's extraordinary design for a helical helicopter and even the cosmic motion of the solar system itself is helical.

The first thoughts that came to mind were the vortexian experiments of Viktor Schauberger, an Austrian forester, inventor and bio-mimicry experimenter. The inventor of what he called "implosion technology", Schauberger developed his own theories based on fluidic vortices and movement in nature. He built actuators for airplanes, ships, silent turbines, self-cleaning pipes and equipment for the cleansing and so-called "refinement" of water to create spring water, which he used as a healing remedy.

I am currently re-reading Callum Coates' books on Schauberger's works and am planning to print a number of items based on his extraordinary devices. These will probably begin with a selection of helical water pipes, utilising his vortextian theories to cleanse and re-energise a wide range of fluids. The manufacture of such pipes was previously quite difficult, requiring sheets of copper to be carefully cut into harmonious measures, and then welded lengthways to embody the irregular ovoid design described by Schauberger. Nature uses the spiral in many ways: hurricanes, twisters, tornadoes, streams and ocean currents and yet up until now, our manufacturing processes have not easily been able to take advantage of these forces. If these devices do actually work, then I am keen to progress onto more complicated designs such as those incorporating implosion technologies, rotational physics, centripetal forces and the coanda effect. With the rapid growth of autonomous underwater explorers I am keen to build a model with a propulsion system based on the lenticular forces that Schauberger ascribed to swimming trout.

A more conventional use of the helical furniture introduced by edrawle is popular among model railway enthusiasts who often use helical systems for storage. As can be seen from the following forum discussion, these can be very expensive and would certainly be much cheaper if some of the parts were made with a 3D printer:
http://www.modelrailforum.com/forums/index.php?showtopic=24242

Prices start at €225 for the smaller 39cm versions and go up to €590 for the 50cm version. These examples use medium density fibreboards (MDF) which is often needs extra support because it is inclined to dip in the middle, but perhaps this could be resolved with acrylics or a little redesign. It is certainly a very niche market, but at these prices, one that would see well worth investigating.

A more conventional technology that I am also keen to explore with my 3D printer is the manufacture of complex gear mechanisms. My interests in this area include epicyclic or planetary gears, harmonic drives and cycloidal drives. Most of all, I am fascinated by double helical gears, or herringbone gears. Precision herringbone gears are more difficult to manufacture than equivalent spur or helical gears, and consequently much more expensive. They cannot be cut by simple gear hobbing machines, as the cutter would run into the other half of the gear, but this is no longer a problem with 3D printers.

Reprap Herringbone Gears

Herringbone gears overcome the problem of axial thrust presented by "single" helical gears, by having two sets of teeth that are set in a V shape. This arrangement cancels out the net axial thrust, since each half of the gear thrusts in the opposite direction. Like helical gears, they have the advantage of transferring power smoothly as multiple gear teeth engage and disengage simultaneously. Their advantage over helical gears is that the side-thrust of one half is balanced by that of the other half. The logo of the car maker Citroën is a graphic representation of a herringbone gear, reflecting André Citroën's earlier involvement in their manufacture. As can be seen in the photo above, the maker community is already putting these precision gears to good use in the latest iterations of the open source RepRaps, but I am sure that there are many far more mind blowing uses, of which I would never have imagined.

27

Plastic Covers

While I have written extensively about niche markets so small that most people do not even know they exist, this does not mean that I think the more obvious mainstream products should be ignored, especially if there is a good local market for them. I want to look at two products specifically before I wrap up this section.

Some of the most innovative 3D printer products out there at the moment are for iPhone Covers. If I could gain access to a small shop in a popular tourist town then these would make ideal products for all those shopping-crazy visitors.

My favourite so far is the Eye of Sauron iPhone 5 (www.cultofmac.com/198087/this-eye-of-sauron-case-is-the-ultimate-iphone-5-case-for-lord-of-the-rings-fans/) case designed by Shapeways user joabaldiwn, "An iPhone 5 case for Lord of the Rings fans, in which the Apple logo becomes the evil eye of Sauron, in the tower of Barad-Dûr, by the fiery pits of Cupertino... I mean, Mordor. Succumb to the powers of the all-seeing eye, rejoice in mass surveillance by your masters at Apple, give in to your inner Nazgûl." I am not really sure that I can improve on a description like that.

Another design that I love to bits is the iPhone Cover for Engineers www.instructables.com/id/IPhone-Cover-for-Engineers/ by Danny Tas of Australia. Designed specifically for engineering/ mechanical students, this cover comes with all gears embossed with the number of teeth so users can work out ratios, without even having to turn on the phone. This might well be the very first analogue iPhone app and everybody that sees it will want to touch it, feel it and spin those little 1.25 module gears.

Shapeways have recently teamed up with SoundCloud to take a

favourite song or voice recording and turn it into an iPhone case. The SoundCloud app creates a picture of any audio clip, known as a waveform. Shapeways's will then print out an iPhone case that captures the unique hills and valleys of this waveform for $25. The only limit here is your imagination. Your case could feature your dog's bark or perhaps your lover's cries of passion. French 3D-printing company Sculpteo also now features an app that allows users to design their own iPhone cases. 3DPCase allows users choose from one of five available templates—there are more in the works—and customize the design by tweaking the shape, switching the colours, or adding images and text. The entire process can take less than a minute, and prices start at $14.99. Various design firms helped create the templates, such as the Society for Printable Geography, who designed the concept for the terrain map "Geography" case.

Shapeways recently held a competition for the most creative iPhone case design and there are nearly seventy entries up on the site from which you can take inspiration.

Australia has just passed new legislation requiring all packets of cigarettes to feature gruesome pictures of smoking related illnesses and deformities. This is a law that has long been in place in Thailand, and now looks set to spread to the UK and the US. This means that there will soon be a very large market for attractive cigarette pack covers to keep these revolting images hidden. There is no point in having a designer handbag, only to pull out a packet of smokes emblazoned with a gangrenous pair of rotting lungs. Only a small handful of Chinese producers are manufacturing silicone covers as yet, and so there is still a limited window for 3D printer owners to take a foothold in this market, with some suitably attractive designs. A two-piece box lasts much longer than the flip-up style, and a quick look at iPhone cases should give some suitable inspiration for places to begin. My favourites so far are boxes with devillike faces and satanic horns.

And on that dark note, we conclude this trip through the fantastic possibilities open to the budding entrepreneur. There is a wealth of opportunity in the 3D printing marketplace that requires only an imagination to exploit and profit. The ideas listed here are just the tip of the iceberg. Our modern world, flooded with individualism, extended adolescence, high-speed communication, disposable income and boundless curiosity is one of truly endless wonderment.

PART III

Storm Clouds on the Horizon

28

Overcoming Negativity

Long before computers became a ubiquitous part of modern society, an abundance of industry experts planted both feet in their mouths with statements that look incredibly misguided with hindsight. You might even be familiar some of these:

> *Everything that can be invented has been invented.*—Charles H. Duell, Commissioner, U.S. Office of Patents, 1899

> *I think there is a world market for maybe five computers.*—IBM Chairman, Thomas Watson, 1943

> *I have traveled the length and breadth of this country and talked with the best people, and I can assure you that data processing is a fad that won't last out the year.*—The editor in charge of business books for Prentice Hall, 1957

> *But what... is it good for?*—An engineer at the Advanced Computing Systems Division of IBM, commenting on the microchip in 1968.

> *No one will need more than 637 kb of memory for a personal computer. 640K ought to be enough for anybody.*—Bill Gates,

founder of Microsoft, 1981

Two years from now, spam will be solved.—Bill Gates, World Economic Forum 2004

Many transformative technologies were initially greeted with skepticism. A McKinsey report in 1980 advised AT&T that mobile phones would remain a niche technology and have little widespread impact. Even now there are plenty of self-proclaimed experts making similarly negative claims, in fact many more than ever before, thanks to the appearance of blogs, forums, Twitter and Facebook. Some, for example, claim the 3D printers they have seen so far are all good fun, but nothing that could actually be useful in everyday life. This myopic viewpoint prevents many people from seeing the possibilities; these machines print out custom items tailored to the needs of the individual. By definition, what is essential to one person may not be useful at all to another. In fact, the internet is full of critics and pundits with varying credentials who insist that 3D printed products are hit and miss affairs, very brittle, extremely time consuming, messy and being good only for prototyping, not manufacturing. Arguments commonly begin with phrases along the lines of "As a practicing engineer..." or when addressing an enthusiast, condescension is evident: "Spoken by someone who, I am willing to guess, has never actually worked in manufacturing..." There are numerous comments along the lines of "Please get advice from expert engineers etc. before writing such utter tosh." One must wonder if Gutenberg had to put up with similar criticisms from squinting scribes that could not see beyond the end of their quills. Maybe they made similar complaints that the new-fangled printers were monstrous, lumbering goliaths, completely incapable of illuminating a manuscript to the level required for the Lord's own book. Perhaps they argued that high volume printing only devalued literary work, or that time spent carving inkblocks was a complete waste when it should be used to apply gold leaf to the word of God. Humankind has always been resistant to change and will always be that way, it is quite likely that there were grunted arguments about the potential of flint over traditional sharpened sticks.

Of course, the latest batch of printed items is still somewhat basic and brittle, compared to the products of advanced and refined mass manufacturing. Home brew machines are especially adept at making examples out of a somewhat weak plastic, (it isn't super fragile, but it isn't high-impact either) but the technology is barely out of infancy. Our growing understanding of complex geometry will quickly ensure that strength and substance meet the requirements of the use of the product. Those who say that 3D printers are useless for manufacturing make it clear that they have not grasped the most basic concept of all. When anybody can print off any item desired, in the comfort of their own home, then mass production manufacturing no longer serves any useful purpose.

While it is true that 3D printers cannot compete cost wise or in production efficiency with industrial mass production manufacturing on a large scale, their real strength lies in limited small batch production and custom one-of-a-kind, just-in-time, in-house design. But mass production has built-in overheads and minimums. The ability to make only what is necessary, and to make it quickly, makes digital manufacturing a clear choice for many.

Many entrenched thinkers are saying that 3D printing is only good for prototyping. The real point is that it makes prototyping so much easier and cheaper. When we reduce the time required to design, build and test manufactured products by a factor of five or ten, then we will, at the same time dramatically increase the number of product designers and entrepreneurs who make things. Until now, where was the motivation to envision and design your own products? Unless you had access to a multi-million-dollar production line, how would you ever lift your ideas off the drawing board? Even if you were willing to fly all the way out to Hong Kong and convince a factory owner of the inherent benefits of your new design, chances are that you would need to place a minimum order of ten thousand just to get the process underway. Chris Anderson of *Wired* Magazine makes the idea of outsourcing for citizen industrialists' sound so easy. As he says, "Anybody with an idea and a little expertise can set assembly lines in China into motion with nothing more than some keystrokes on their laptop." With comments like this, it is doubtful that he has even seen the inside of an average Chinese factory, let alone make it actually produce something. Anybody that believes dealing with Chinese factories is an easy process should read 'Poorly Made in China' by Paul Midler. Having been though this purgatory many times myself, I can vouch for almost everything the book describes, from incompetent and dishonest owners to non-existent quality control. If you arrive in Guangdong as a small entrepreneur rather than a vaunted executive from Apple (or perhaps a journalist from a glamorous Conde Nast publication such as *Wired*), then you quickly learn to accept lies, and deception as the natural way of doing business. I would even venture that so many repeated disappointments with Chinese factories that have made me an evangelist for 3D Printers. With the advent of desktop manufacturing, if you have an idea for a new product, it does not matter how zany or fruit-cakey it might be. If a 3D printer can knock out just one, then suddenly you have a working prototype.

Traditional mass production is based upon the economy-of-scale model. This means that the manufacturing industry is stuck in a trend, moving towards gradual refinement of processes and of products. Vertical integration, a process where manufacturing begins to take control of both supply and demand, has also reduced the number of choices, and the amount of diversity in the marketplace. Even today, you can visit any one of a number of manufacturing facilities and be confronted with the same processes, the same standards, even the exact same machinery. No longer is there a need to consider a product based on it's merits, all products are the same. The only factors now are turnaround time and price. This has inevitably left the manufacturing industry catering only to a statistical minority of potential clients, inadvertently creating a new market out of what is likely to be one-third of the world's population.

With three billion people who are potential customers, distributed digital manufacturing has the power to capitalize on fads and trends faster than mass manufacturing ever could. In fact vertical integration includes, in the bigger picture, manipulation of these trends and fads to ensure fortuitous timing. We don't need to corner the market on product in a global sense any more, just the one in which we live and work.

Of all the contemporary bottlenecks of 3D printing, size is possibly the biggest, but this limitation never dented the popularity of Lego or Meccano. We can always build big things out of small pieces, as long as we design the parts correctly in the first place. Once the cumbersome processes involved in mass manufacturing are eliminated from the equation, it does not cost any extra to over-engineer, so there will be longevity gains in that respect, compared to most of the shoddy products we currently buy based on low prices provided by traditional mass manufacturing. It might turn out that few items need to be serviceable and why should it be, when you can print out a replacement? But that does not mean that waste will inevitably go up. Could we not process our own plastic rubbish to 'feed' this? How difficult would it be to melt everyday plastics into some form of 'injection rod'?

An inline recycling unit is feasible. Something breaks—junk in, replacement part out. The base materials for plastics being a finite resource, then additive manufacturing allows us to be far more frugal with them. Those base materials aren't necessarily even finite; it is not out of the question to picture a zero-transport production chain, where a crop is grown in the garden, processed into a polymer and then fed into the printer in your living room. Then, when you no longer need it, you can simply grind it up and make something you do need. With organic plastics, waste can be composted to feed the next batch of PLA crops. Part of the problem here—as already exists with current recycling initiatives—is that for no very good reason, six or seven hundred different types of plastic are currently used in manufacturing and you cannot just melt them all down together.

3D printing technology is certainly new, glitchy, and not quite ready for prime time, but that does not mean that it should simply be dismissed as an expensive toy. The potential of this technology to cut energy and materials waste in production is extremely promising. We are going to need to use more advanced lightweight plastics in the future in manufacturing of all types of vehicles for example. The lighter the vehicles, the less energy they require. This process not only allows us to use less plastic in the manufacturing process, it also allows the manufacture of designs that would have been impossible with traditional techniques.

Conventional production is currently being subsidised by sweat shop Chinese labour that works without health and safety regulation or basic forms of worker's rights. Energy and materials are available at prices that are magnitudes below their replacement costs, and the added costs of pollution, environmental damage and waste are completely externalised, as though they do not even exist. Even the most deluded economist can see that this cannot last forever. The damage done by production doesn't include the environmental impact of shipping everything halfway across the planet. A recent study found that one large container ship emits almost the same amount of cancer and asthma-causing chemicals as fifty million cars.

Anybody thinking of printing coat hangers, shower rings and spatulas has obviously failed to grasp the concept of additive manufacturing at all. This technology will revolutionise high-end items, such as complex aerospace parts and components for bespoke under sea pumps. 3D printers can produce complex internal structures and mix multiple materials in precise ratios and patterns, so a wide range of properties is combined in a single object. A simple example would be printing a mallet; the handle would be full of a honeycomb structure to make it light, and the head would be semi solid to give it weight, or even filled with pellets to make a dead-blow mallet. Another trick is making ball bearings, which these machines can build as single pieces. The printer creates the ring around the bearings (with a thin piece of connecting plastic that is snapped off). The bearings are not aircraft-quality just yet, but for many applications, they are quite servicable.

The current generation of DIY machines certainly have their drawbacks but they themselves are little more than prototypes, and will soon evolve into something much more useful and efficient. The first generation of 2D desktop printers was horrible. For the price of thousands of dollars, we got lo-res dot matrix printouts on paper that had tractor-feed holes punched into the margins. It was not pretty, but those early models paved the way for high-resolution, low-cost laser printing. I would be the first to list of some of the many criticisms of current machines. Build times are excessive. Leveling and squaring can still be extremely difficult. Machine vibration can cause the screws to loosen which requires constant maintenance, in fact, a single fastener, not properly tightened, can lead to misprinted parts, cause instability in the printer, and worse yet, cause other fasteners to shake loose. Despite these problems, we can all see that these are little more than teething troubles. These are hiccups and glitches that one must expect when pushing the envelope, but not inherent faults of the technology itself. These problems are part of the learning curve of an industry.

Just as there were those who said the computer would amount to nothing, there is now a new generation of naysayers claiming that additive manufacturing is fine for keynote speeches and think tank prognostications, but not the sort of thing you would expect to turn quickly into a profitable business. I hope that the previous section has shown you that there are far more opportunities to quickly re-coup the costs of buying the 3D printer than you have perhaps so far imagined.

29

Some Interesting Analogies

The *Economist* states that 3D printing will "disrupt every field in touches." Business Insider calls it "the next trillion-dollar industry." With such a media feeding frenzy already in progress, every journalist and his dog are coming up with imaginative analogies to illustrate the impacts of this amazing new technology. Many of them are quite eye opening.

Some claim that the 3D printer of today is a lot like the VCR, or maybe even a high end sewing machine. It has elements of robotics, complex control circuitry, and many now also have an on-board LCD interface. But with all that technological brilliance, it is what it does that matters the most. To watch a 3D printer in action, is like witnessing art, science and engineering all working together in glorious unison.

Could physical products take the same route as recorded music? Even with a slow dialup internet connection, the value of a CD went from $15 to almost zero practically overnight. Just as Napster and Torrents made the entire music archive available for anybody with the knowledge to download it, the same might very well happen with high-end designer products. How far away are we from a time when even the scruffiest of mutts has a Le Corbusier dog kennel? Will it be same as LV handbags and Ralph Lauren polo shirts, churned out in boatloads from Chinese sweatshops, but with absolutely everything?

Peer to peer sharing, the kind that began in earnest with Napster, is a platform that does share some similarities with the 3D printing world and one of it's features in particular has a striking parallel; many efforts have been led to curb the practice, including massive campaigns by government and industry. In spite of these efforts, the platform remains, like a hydra, when one head is cut off another takes its place. This is because the peer-to-peer platform is dependent upon the users. The various websites merely track the availability of a file. 3D printing is a part of the distributed production spectrum, which makes it a robust industry because it is not based on central facilities that are being located farther and farther away from the marketplace with massive overheads and the economic inefficiency of the mass production system. It is a dynamic, responsive production system that uses common materials and works in an almost surgical fashion, making only what is required.

A comparison can be made with the effect that digital cameras have had on photography. In terms of new designs, will anybody be able to stand out, when the market is flooded by enthusiastic students and amateurs just trying to be seen, making their portfolios available for free? Will we be so spoiled for choice by the free stuff that there will no longer be any need to buy anything? Just think about stock photos today—the skilled photographers with 99 percent brilliant photos in their portfolio are often impossible to find among the millions with one good shot to their name, driving the prices down, as they are desperate to sell that one photo so they can feel like 'pro'. Even if you do find them, why pay them enough to be a full time photographer, when you can pay pennies to an accountant who happened to take a good photo while on holiday once? There is another side to this, however; in a sea of mediocrity a gem is much easier to spot, competition allows the customer to see the difference between each choice available to them.

3D printing is a new paradigm whose potential is just being noticed. The RepRaps and Tinkerines are at the scratchy vinyl and typewritten fanzine level, but they will bring us their own equivalents of Ian Dury, Vivienne Westwood, or Malcom McClaren. Later, they will inspire a completely new generation to combine spontaneous, ubiquitous cheap tech with old-school creative education. On $100,000 high end Objet machines, the PhD laden equivalents of bands like Queen and Yes will still be churning out design styles similar to the overly intellectualised, self-indulgent prog rock of the seventies. RepRappers and their successors, the rebels of this story, will be coming up with entirely new genres. The digital design equivalents of rap, thrash, house, ska and hip-hop will open up entirely new avenues of which we cannot currently even conceive.

One interesting industry that might show us where 3D printing is heading in the future is that of micro brewing. Although the term "microbrewery" is generally used in relation to size, it has gradually come to reflect an alternative attitude and approach to brewing: flexibility, adaptability, experimentation and customer service. Despite a backdrop of continuing pub closures in the UK for example, (almost ten thousand pubs have closed in the past decade) the Campaign for Real Ale (Camra) says there are now one thousand breweries in the UK - the highest figure for 70 years. One hundred fifty-eight new breweries opened in the past year alone, the highest number ever recorded in the lobby group's annual Good Beer Guide.

Micro or craft breweries have adopted a marketing strategy quite different to that of large, mass-market breweries, offering products that compete on the basis of quality and diversity, instead of low price and advertising. Their influence has been much greater than their market share (which amounts to only 2 percent in the UK), indicated by the fact that large commercial breweries have introduced new brands intended to compete in the same market as microbrews. When this strategy failed, they invested in microbreweries; or in many cases bought them outright.

Twenty million pints of beer are consumed every day in the UK and almost nine out of ten are brewed in the UK, supporting around a million jobs in total. The boom in new breweries has, in many cases, made the term 'micro' obsolete, with some small brewers having become remarkably large, installing new equipment and repeatedly doubling production to keep up with demand. Are these the patterns that we are going to see with 3D printing?

While I have presented a number of contemporary analogies, I would also like to look at some important historical events. These seem to share more than a coincidental similarity with the situation that we are currently seeing with 3D printers.

For his development of the first movable-type printing press, it is now widely agreed that Johann Gutenberg was the greatest inventor of the millennium, and that his printing of the first Bible, was a critical building block of our modern civilisation. Thanks to his genius, labouring for two weeks to hand copy even the simplest of books quickly became a thing of the past. Previously, a hand written book such as the Bible was far beyond the reach of the common person, costing an astounding $1 million dollars in current terms. The Black Death had just ravaged Europe, killing as many as twenty-five million people (approximately one-third of the population) including many of the all-important monastic scribes. Gutenberg's invention therefore came at an important convergence point in human history that literally shaped the modern world. Crusaders were returning from the Holy Lands with a wealth of ancient knowledge that had been completely lost to educated Europe since the fall of the Roman Empire, over a thousand years before. Scholasticism in the form of the first universities was just gaining its first foothold, and all this new learning needed a way to be easily disseminated. In fact, by 1470, just twenty years after the introduction of the first printing presses, it is estimated that there were already more than ten million books in existence, twenty million by 1500, and the knock-on effects ever since, have changed our society beyond recognition. Literacy in Northern Germany at the time of Gutenberg was estimated to be a mere four percent of the population. It has now jumped to almost universal levels all over Europe. At the beginning of the fifteenth century, the prestigious Cambridge University had a grand total of 300 books. This one university alone now houses more than 5.5 million volumes. The British Library in comparison houses more than 625 kilometres of bookshelves and has to add an additional nine kilometres every single year. What about the original Bibles that were the very first books off the very first press? Bill Gates recently picked one up at auction for a whopping $30.8 million.

Of course, this great invention that has so benefited the entirety of humankind was not without its early detractors. The corrupt rulers of medieval Europe saw knowledge as power, and were terrified at losing their monopoly on education due to the spread of knowledge into the hands of the unwashed masses. Along with the Church, who controlled the universities of the time, they quickly became the most powerful bastion of resistance to change and the heaviest-handed censors. At the time, the Bible was available only in Latin, and the clergy had absolute control on what the public thought and believed. The printed text led directly to the Protestant Reformation, even though the Church denounced printing as a 'black art.' It even gave second wind to the Inquisition who specifically targeted printers, while ironically using the same technology to publish their own *Index Librorum Prohibitorum* (list of banned books). Henry VIII did everything that he could to prevent the expansion of this new technology, and introduced a plethora of laws on censorship and prohibition. When Oxford Scholar, William Tyndale travelled to the Netherlands to publish a translation of the Bible into English, he was arrested upon his return for smuggling copies back into England. Tried by the Royal Court in 1535, he was sentenced to be publicly strangled and burned at the stake for his crimes.

Perhaps the most vociferous opposition came from the guilds of calligraphers and illuminators, who were petrified that this new fangled wonder would put them all out of business. It is therefore especially interesting to note that exactly the opposite came to pass, and that historians now universally agree that the sixteenth century became the golden age for illuminated manuscripts. As more and more people learned to read, obviously more people learned to write, and we saw great works of art created as part of this new information revolution. Barely fifty years after Gutenberg's initial print run, book fairs began to spring up all over the continent, and entirely new professions came into existence that were previously unheard of. Printers, editors, booksellers and journalists began to gain influence, not to mention those whom we know today as writers. The very first best-selling author was Erasmus. His *Moriae Encomium*, (Praise of Folly) printed in 1509, was a satirisation of church abuses and ecclesiastical ignorance, and went into forty-three editions in his own lifetime.

What important convergences are taking place today that will have equally dramatic effects on 3D printing? Without truly psychic powers, it is impossible to say but there are certainly a number of plausible contenders. I have written earlier about the importance of open source. I have also spoken of crowd-funding, crowd-sourcing and micro-tasking. I am especially interested in the concept of distributed networking. With so many game-changing influences all coming together at once I wonder how long it will be before the Internet is superseded by the Digital Matter-Net?

Despite all this over optimistic gushing, it is important to note that every technological advance has a sinister side. The discovery of rocket science gave us the opportunity to land on the moon but also gave us increasing political instability, the Cold War and Mutually Assured Destruction. To quote Einstein; "Only two things are infinite, the universe and human stupidity, and I'm not sure about the former."

30

Printing on a Larger Scale

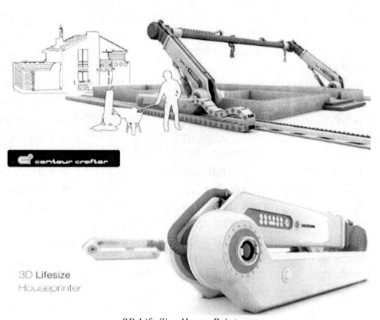

3D Life Size House Printer

Not everybody is printing at the smaller scales. Enrico Dini for example, is using his prototype D-Shape printer to create buildings made of stone and eventually, moon dust. Dini claims the printer is four times faster than conventional building methods, costs one-third to one-half the price of Portland cement and creates very little waste, so it's better for the environment. The printing process starts with a thin layer of sand. The printer then sprays the sand with magnesium-based glue from hundreds of nozzles, which binds the sand into rock. That rock is then built up layer by layer, eventually taking shape of whatever object it is destined to become, be it a curvy Roger Dean inspired sci-fi dwelling or an entire gothic cathedral.

Although it is still in its early stages, the IAAC Stone Spray Robot shows great potential for 3D printing ecologically friendly structures. The Institute for Advanced Architecture of Catalonia, a research and education centre in Spain developed this robot, similar to Dini's. Dedicated to the development of sustainable architecture, they hope to "push further the boundaries of digital manufacturing and explore the possibilities of on-site fabrication machines." The robotic device blends soil sourced on-site with a binder (which is composed of LEED-Certified components), and then sprays the mixture onto a surface. The soil solidifies as the machine works, which allows it to create sculptural forms. The robot is computer controlled and, unlike other 3D printers, the device runs on solar power.

Inventor and USC engineering professor Behrokh Khoshnevis has developed a contour crafting machine which will allow him to "print" a house out of concrete in twenty-four hours. This is really a 3D printer on steroids, with a gantry crane and a computer-guided cement nozzle on rails attached to it. The USC engineering professor was inspired to build this machine after witnessing the devastation of an earthquake that destroyed the city of Bam, in his native Iran. A typical American house takes at least six months to complete, generating about four tons of waste. It's believed the contour crafter will be able to erect most structures in about a day, generating far less waste in the process.

Furthermore, by automating the process, architects are free to create some pretty wild designs—curved walls are just as easy to create as flat ones and structurally just as sound. The professor explained the process in a speech at the TEDx conference, which you can watch. (Start at 4:30 to see the animation demo.) In the video, the professor demonstrates how the machine lays down a concrete foundation, puts up walls, even inserts wiring and plumbing, and eventually constructs an entire building. Khoshnevis believes that the contour crafter will ultimately be able to create structures using adobe, mud and straw dried by the sun rather than cement.

NASA recently awarded a team led by Khoshnevis $100,000 to test the concept of 3D printing structures on the moon, including landing pads, roads, shade walls, and dust barriers. In the lunar project, a mixture of lunar regolith (moon dust), water, and cement (made from lunar rock with high calcium) would be used to create walls and other structures, made out of 'mooncrete.'

A South Africa-based company, Aerosud is working hard on realizing the world's fastest and largest prototype 3D printer. The printer will use powdered titanium to make aircraft components ten times faster and forty-six times larger than any other metal 3D printer. They are working with Council for Scientific and Industrial Research's (CSIR's) National Laser Centre, and now Airbus.

Airbus designer Bastian Schafer has been working on a new concept plane that would largely be "printed" using a hangar-sized 3D printer. "It would have to be about 80 by 80 meters," he told reporters. Apart from significant cost savings, it would also allow for parts that are 65 percent lighter than those made with traditional manufacturing methods. Naturally, the concept plane itself is also a showpiece for a raft of other new technologies, including a transparent wall membrane, a 100 percent recyclable cabin, and "morphing" seats that could harvest body heat from passengers.

Not wanting to be left behind, Boeing has used additive manufacturing processes to produce more than twenty thousand parts that are utilised on military platforms, according to Daryl Stephenson, a company spokesman. Some of those parts have been designed to be lighter. By reducing an airplane's weight by just one kilogram, an airline can save $1,300 in fuel costs per year, according to an IBISWorld report. If it were possible to reduce the mass of a commercial jet by just one hundred kilograms, it would save 4.5 million litres of aviation fuel over its lifetime.

The expense of carrying equipment into outer space is even higher, currently coming in at about $10,000 just to bring one pound of equipment into orbit, if one takes into account both the costs of fuel and the complexities of a full-scale rocket launch.

Think back for a moment to Ron Howard's Oscar-winning movie *Apollo 13*. In response to the disastrous carbon dioxide removal malfunction, that threatened the life of the crew, engineers at ground control used materials they knew were on the craft to jerry-rig a solution. They then shared this information with the astronauts. If the spacecraft had been equipped with a 3D printer, things would have been very different. Instead of "Houston, we have a problem! it would have been, 'Houston, we have a problem, but send up a couple of CAD files and we will be back on schedule in a few minutes."

31

Printing Materials

The Nurdler

As we have seen, there are many choices of materials that can be utilised with 3D printers. At the smaller scales this is mostly some kind of plastic filament, usually made from fossil fuels. Fortunately there are many alternatives springing up, especially in the area of recycled plastics. Imagine how much more profitable end products would be if they only used filament from recycled bottles and other plastic products.

A recent Kickstarter project known as the Filabot raised $32,000, three times its original $10,000 request. The "big idea" here is the ability to take recycled plastic materials and turn it into filament that you can use with your 3D Printer. Although the demo was a little basic, the idea is on the winning track. The price will be $350 for an un-assembled kit.

The Desktop Factory Challenge on the other hand is a partnership between business competition aggregator iStart and online fab supplies store Inventables.com. This is a competition to build an open source filament extruder for less than $250 in components that can take ABS or PLA resin pellets, mix them with colorant, and extrude enough 1.75mm diameter +/- .05mm filament that can be wrapped on a 1kg spool. The prize available is $40,000 from the Kauffman Foundation and a Desktop Fabrication Lab (a 3D printer, an FS Laser Cutter, and a Shapeoko CNC Mill).

Making filament is not that hard, but doing so consistently is much more of a challenge, especially making it stay as a straight filament until it cools and can be wound onto a spool. This is why extruded plastic filament can cost five to ten times the cost of the raw resin pellets. There are China-based sellers that offer lower prices but the quality is inconsistent.

Detractors claim that it is very inefficient to melt pellets into a straight filament just to be melted again when coming out of the hot tip. A better solution might be to make 3D printers that can accept pellets and colour as needed, with an open source colour print head.

Although the contest does not close until May of 2013, a number of entries have already been posted on Thingiverse. One of these is the Lyman Filament Extruder which extrudes filament of 1.75mm and 3mm, with easy nozzle exchange. Another, the Bottleworks entry, has a larger hot end with a 350-Watt heater, automatic timing, fan ducting and adjustable motor speed on the control panel, despite the fact that is constructed mainly form discarded parts.

Full details are available at:

http://desktopfactory2012.istart.org/

All of the design competitions that we have been seeing, the 3D4D challenge, GrabCAD's design challenges, EvD's Design challenges, are quite reminiscent of the early 1900s, which saw the rapid development of the airplane. Just a century ago, newspapers and wealthy sponsors were offering large cash prizes to aviators, hoping that they could make planes fly further and faster than ever before. These competitions made instant celebrities out of pioneers such as Charles Lindbergh, Amelia Earhart, and Louis Blériot.

Every week we recycle dozens of bottles and we hope that the recycling plant does not simply throw them in the garbage. What we really need is a machine where plastic bottles are dropped into one end, shredded, then turned into usable filament at the other. This way Earth Cleanup Day will not just be about cleanup, it will be essential for restocking our bulk plastic piles.

Users are looking forward to being able to reuse milk jugs, detergent bottles, soda bottles, shampoo bottles, product packaging, and many more. The three most common types of plastic that can be recycled are as follows:

PET or PETE is the most common type of plastic used in drinks bottles.

PE-HD or HDPE is used in milk jugs, five-gallon buckets, water pipes, juice bottles.

PE-LD or LDPE is used in parts that require flexibility such as snap-on lids and six pack rings.

Perhaps our largest recyclable plastic resource is the North Pacific Gyre, or as it is rapidly becoming better known, the Great Pacific Garbage Patch, an enormous 'plastic soup' mass of marine litter trapped in the swirling vortex of currents of the Pacific Ocean. Recent studies estimate an average of 46,000 pieces of plastic litter every single square kilometre of the world's oceans. The number of plastic pieces in the Pacific Ocean has tripled in the last ten years to what the UN estimates at one hundred million tons worldwide, with current trajectories predicting this figure to double in the next ten years.

Contrary to common expectations, the fact that plastic breaks down has far more harmful consequences to the marine environment than most of us imagine. Plastic fragments act as sponges for harmful hydrophobic chemicals such as pesticides and fertilisers; with concentrations of up to a million times greater than the surrounding seawater, they form little toxic pills. The plastic resembles small sea creatures and enters the food chain leaching chemicals into fishes' fats and raising the toxicity of marine life. Samples from the Pacific Gyre have shown a ratio of six pounds of plastic to one pound of plankton. It is estimated that as much as 98 percent of this pollution is made up of nurdles. Although cricketers might be familiar with the verb form of nurdle, much of the rest of the population are unfamiliar with this material, despite its enormous effect on the environment.

Nurdles cover a wide range of micro plastic products ranging from the tiny plastic pellets used in injection moulding, to the broken down remnants of plastic litter. Sometimes also known as 'mermaid's tears,' many nurdles are simply lost through spillage, such as the containers that were whipped offshore in Hong Kong by Typhoon

Vincente in 2012, but more often, it is simply a case of poor storage and lack of regulations. More than 250 quadrillion (27 million tonnes) nurdles will be made this year and the United Nations states that thirteen thousand nurdles are floating in every square mile of the ocean. The pellets are around 4mm in diameter, and their tiny size means they are not picked up by waste systems. Being buoyant, they will float on the sea surface taking over a thousand years to biodegrade, all the while resembling fish eggs.

Taking their inspiration from early Cornish miners, inventors in the South West of England have come up with a design known as the Nurdler, a sluice-like contraption that allows the sorting of vast quantities of marine debris quickly and efficiently. The Nurdler consists of a hand-powered water pump and a sluice that sorts the micro plastic collected from the strand line, or high water mark, the area at the top of a beach where debris is deposited. Particulates are graded by size and pass through a floatation tank to separate materials by density, enabling users to separate the elusive plastic fragments to be recycled. The Nurdler (also known as the Sea Chair) is being tested on Cornish beaches, many of which are sink beaches facing the vast North Atlantic, from which great swells bring in a enormous daily tide of exotic rubbish, revealing the true state of our marine environment. Porthtowan Beach in beautiful Cornwall for example, is currently the UK's most polluted beach for micro plastic.

The Nurdler could be very useful in the recently unveiled EU plans to pay fisherman for plastic by-catch. A 'fishing for litter' campaign involved fisherman from Sweden, Denmark, the Netherlands and the UK who returned all litter caught in their net to the shore, landing some five hundred tonnes from sixty boats in 2004. By diversifying modern fishermen's skills to restore our ocean environment, it is hoped that schemes like this will help regenerate Britain's once strong fishing community.

The Nurdler is made entirely from recovered plastic has been constructed with simple moulds and tools that would enable production at sea; the chair is tagged according to its geographical coordinates and production number. After sorting the marine debris, users are left with roughly a quarter of organic material such as seaweed and wood. This can be compressed with a simple hydraulic press that fits on a small fishing vessel, into briquettes to burn as a bio fuel for melting the plastic.

Of course, that is not to say that some 3D printers are not already utilising recycled plastics.

Student members of the University of Washington Fabbers, the UW's 3D printing student club, created the world's first boat via a 3D printer and they entered it in Seattle's annual Milk Carton Derby. The 7-foot boat was made from recycled, melted and extruded milk cartons that the students collected, and then ran through a large, custom-designed 3D printer in the UW's Mechanical Engineering Building. They spent the last two months researching, engineering, extruding, printing, and dumpster diving for the greater good, and eventually produced a 40-pound (approximately 250 one-gallon milk jugs) "canoeyak" capable of supporting 150 pounds.

The club aimed to be the first to print a seaworthy craft, but the judges of the Derby weren't sure what to make of their creation. Qualification was a problem as the engineers had used recycled milk cartons for its buoyancy, but not quite in the way that contest organizers had originally envisioned. It was eventually decided that the boat should be entered as "an unofficial entry in the adult open category", and it eventually placed overall second in the race.

In a separate venture, two transparent Ultimakers at the Lowlands 2012 exhibition were used to create objects from disposable cups. As well as enabling people to recycle on the spot, visitors were able to go through the whole working process from washing, drying, shredding and melting of the disposable cups to the final step of extruding the recycled melted material with the Ultimaker.

Even this does not match up to the Dutch artist, Wieki Somers who is using the ashes of dead people to create common household objects using a 3D industrial printer. "We may offer Grandpa a second life as a useful rocking chair or even as a vacuum cleaner or a toaster," she said. "Would we then become more attached to these products?" The artist claims that in excess of 465,000 litres of human ashes are produced every day worldwide and that this is an alternative to the traditional scattering.

Freedom of Creation recently announced a new 3D printing technique that transforms sawdust into objects that closely resemble real wood. Using a special glue to bind the sawdust together, the result is a solid object that is every bit as strong as medium density fibreboard. Unfortunately, despite lots of tweaking, the researchers have found that not all wood prints equally. They can work wonders with teak and mahogany, but sawdust from soft woods does not spread so evenly on the printer.

Mcor Technologies recently launched a brand new rapid

prototyping machine, The Mcor Matrix, capable of using plain or recycled A4 paper and water-based adhesive. The machine selectively deposits glue on the sheet of paper: more glue on the cross-section, less on the waste. It then uses a blade to cut out the part profile. The vertical resolution is determined by the paper thickness. It can use either twenty-pound paper, which has a thickness of .1mm, or forty-pound, which is twice as thick, so it will build twice as fast. The final part can be sanded and painted like wood. The idea is similar to LOM (laminated object manufacturing), but those machines require specialized paper. It is very refreshing to see a company intentionally target a lower cost of ownership, but if they had used a laser, we would only have to worry about sourcing the glue." The *Irish Times* newspaper gives a pre sale price point of $25,000.

Markus Kayser's Solar Sinter is a remarkable 3D printer that uses only Saharan sand and sun to make actual objects. Instead of using one of the regular polymers, this device ingeniously makes use of the deserts other most plentiful feature—sand. While this is a fantastic example of sustainable innovation, it is still more art installation and ingenious hack than commercial project, but it certainly does open up the future possibilities of the industry.

The next step will be the simplification of combining multiple materials to create products that are more complex. Just as regular 2D printers mix red, green and blue to print full colour, it will be a major breakthrough when we can use a similarly small palette to create a wide variety of different substances.

According to extremetech.com writer John Hewitt "Most plastics are relatively soft materials with low compressive and tensile strengths, low melting points, and poor chemical resistance. Even the more expensive formulations like polyimide or polyether ether ketone (PEEK) give only modest improvements relative to metals. Plastics also become brittle when cold, and quickly age through exposure to UV light from the sun. Their lack of hardness also means that fine details cannot be rendered by traditional methods of manufacture since they do not hold up to the forces required to create them. Fine detail is also quickly degraded by repetitive use."

The community is already experimenting with alternatives. Hackaday.com features many articles related to the field, including the following: "Most extrusion printers are designed to print with ABS (a very hard plastic that melts around 220-230° C) or PLA (a somewhat softer plastic that melts at about 180° C). One member of the Instructables site is working with Nylon 6, a very slippery and bendable plastic that melts around 320° C (about 600° F). He's doing this with a hot end of his own design and a 'spiky' extruder bolt that allows high-temperature thermoplastics to be extruded into any shape imaginable."

The benefits of using low-temperature thermoplastics such as PLA and ABS are obvious. Spools of filament are easily sourced, and the low melting point of these plastics makes building a printer easier and safer. If we can crack the higher temperature nut, then we can expect a much greater choice of material to run in our printers, from easily machined Delrin to transparent Polycarbonate. In the meantime, there are other obstacles to overcome.

One of the biggest problems is that melting nylon smells revolting and emits hydrogen cyanide, carbon monoxide and other nasties. At the very minimum the printer needs to be enclosed in an acrylic box with an exhaust fan and even then, pumping it outside does not make the problem magically go away. It then becomes a problem of poisoning your neighbours. The chemicals emitted are toxic in very low quantities, as little as 10 ppm. This not actually the nylon but the main additive fibreglass, which gives nylon it's strength at high temperatures and low densities. Worse still, it is bio-accumulative, meaning the effects will slowly poison humans over a long period, even in low concentrations. Fiberglass is cheap and as an additive, it reduces the overall costs of the part being made. A win/win for injection moulding but not so much for 3D Printers. The fibreglass and other chemicals added actually raise the temperature needed to way beyond what raw nylon normally requires and at those temperatures, all plastics become unstable. Add fibreglass to ABS, PLA, PET, even PVC and it will burn and boil the base plastic.

While some complain that the resins most commonly used in 3D are quite fragile, resin technology is quickly becoming more sophisticated, and many other materials are now being used to make lightweight, high-strength and functional components. There are now over twenty metal alloys commonly used for additive manufacturing including titanium alloys, nickel super-alloys, aluminium alloys, steels and others. New alloys are released for use on an almost monthly basis. It is reasonable to project that by 2015, there may be a hundred or more alloys in common use and still rising.

Plastics of course are just the beginning. We are now beginning to see the introduction of low-cost metal powder additive machines.

Unlike other UV-bonded powder machines that currently cost about $50,000 or E-beam deposition machines that are even more expensive, the Danish Blueprinter uses a selective heat sintering technology in an office 3D printer that costs just €9,995. The technique is similar to laser sintering, but instead of using a laser, SHS uses a thermal print head. The powder bed is held at an elevated temperature so the mechanically-scanned head only has to elevate the temperature slightly above the powder's melting temperature to selectively bond it.

For hobbyists there are at least two open source powder printers currently available at around a tenth of the price of the Blueprinter. The Open3Dprinter project in Russia has precious little information in English available just yet, but desktop laser sintering is just on the horizon in the form of the Pwdr, an open source powder-based rapid prototyping machine developed at The University of Twente. A whole new range of materials becomes available for experimenting with open-source rapid-prototyping; for example, when using the 3DP process: gypsum, ceramics, concrete, sugar, etc. When the SLS process is fully supported, plastic materials like ABS, PP, Nylon and metals will become available as building material. A Hewlett Packard inkjet cartridge is used for the deposition of binder. The cartridge can be refilled with custom binders using a syringe. A custom binder of 20 percent alcohol and 80 percent water has proven to work. The printer consists entirely of off-the-shelf components and can be built for about €1000. Although it is very much a prototype, if it evolves at the same rapid pace of the Reprap then we will likely see massive changes in the desktop 3D Printing ecosphere. Look forward not only to cheap aluminium or expensive titanium as a base metal, but stainless steel, sitanium, cobalt chrome-moly, or nickel alloy, are all of which are available on laser sintering machines.

DLS (digital laser sintering) is not new, most modern jet engines use parts made this way, and it produces good results. These technologies, can print in metals and give material properties superior to those of cast components, but inferior to wrought metal. These processes allow superior geometry in the design and speed in the production process.

Even if a casting made by a local foundry is required, rapid prototyping can dramatically cut the cost of pattern making. At least one 3D printing company offers 'printing' in brass, bronze and titanium, even in gold and silver. They use a very old and well-known technique, the lost wax method - but the wax is printed with a 3D printer. This is not only an amazing evolution on an existing technology, but because the final products are not built up layer by layer, they are structurally equivalent to anything coming out of a foundry.

High detailed stainless steel is already available from i.materialise, with the strength of titanium but significantly less expensive. This material is suitable for small, detailed, strong, and weatherproof models where accuracy is not yet the initial concern, such as board game figures, miniatures, key chains, jewellery and bolts. The stainless steel powder is deposited with a binder, through a precision ink jet printer; the object is then depowdered and sintered in an oven at around 1300 degrees. After cooling down the object is mechanically polished before being sent to customer. Models need to be at least 3 x 3 x 3 mm, up to a maximum of 40 x 40 x 35 mm, while detail resolution is 0.3 mm and wall thickness 1.0 mm. As a guideline to pricing, a model of 10 x 10 x 10 mm will cost just over €18, while a ring of 23 x 23 x 5 mm comes in at around €35.

There is even more interesting work being done in ceramic 3D printing, the result being a product robust enough to work in jet engines. Ceramic particles in a fluid suspension have a laser shined on the surface in the relevant shape. This fuses the ceramic layer, the object is lowered a tiny amount and then the process is repeated for the next layer. It is a few years off but will be revolutionary. Just imagine the potential of creating semiconductor substrates in your own workshop. If the home kit includes baking at controlled temperatures with a way to exclude impurities, then away we go!

When some bright spark manages to 'print' using carbon rather than ordinary plastic then the fun will really begin. The development of 'printed' solar cells and 'printed' computer memory is cracking on and it looks like 'printed' stuff is definitely going to be the next big thing. Exciting stuff—especially the prospects for graphene and printable electronics

32

Legal Issues

The Botmill Reprap Glider 3.0

Intellectual property rights are intrinsically linked to 3D printing. The very nature of the business is that a digital file will be printed as an object. This makes it very clear that it is the file which is important, rather than the printer.

Powerful tools of production are now in the hands of anyone who cares to buy or make a machine, and the dissemination of information over the internet means that the knowledge required to build a 3D printer is minimal. This change in technology alone will make things more complicated than ever before. There are some simple facts relating to copyright that suddenly become very important. The most notable of these is that whoever owns the copyright owns the right to use the material and the right to prosecute violators. This rather tragic circumstance arises from continued industry attempts to change copyright in ways to benefit themselves, and the core of it always is about money, or controlling the flow of it.

As the subject relates to 3D printing, what the reader, the prospective contract manufacturer, has to consider is whether or not they will respect these laws that have been forced through to protect large vested interests. Small businesses in the additive manufacturing spotlight will need to have a solid knowledge of what they can and cannot do as far as copyright is concerned, and it is essential that 3D fabbers arm themselves with appropriate information.

There is also another angle to consider here, that of the 3D manufacturer as the originator of a design. What can be done if you design something and want to protect it? The legal protection is automatic, but supporting that protection with evidence and backing it up with legal muscle is often the province of massive, multi-billion dollar corporations, so what can a humble individual do? Useful resources include the American Intellectual Property Law Association (http://www.aipla.org), who offer a thorough guidebook covering many aspects of innovation and creativity and how they interact with the law.

Copyright and patent law, both of which apply to the world of 3D printing, are complex and riddled with grey areas lacking any precise definition.

A review of the history of copyright reveals a simple pattern. New and revolutionary technologies arrive, technologies that permit the easy copying of materials. These include the photocopier, the cassette recorder, audio and video codecs and now digital manufacturing technologies. Historically we have seen hysterical reactions to the kinds of activities that these technologies bring with them—Crackdowns on unauthorised music recordings and copy DVDs, increasingly more policed internet connections and DRM/DMCA takedown notices for websites that host user-contributed content. This book is itself a fine example of how the realm of copyright is changing. No longer does the author need a printing press, a publisher or any other form of traditional printing industry.

Activities that prompt these legal actions are widespread, and will continue regardless of attempts to curb them by industries seeking to delay the inevitable. The purpose of this chapter is to provide you, the prospective entrepreneur, with an overview of the legal arena being entered and some advice to help avoid troubles down the line, as well as an understanding of the impact that copyright law has on creative endeavours.

Copyright law covers all variety of ideas; music, literature, art and any form thereof. Almost anything can be copyrighted and the protection is automatic once the idea is "fixed in a tangible medium". Patents, however, could be described as protecting functional systems without regard to the design. A copyrighted design may be affixed to a medium that is independent of the medium itself, such as a pattern on a piece of cloth, an image printed on paper or an aesthetic styling of an everyday product like a car or a television. Remove the unique design elements and all that is left with the medium. If we take all of the unique styling away from a Jaguar car we still have a car—four wheels, an engine and so forth. If we take an image of Mickey Mouse away from a poster, we are still left with a piece of poster paper. What a patent does is to protect the medium. The operational concept of a television could be patented, and as long as the manufacture conforms to those principles it does not matter what it looks like, it is still a patented product.

While some organisations are already seeking other ways of protecting intellectual property, with ideas including Digital Rights Management (DRM) built into 3D printers as well as monitoring of the internet for violations, but ultimately it will be up to the individual to decide whether to commit a violation. We have speed limits the world over, and vehicles are capable of breaking them, it is only a matter of the will to do so.

Copyright is sadly touted as a protection for the artist creating the material, but the truth is that copyright protects the profits of those who produce and distribute the material. It remains an important method of controlling the marketplace and the flow of profits.

All art, whether it be music, the written word or that strange lamp design you just saw on the internet over your morning coffee, all art is communication. Its purpose is to use the language of form to communicate thoughts and feelings. This communication comes in so many different shapes and sizes, but the whole point, the whole purpose is to make information available to other people. That point is lost when the purpose of creating becomes solely about money. When the bottom line dominates, the laws of economics take over and begin to change the process. Record companies will sign artists for multiple album deals spanning a set period, publishers will offer up advances for books. Many forms of inducement serve to use financial rewards and contractual obligations to direct an artist towards creating a product, yet once the artist has created the work, it instantly becomes the property of the producer or publisher. Just look at the back of one of your CDs, does it say "Copyright 2008" and the artists name? No, its says; "The copyright in this sound recording belongs to XL Recordings" or words to a similar effect. How can copyright laws, in their modern iteration, be truly said to protect an artist? Publishers and music companies obtain the copyright to these works through literally bribing the artist with what every artist wants: to reach people, as many as possible.

Copyright law has changed so much that it is now possible for someone else to own the rights to your work forever, and this is the problem, one which will likely become a major issue in the 3D printing community very quickly. Copyright should always belong to the creator, the originator of a work, and be controlled by them, it should be non-transferrable. It can be licensed out to others who think they can make money, but the ownership and the choice about the fate of the product in question should always remain with the person that created it.

What follows are some examples of the copyright system in action, some of which appear to be questionable to anyone with a modicum of common sense.

Miniature war machines

One good example of these ideas is the case of Games Workshop, Ltd. issuing a takedown notice to Thingiverse for a 'Sentinel' war machine 3D file uploaded by a user. The Sentinel was an almost exact copy of Games Workshop's own Imperial Guard Sentinel miniature, which meant that users were able to create this model without due credit or payment to the owner. This illustrates one of the very fine lines of the law; the Sentinel is a copyrighted design produced by Games Workshop, but the casual observer might find themselves asking "Why didn't George Lucas take action against Games Workshop?", because the Sentinel is a very similar machine to the AT-ST walker featured in the Star Wars universe. This question is complicated and requires a little background to answer. Firstly, the Sentinel design falls under the realm of copyright law because it is a design, one of many possible variations of walking war machine. Were the idea of a walking war machine central to the question it might fall under patent law. There is a history of walking war machines that greatly predates Games Workshop and George Lucas, whether they be the android Cybermen from Doctor Who, ED-209 from the Robocop series, H.G. Wells Martian invaders of War of the Worlds fame. We could even include the legendary Golem in this categorization, and the Trojan Horse, the possible basis of the four-legged AT-AT walker?

Had the user on Thingiverse created a walking war machine of his own design for use in tabletop war games, even if it resembled the Sentinel in that it had two legs, no arms and an armoured cab, then he would have been in the clear, legally speaking. Copyright law allows for simultaneous creation of works and only applies to a specific design. You can remove the design from the underlying structure in this case and still have a two-legged walking war machine, much like the users' other upload, a copy of the Leman Russ battle tank from the same range of models. A battle tank is not a new concept, not one that is protected in any way, but the Leman Russ battle tank is the intellectual property of Games Workshop, and to make a copy, digital or real, and distribute it would be a clear violation of copyright law.

This illustration is not here for any moral or political purpose, it is merely an explanation of what will put you into legal hot water. The same company mentioned above, Games Workshop, Ltd, also publishes a magazine and a website, both of which encourage hobbyists to make their own models from scratch; war machines, soldiers or terrain features. Their publications offer step by step instructions for making, converting and painting miniatures and there is a thriving market for painted models that are painted in schemes created and copyrighted by Games Workshop. While moral protest is fine, I cannot encourage you to break the law BUT I do strongly urge you to become engaged in, and instrumental in changing the way the intellectual property inherent in design is administered.

Continuing with the science fiction theme we can also look at the case of the Stormtrooper helmets. This case is interesting because it involved two countries with different laws. The maker of the Stormtrooper helmets claimed to have unearthed a set of original moulds for the helmet and began production of replicas. He was successfully sued in California, but when Lucasfilm tried to follow up in the UK the helmets were found to be protected differently from other forms of artwork because they were film props. These are protected for fifteen years in the UK and the helmets are still for sale, legally, in England. The most interesting facet of this case is that the US courts defined the helmets as sculpture, art in and of themselves, whereas the British courts found the film in which they featured to be the work of art, and the helmets to be little more than a production tool. This highlights the differences between the laws of the two countries as well as bringing up the important question about the vague nature of US copyright law.

What is most important about this case, though, is that the helmets were specifically defined as not being sculptural works in and of themselves, but utilitarian forms used to create the artistic work that is Star Wars. As copyright law evolves, we can only hope that more nations will adopt standards that do not offer blanket copyright protection to everything, thereby allowing market innovations and a further spread of creativity and deeper enjoyment of more works.

Much like charity and social safety nets, this aspect of life is rife with the possibilities of abuse, but much like those same ventures I do not think that it is possible for us to have an economic system of any kind without some number of innocent or dishonest people seeing and implementing ways to make or save a few bucks by abusing trust. No matter what draconian measures are taken, there will always be instances of abuse, theft and other criminal activity. Enacting protections such as the notion of a BIOS DRM system in every 3D printer is an over-reaction that will do more harm than good in the long run and in a larger perspective. One also has to question the justification for such actions, some of which seem reasonable on the surface but are decidedly deceitful once numbers and evidence are examined. The strongest example of this is the music industry, which claims file sharing has heavily damaged its profits, but an examination of the facts points towards the business model of the music industry, the industrial mass-production of music, as the real culprit. In any industry attempting to adopt an economy of scale, it is inevitable that the variety of products will diminish until only the most profitable remain, and that those most profitable products will become so heavily commoditized that there is no longer any substantial differentiation between them. Let's not let this model take over the digital manufacturing industry, an industry which has the potential to unlock, nourish and sustain human creativity in ways that few other technological advances have ever done.

33

The Printed Gun Controversy

The Virtual Handgun

Ever since second-year Texas law student Cody Wilson announced his intentions to design and print firearms using a 3D printer, debate has raged on the subject. This is hardly surprising when it encompasses discussions as divisive and partisan as gun control, censorship and personal liberties. Regardless of the current impracticalities of the project, I would like to devote a few paragraphs to it, simply because the discussions are often interesting, and sometimes even quite enlightening.

To begin with, let us be quite clear, just about anything can and has been used to make a gun. There have even been instances where prisoners escaped from jail by fabricating facsimiles of pistols from soap. Of course, they did not have fully functioning firing mechanisms, but this has never stopped criminals from using toy guns to hold up banks in the past.

People have made weapons out of blocks of stone, but does that mean that we should outlaw building stone or concrete houses? Should we be nervous that any Tom, Dick or Harry can head down to the hardware store and legally buy steel piping with which to produce a zip gun or other kind of improvised firearms. The Wikipedia entry on this subject is especially enlightening. http://en.wikipedia.org/wiki/Improvised_firearm

When Glocks were first released there were articles full of "The Plastic Pistol," stating that bad people would use them to evade security and metal detectors. There is little mention of the fact that the metal spring is huge, and the barrel is a large chunk of metal that is especially hard to miss. Hollywood has perpetuated a similar myth regarding ceramic pistols. While I rarely fly, my ceramic fruit knife is nearly always picked up by the X-ray machines at train and bus stations.

Of course, the ammunition is the part that does the actual launching of the projectile, the gun itself is just there to hold the mechanism and the bullets together while they are being fired. It is almost like putting serial numbers on hypodermic needles, but making heroin legal to sell at Walmart.

The real irony is that anybody can order a whole plethora of books, DVDs, and full-scale schematics detailing almost any firearm ever made, along with complete instructions on how to make them, from a huge selection of online stores and mail order companies.

Cody Wilson's plan is to create a Wiki Weapons' page and use the Defense Distributed brand to create an open-source schematic for a "WIKIWEP A," handgun that anyone can download. He has already used a 3D printer to make the lower receiver of a semi automatic rifle, the AR-15, the civilian version of the standard US army issue rifle. The lower receiver is the only part with a serial number, every other part can be freely purchased in USA. This heavily regulated part holds the bullets and is the only part that is legally considered a "firearm," even though it takes the least amount of stress, and is already quite cheap, costing from $50 for a basic stamped lower to $150 for a nicely machined example. Interestingly, anybody can buy the rest of the parts such as triggers, barrels, etc. completely off the books with no controls whatsoever. It is also relatively easy to buy all the machine tools and heat treat ovens second-hand, to make your own real guns at home.

In practice, it is much more of a challenge to 3D print a barrel and chamber, the business end of a gun, since it has to be made of something with the strength of steel in order to contain the tens of thousands of PSI generated by off-the-shelf ammunition. For the time being, printing guns simply is not practical. The closest realistic option with the available technology would be to print components required to reactivate deactivated guns.

Even so, there are always armchair commentators on the internet, intent on adding their own two cents. Statements like the following are quite common.

"When 3D printers can print rifled plastic at less than a twentieth the cost of traditionally machined steel at the same strength I'll start worrying about it." Or how about this:

"I fear that we now have a generation brought up with computers and plastic junk who simply don't appreciate the importance of a material's physical properties. They don't understand that even if their plastic firing pin did manage to fire a bullet, their plastic barrel and chamber will be turned into instant mush by gas pressure, friction and heat."

Some detractors appear to be dismissing the danger of this gun due to its plastic construction. One of the plastics that 3D printers can use is polyphenylsulfone, which has a very high melting point, has a tensile strength of around 8000 psi and is used in aerospace projects. Varieties of plastics are available for 3D printers, and their properties vary greatly depending on the mix. Plastics are amazingly useful and flexible materials. I am not saying that a plastic gun would continue to work after repeated firings, but just a few successful shots could be very dangerous.

For those who might pose the question "What about laser sintered printed weapons?" there is a great deal of strength difference between sintered "technically a metal, but barely" and a properly forged and heat-treated alloy. Unless the technology improves substantially, 3D printed guns are only going to succeed in stimulating the market for guns that are operable with multiple missing fingers.

The forums on Slashdot.org were alive with debate on this subject, and surprisingly informative:

In an ironic turnaround, Wilson's project suffered a decidedly non-technical setback, when printer manufacturer Stratasys revoked the lease on, and immediately repossessed his uPrint SE 3D printer. According to New Scientist, the manufacturer cited Wilson's lack of a federal firearms manufacturer's license as their reason for the repossession. Homemade firearms are not (in the U.S.) illegal, per se, on a federal basis, though states have varying degrees of regulation.

"It is the policy of Stratasys not to knowingly allow its printers to be used for illegal purposes," the company's legal counsel wrote in a letter, although this probably translates more accurately into Stratasys being fearful of getting a bad reputation as an enabler of terrorist groups and crazies. Regardless of legality and logic, this is a serious public relations/political policy landmine the company does not wish to step on. They probably have legitimate reason to be concerned, the media will sensationalize these stories, and then people will write to their Congressmen, suggesting we need government regulation of 3D printers.

One net commentator joked that reading between the lines of Stratasys' statement, the company's president clearly says:

> *"For the love of god please don't give us this kind of press. If we don't shut this down now I'm going to have Homeland Security all over my ass. Don't ever use gun and printed in the same sentence again. My hands are too delicate for jail. Why are you doing this to me I'd like to continue selling these machines without mountains of paperwork. If you're going to print something illicit, please do it quietly, and make sure that you own the printer you're using." (There were, of course, plenty of witty suggestions that the joke was on Stratasys, as the machine seized was a clone that Wilson made with his 3D printer.)*

Despite the humour, this really is a legal minefield. Under federal law, hobbyists creating pistols, handguns and some rifles do not have to register their creations with the bureau of alcohol, tobacco, firearms and explosives (ATF) as long as they do not sell, trade or share their weapons. Since 3D printing technology is so new, even the ATF does not have an answer for what the legal status of a Wiki

Weapon would be.

Despite the setback, Defense Distributed plans to press on with the project, albeit on a different path. To protect them from prosecution Wilson has decided to obtain a manufacturer's license and incorporate Defense Distributed into a company. The paperwork will likely take a few months and cost a couple thousand dollars, but Wilson said he would rather do that than risk going to prison. This has not stopped the group, who test fired a 3D printed gun to destruction in early December. The item was printed on a newly obtained Objet printer, ironic considering that Stratasys had just announced the long awaited approval on their proposed merger with Objet from the Committee on Foreign Investment in the United States (CFIUS).

This is the second delay the project has encountered since it started. The crowdsource funding website Indiegogo froze the Defense Distributed account earlier this year, claiming the project related to the sale of firearms. Shortly afterwards Defense Distributed secured the $20,000 it needed by using the direct distribution platform Bitcoin.

It has been argued that the project was not just about printing a gun, but a test of the limits of this particular emergent technology, and how it can be applied to the specific domain. If the goal was just to obtain guns, there are shops all over the country. There were even comments that the actions of Stratysys were the equivalent of Toyota reclaiming your car because you drove to a bar and you 'might' not be of drinking age in 'some' places, regardless of whether or not you are of age where you live.

In reality, it is more akin to the directors saying "He's doing what? Is that legal? (Gets seven different contradictory answers) Oh shit, we do not want to be involved with this."

Can we really blame the company here, when there are lawsuits every time someone sneezes in the USA?

As an aside, it did raise an interesting little fact about 2D paper printers that most people do not know. If you try to counterfeit currency, some colour copiers can shut down automatically, resulting in the need to call a technician to come and reset the printer. Many higher quality copy machines and scanners have built-in firmware that will recognize currency and refuse to scan it. (This news is going to lead to an awful lot of tedious April Fools prank next year.) Could this be the direction in which 3D printing is heading?

Debates about the legality of guns, receivers and 3D files

continue unabated and there will always be a voice of dissention claiming that many items are never going to be printable, eg: CPUs and items requiring high strength. These could end up as famous last words that may sound familiar. Remember this? "There is no reason anyone would want a computer in their home."—Ken Olson, president, chairman and founder of Digital Equipment Corp. (DEC), maker of big business mainframe computers, arguing against the PC way back in 1977.

On a personal note, it was a Glock promotional T-shirt that finally decided my own stance about the ongoing gun control debate. I was on a visit to Bangkok, and had just spent a relaxing morning exploring Wat Suthat, one of the most beautiful temples in the city, a natural sanctuary away from the suffocating heat and traffic, with some of the most beautiful Buddhist murals that I have ever seen. Exiting this haven, I found myself on a street entirely devoted to the sale of guns, everything from Taurus pistols, all the way up to fully automatic machine guns, hardly what I was expecting in the country known throughout the world as the 'Land of Smiles'. What really caught my eye was the aforementioned T-Shirt with a big Glock logo and the slogan, 'For those occasions when you absolutely, positively have to shoot some c*nt in the face!' I later learned that Thailand ranked third in the world in terms of firearms homicide, following only South Africa and Colombia. Still, while many people argue that "Guns don't kill people", they certainly do make it very easy. Haven't we all read of cases, where what would ordinarily have been a black eye turns into a homicide because some damn fool had a gun?

34

3D Printing in the Third World

The Lagos Maker Faire

Despite my own philanthropic leanings, much of this book is about using 3D printing technology for personal gratification and personal profit, rather than the more pressing needs of relieving poverty and encouraging innovation. When these developments are given names such as personal fabricators and home replicators, it is very easy to be caught up in the fantasy of what we would like to make only for ourselves, and temporarily forget about the bigger picture.

While Makerbot have received a fair amount of negative press recently, it should not be forgotten that they have been heavily involved in solving Third World problems with third world ingenuity. They recently donated a printer to the Centre for Social Innovation and Entrepreneurship (CSIE) at the Indian Institute of Technology (IIT) in Chennai, India. They also support the 3D4D Challenge, a competition that awarded Washington Open Object Fabricators (WOOF) a prize of $100,000 to develop a recycling process that will enable waste plastic to be used as filament for 3D printing machines. The project is focusing on recycling high-density polyethylene, the plastic used in milk cartons, but the requests for finished products have been slightly different to what might have been expected. You could be forgiven for thinking that many Africans would want more mass-produced items such as buckets and plastic bowls. However the project coordinators doubt that a 3D-printed bucket—even one made from milk bottles—will ever be cheaper than one made in a factory. The surprising alternative to buckets is actually boats. Most small vessels in West Africa are made from hardwood trees, such as teak, that are becoming increasingly scarce. Making them from waste plastic instead is an environmental win/win: rare species are conserved and less rubbish thrown away. The team estimated that if they had printed a boat from commercial plastic filament it would have cost them $800. Instead, 250 clean, empty milk bottles set them back just $3.20. With our Western cultural bias, it is often easy for us to think that we know what is best for those in the Third World, but this is a perfect example of why we need to keep a more open mind.

Other suggested printable products have similarly come as a surprise to Western observers. Who in America or Europe could have guessed that one of the most useful items would be specially designed and printed shoes to be worn by individuals suffering from foot deformities caused by the growing problem of jigger fly infestation? There is often a vast chasm of thinking between educated Western urbanites and those still trapped in rural poverty. For example, when we think of shoes, we imagine a pair of expensive Nikes, manufactured from a wide range of complex synthetics. In remote Chinese or sub Saharan villages, acceptable shoes are more likely a simple pair of plastic sandals, something that is both affordable and a step up from their current barefoot status. 3D-printers are ideal for this kind of product.

Other printables are being introduced, but local partners are essential in establishing which products are needed and how much local people are prepared and able to pay. So far, these include toilets, water collectors and simple, 3D printed solar trackers that work for both solar ovens and photovoltaic electricity production.

South Africa's 'The Star' reports that The Vaal University of Technology (South Africa) is developing a self-help laboratory that will be equipped with numerous 3D printers with installed designing software. The objective of the laboratory is to empower students, staff members and the community to develop their innovative ideas into prototypes. How long will it be before we see the 'Made in Africa' brand or label for products, for sale on the streets of London or New York? Africa already has a $1.8 trillion economy, and is forecast to have a population of 1.3 billion by 2020. With the growth of the African middle class, consumer demand is already very high.

It is widely known that the Chinese are investing all over Africa, estimated at $15bn over the past decade, but is it the right kind of investment? All over the continent, China has built roads, railways, bridges and airports, focusing primarily on hardware and infrastructure. The rehabilitated 840-mile Benguela railway line, which now connects Angola's Atlantic coast with the Democratic Republic of Congo and Zambia, and the newly announced coastal highway that will connect ten West African nations are just the kinds of projects that match Chinese expertise rather than meet African people's needs. These projects enable China to export more raw materials such as crude oil and copper, products with profits that tend to benefit large corporations and ruling elites rather than people and communities. At the same time, China is a major importer of cheap manufactured goods to Africa, such as electronics and clothes, causing some to accuse the Chinese of taking a neo-colonialist approach to the continent, simply to exploit its rich natural resources, much like the US has done with Asian labour. Many African nations now want China to export much more than just resources.

While Chinese companies have invested heavily in Africa, they have not always had a smooth time of it. One of the low points came in 2010 when a Chinese mining boss in Zambia shot nearly a dozen local miners during a labour protest. The Chinese industry focus on economic prosperity has led to massacres and violent backlash in Indonesia, Myanmar and many other countries. While Tibetan and Uighur resentment is well publicised in the west, similar actions in Africa are not so well documented. While China has recently introduced several measures to help rebalance trade ties, including zero tariffs for an expanded range of African products and more trade expos to display African merchandise, continuing to build mines and airports is unlikely to benefit few except Chinese investors and their local cronies.

Africa needs a combination of improvements before it can begin to make real headway. A legal framework to create a more hospitable environment is perhaps the most obvious, but financing also plays an important role. Micro-finance is growing rapidly, enabling grass roots entrepreneurship. Even so, it usually tops out at about $500, so ventures in the next tiers that need $1,000 to $100,000 go unfunded. The global availability of venture capital and private equity, according to last year's figures, was about 3 percent of GDP; in Kenya it was a measly .07 percent; Uganda .05 percent. This suggests that, in East Africa alone, a financing gap of $100 million a year still exists, which will equate to more than $1 billion over the next decade, a figure that in some respects seems small, but on a local basis is insurmountable.

This potential democratisation of the manufacturing industry is an exciting thought in the context of the West, but in the developing world, this idea could be even more worthwhile. 3D printing could help countries to 'leapfrog' into new, distributed forms of production that create opportunities for better, environmentally sustainable and more just forms of economic development, avoiding some of the pitfalls our own economic model has uncovered.

In the same way that we are seeing the breaking down of the barriers between an object, and the information carried within an object , we will also see 3D printers and scanners as democratizing tools, where consumers assume the role of designers copying, "tweaking," and customizing existing designs. If consumers can easily wield the software to modify an openly shared design, they are no longer forced into incentive to purchase an original one. Not that "democratization" of design will kill design or that designers will cease to be relevant. On the contrary, this technology will allow innovative designers to evolve and improve their craft. 3D printer technology permits us to manifest what would otherwise have stayed firmly in the mind. We are already seeing a new wave of innovation and creativity driven by the ability of the average person to make whatever they can imagine. Parts of the internet will quickly mutate into global suggestion boxes for online designers, so that we can all contribute to eliminating those irritating design features that annoy us so much.

There is of course the risk that the "democratization" of design will slow innovation if it moves towards the current Western democratic dialog, where a small lobby uses the illusion of democratic choice to create divisiveness and partisanship. This does not only mean contractors and builders on one side yelling at architects and designers on the other. I am thinking more of the heavily entrenched interests fighting hard to maintain the status quo. This has been clear in the areas of digital photography, desktop publishing, and digital music creation, where myths such as piracy have been introduced and popularised to create the impression that this change is damaging and dangerous.

Huge sums are paid to lobbyists and lawyers, as content owners wage war on their very best customers. Once these industries realize that it is much more sensible to swim with the current, they begin to experience rapid growth as suddenly everyone wants to try the technology, be it digital garage recording, digital photography etc,. When most people realize that they do not have superior talent in that medium, there is a spike in legal and illegal "clip art" and "sampling" use. Soon thereafter, things settle down to a new normal where most people respect the rights of others.

We then begin the process of finding more constructive ways to innovate that value design, while promoting and not penalizing risk taking in fabrication.

In *Small Is Beautiful*, British economist E. F. Schumacher stated "the poor of the world cannot be helped by mass production, only by production of the masses." While the *Times Literary Supplement* ranked *Small Is Beautiful* among the one hundred most influential books published since World War II, it has so far had little impact on mainstream economic thinking. Schumacher believed that the modern industrial technology of the production line had deskilled and dehumanised work, rendering it meaningless. 3D printing could have the power to reverse this. In conjunction with other technological developments, such as distributed energy generation and the expansion of the internet, 3D printing could provide local communities with the access to facilities they need to produce and market their own products.

This kind of revolution seems much likelier to find traction in the developing world where communities can start their own local economies from scratch. The best parts of Neil Gershenfeld's book, Fab: The Coming Revolution on Your Desktop—from Personal Computers to Personal Fabrication' describe his adventures setting up experimental fab labs in places like Ghana and India. Encouraging locals to try making tools that are unavailable or unaffordable;

portable solar collectors that can turn shafts and wheels, inexpensive electronic gauges farmers can use to measure the quality of their crops, giving them an edge when they haggle with the brokers. It is clear that 3D printing could have a very interesting Third-World dimension, one that might even revolutionise manufacturing in many Third World nations. 3D printing could provide local communities with the access to facilities they need to produce and market their own products.

There is good reason to be optimistic: A successful Maker Faire event was recently held in Lagos, the capital of Nigeria and the largest city in Africa. For those that are interested to see how this plays out, an interesting site to watch is Afrigadget.com, which features creative ideas and innovative technologies coming out of Africa today. Created by a group of African bloggers from around the continent, Afrigadget.com chronicles everyday people making extraordinary contributions to their community and the larger world. Much of the international development news that occurs in Africa does not make it to the big networks such as the BBC, Fox and CNN, who are more interested in stories that are closer to home than sustainable inventions taking place in Africa. Recent entries have covered 3D printing developments, along with efforts to create biodiesel fuel out of local pine nuts in Sierra Leone, and a deceptively simple device designed by four schoolgirls that successfully extracts usable fuel from urine. For other good sites addressing sustainable development in Africa check out the African Uptimist and Timbuktu Chronicles.

35

The Disruptive Power of 3D Printers

The 3D printers available today are still rather primitive in comparison to our personal computers, and hardly anybody actually 'needs' one, but what about ten years from now? Many tradespeople will see their industries completely upended. Old school sign painters were just one small group who had to face competition from relatively unskilled newcomers with personal computers and a vinyl cutter. Skills that took a lifetime to learn no longer provided any competitive advantage. The 3D printing revolution promises to be similarly wrenching. "It's like a new industrial revolution," claims Siert Wijnia, a founder of Netherlands-based Ultimaker. "[3D printers] are where the microcomputer was 30 years ago."As a technology it is disruptive, energetic and cannot be ignored. Why? Because up until now, the domineering forces in manufacturing have been economies of scale. The upfront costs of "tooling up" to manufacture anything—whether it is roller bearings or automobiles—using conventional materials and assembly methods are huge, so factories must stamp out many thousands of identical products in order to bring the individual price down to a reasonable level. With 3D printing, the tooling-up costs are much less—essentially consisting of the costs of building the computer model of the product. Since it is becoming so easy to tweak a computer model—it is just software, after all—small production runs suddenly become economic. This technology could enable a shift from the mass production bequeathed to us by Henry Ford to what some people call "mass customisation". Actually, attributing this advance to Henry ford is almost as misleading as ascribing the invention of the light bulb to Edison. Mass production was given to us by

Maudslay and Brunel in the Portsmouth Blockmaking factory a century or so before Henry Ford was even born. It really does not matter how much we argue about who the founding fathers of traditional manufacturing were if it all becomes a bygone technology in the next twenty years.

The disruptive significance of this has yet to dawn on many governments and corporations, but some observers—for example, writers for that great cheerleader of capitalism, the *Economist* – are trying to attract their attention by dubbing digital-driven manufacturing the "third industrial revolution". "Three-dimensional printing ... may have as profound an impact on the world as the coming of the factory did," and "Digital technology has already rocked the media and retailing industries," it continues, "just as cotton mills crushed hand looms and the Model T put farriers out of work. Many people will look at the factories of the future and shudder. They will not be full of grimy machines manned by men in oily overalls. Many will be squeaky clean – and almost deserted... Most jobs will not be on the factory floor but in the offices nearby, which will be full of designers, engineers, IT specialists, logistics experts, marketing staff and other professionals. The manufacturing jobs of the future will require more skills. Many dull, repetitive tasks will become obsolete: you no longer need riveters when a product has no rivets."

The whole notion of industry changes if we no longer have big manufacturing facilities any more, but instead new micro-distributive facilities. This may all take place in just a few short steps. It will start with the larger manufacturers expanding the use of 3D printing, and then the shift to smaller and mid-sized manufacturers. Then we may see things like auto-body shops and parts suppliers begin to move into the realm. At least for the next ten years, it may be more of a Kinkos model where we will see small, franchised 3D print shops that print up components and parts for the general public. Perhaps these are niches into which all the new hackerspaces will evolve?

Just suppose for a moment, that the *Economist* is correct – that digital manufacturing really does wipe out the low-level manufacturing jobs currently provided, here and overseas, by older technology. What then happens to the hundreds of millions of people who will have no employment (not everyone can become "designers, engineers, IT specialists, logistics experts", after all), and who, incidentally, will have the disposable income to purchase the wonderful products created by digital manufacturing?

More importantly, if mass production and economies of scale are no longer necessary in order to produce something at a low enough price, and if unskilled labour no longer figures in the cost equation, then there is no need to outsource manufacturing abroad. Just think how this affects children's toys for example. No more Chinese labour, lead paint and international container shipping. Many of the jobs this type of manufacturing would replace are now based in China. Developing a domestic infrastructure using cutting-edge rapid prototype machines would probably create more jobs in Europe and the US than lose them. Will this finally put an end to seeing all those "Made in China" labels? Some might argue that China is more capable of adapting than the US, because China is not yet a fully developed country. Those who have spent any length of time on the Mainland might not be so optimistic.

3D printing might not be cheaper then a factory, but it could be cheaper then a factory and its distribution network. The cost of keeping small piles of stock far from the factory is immense, and this alone makes 3D printing cheaper. Printing also saves time, as I can print a coat-hook or washer faster than I can go and buy one from the shops. We will still need to transport the plastic pellets that 3D printers need to make stuff, but think of all the associated savings involved in local manufacturing. We have already discussed the reduction in waste of the printers themselves, but then there is the cost of shipping the product ten thousand miles to the store, all the packing and packaging required, and the repeated mark ups every time another business is added to the supply chain.

I would like to take a moment here to explain how many of the costs involved in manufacturing and mass production remain invisible. We all know about the cost of raw materials and shipping, but what about the unseen human suffering. Brutal working conditions and almost non-existent pay help keep the prices low. If we as consumers want prices to stay low, then 3D printing technology might be the only option, as cheap labour in China may not be able to last much longer. Much of this cost is borne by the workers themselves, many of whom pay with their lives. The exact number of annual work-related deaths in China is unknown, as even Beijing acknowledges, "it is much more cost-effective for owners to buy-off the families ... than risk closure by reporting an accident."

There are many web-based resources attempting to document the full breadth and depth of the horror workers suffer in order to produce our cheap goods for us. FactsandDetails has an entire section devoted to the subject:

Industrial accident and death rates in China are in fact among the highest in the world, killing more than 100,000 people every year, which works out at 380 deaths per day, or almost 50 per hour. The highest number of fatalities is on river barges, in transportation and in mines, but factories are not far behind. Workers have repeatedly died in fires, because owners locked the doors out of fear that the workers would steal the products they were making. According to government statistics thirty workers lose a limb every day in Shenzhen's 10,000 factories alone, just one of Chinas many cities dominated by industrial production. In most cases, the factory owners pay a token compensation and hire new workers for another $50 a month. When off-shoring their production, western companies often ship out their old equipment that would be too expensive to run in the West. These shoddy machines no longer have any maintenance engineers, and quickly become death traps for innocent workers. The China Labour Bulletin recently spoke with a worker who caught a finger in some equipment and was sent to a local hospital. It was cheaper for the company to compensate the unconscious worker than to surgically repair his finger. When the worker woke up in the hospital, he found to his horror that his entire hand was gone.

Factories workers live in cramped dorms, with up to twenty in a room, some saying that prisoners in jail live in better conditions. These conditions are sometime worsening rather than improving. Production companies are responding more to the demands of big retailers such as Wal-Mart to cut costs, rather than calls by human rights groups to improve working conditions. Taiwanese and Korean factory owners have the worst reputations of all, sometimes paying wages as little as 12 cents an hour or $15 a month. The most draconian do not allow their workers to leave the factory compound, deny workers bathroom breaks and demand regular sexual favours. At one prison-like Taiwan-owned factory that had a hundred guards watching 2,700 workers, one worker was killed during an escape attempt. There are endless stories of managers that force workers to work until midnight, fire them when they complain and beat them up if they try to claim their paycheck, often using their police connections to counter any complaints. Dickensian conditions keep prices artificially low. It is hard to imagine workplaces in the twenty-first century where workers are only allowed to shower once a week, and are kept locked inside buildings that have their windows covered and the doors bolted shut. In some cases the meals are cabbage and potato soup served three times a day. Some factories require that workers provide a deposit of two weeks pay and turn over their ID cards. Some Korean employers in China have been accused of beating and humiliating their workers. In one extreme case a woman was locked in a cage with a large dog and put on public display in the factory compound. According to a Chinese newspaper nine out of ten spontaneous strikes in the city of Tianjin occurred at Korean-owned factories.

No-one visiting coastal factory cities like Quanzhou and Wenzhou, will be surprised to learn that many of the shoe factories are filled with fumes ten times above safe levels. While pollution is a fact of life in all Chinese cities, the noxious odours that assail visitors to these industrial concentrations are apparent well beyond the city limits. The same fumes that permeate the entire district poison teenagers that glue soles on shoes. The *Washington Post* interviewed one poor woman who worked gluing sneakers for seventeen hours a day. After only a few months, she began to experience numbness in her fingers and ankles, which quickly spread up her arms and legs. By the time she realized that the glue she was using was destroying her nervous system she was paralyzed from the neck down. In 1995, an explosion at a chemical explosives warehouse in Hunan province killed ninety people, injured four hundred and left a crater one hundred feet in diameter and 30 feet deep. Many of those killed were children playing at a video arcade next door to the warehouse. China has no independent unions, only the All-China Federation of Trade Unions, which generally sides with the state and employers so that workers essentially have no voice. While a good number of us in the West may hate our jobs, none of us are forced to endure conditions such as those which I have just described, many of which are still commonplace in China, Indonesia and Bangladesh. These are the true costs of low prices. Next time some know-it-all claims that 3D printers will never be able to print washers as cheaply as a Chinese factory, remember that human misery far outweighs the petty financial costs to which they are referring.

The longer-term socio-economic reifications of this technology are complex enough to fill an entire book but I would like to touch upon them briefly here. The usual "machines will replace workers, so what about the jobs?" question is an obvious point, brought up countless times for every technological advance. So what happens to the people who lose their jobs on production lines? They cannot all become 3D-printer repairmen.

Surely this is already happening, and has been going on for the last thirty or forty years. We have seen jobs replaced by automation, by internet applications, and Chinese slave labour, and there has been little done to replace them. It is possible that what we are seeing now is not a recession or a depression, but the end of capitalism.

At the risk of sounding Marxist, progressive immiseration of the workers is inevitable, as business increases surplus labour value, here via automation. This began a few decades ago in the West, so we already know how the market for products is maintained and the immiseration concealed: via mounting levels of debt. A business makes itself more "efficient" by automating in the hunt for more profits and increased share prices, forgetting the fact that when you sack a worker you are also sacking your customers. A good illustration of this: Henry Ford showing off a piece of automation at his factory quipped to a visitor "This machine doesn't go on strike." The visitor replied "But the machine won't buy your cars."

Go back a few centuries back rather than a couple of decades and things like pottery, weaving and metalworking were all rapidly turned from small operations in to city-wide industries. Others might also argue that off-shoring was begun around the same time. The use of 'convicts' was just one of many ways to produce things more cheaply overseas, and at the same time deal with a surplus of farm workers. Could it be that this is now coming full circle?

The first two industrial revolutions made people richer and more urban. Now a third revolution is under way. Manufacturing is going digital. This could change not just business, but much else besides. The factory of the future will focus on mass customisation, and may look more like those weavers' cottages than Ford's assembly line. There could be a sort of fragmentation of business into little artisanal operations. Could we be witnessing the revival of a spirit that had been fading since the Industrial Revolution: that of the artisan? While corporations like Microsoft and Oracle were employing droves of programmers to homogenize products for the mass market, these technological craftsmen were working on a personal scale. Crafting their code in home workshops, they enjoyed the same satisfaction that comes from building a bookshelf or caning a chair. Could 3D printing technology continue this trend, returning us to the days before "art became separated from artisans and mass manufacturing turned individuals from creators to consumers"? That is certainly a very romantic but appealing point of view.

Technology has always been about the abolition of mundane activity. It is a waste of any human being to spend their time standing on an assembly line. In reality, the 'right' to work is no more a right than the 'right' to own a slice of the earth we live on. It is all moot when the food, clothes, shelter, infrastructure we need could be provided automatically, and better, than if we try to do it manually. The real question is why has it not happened earlier, and been offered to everyone? (Capitalism/selfishness/greed is the answer, in case I have not made that obvious.) The fact that we need money to survive is an increasingly abstract societal problem. The things we really need to watch for are vested interests attempting to prevent the inevitable by legal suppressive measures, as without scarcity, there is no power. The copyright maximalists that control our government are already resorting to the dirtiest low down tricks in the book to maintain their illegitimate monopoly on a cultural legacy that rightly belongs to us all. This is the elephant in the room that no politician or pundit wants to tackle. Is capitalism so entrenched that we would rather face global collapse than risk replacing it with an improved system?

Of course, there are still some people who feel protective of soul-destroying, mundane "work". Many of these modern day luddites know that overall it will be beneficial, but cannot help lament the loss of manufacturing jobs. After all, who wants to live in a country where we are all cappuccino frothers and insurance salesmen. Perhaps the rest of us will be limited to repairing "Classic Pre-Printables: 1950 - 2015" in the museum. The reality is that jobs are going nowhere, except into oblivion. The biggest threat facing us all is redundancy hitting us at an earlier and earlier age, as one disruptive technology after another picks up speed.

Ever increasing levels of unemployment are in fact just one side of the coin. The other is the rapid ageing of prosperous populations. If our amoral economic systems continue to disenfranchise younger people, who do still actually want to work, how will it react to the growing numbers of society who feel that it is part of their entitlement to work no longer, and instead rely on the contributions of others? In the US, there are currently forty million over sixty-five years of age. In twenty years, barring disaster, it will be eighty million over eighty. If we look at China, it has an even greater ageing population that is unprecedented in human history. Currently, there are 180 million people over age sixty, about an eighth of the population. If we jump ahead twenty years, they will have over 360 million people over age sixty. In 2000 there were six workers for every person over sixty. By 2030, there will be barely two. This makes anti-communitarian ideology increasingly unworkable and even irrelevant.

Another factor is simply the glaring success of managed capitalism in contrast to relatively unmanaged varieties. The arguments about European failure ring increasingly hollow—despite the economic turmoil; the reality is that European managed capitalism continues to deliver the highest standard of living in the world by every meaningful (non-ideological) measure. American politics is deeply dysfunctional, of course, and change will take some time, but there will be increasing impatience, even among conservatives, with economic policies that fail for more than a generation. The word "socialism" will simply be replaced with some alternate formulation such as "managed capitalism" which allows the majority to climb aboard.

3D Printing is an early glimpse into the post-scarcity economy that has the potential to revolutionize our way of life and progress of humankind. In theory, it should release the workers from a life of drudgery and monotony, and herald a new era of advanced technology and eco-inspired architecture. If we look back at the evolution of buildings, bridges, transport and many other familiar objects, we can see a link between manufacturing process, materials and design. If you change one, you have to change the other two, or at least have the opportunity to do so over time. Even if 3D printing is a complement to, rather than a replacement for mass production, it will be important in generating new economic activity—otherwise known as growth. 3D printing technology is developing during a time where we have this archaic, dangerous capitalist model, which threatens the environment, the financial security of millions and leads to increasing resource scarcity in the vain pursuit of "perpetual growth". In practice, will those who possess the means of production, exploit it to boost profit incentive at the expense of human misery? This technology is, by its very essence, labour-augmenting: The reason it makes things cheaper is because it increases the capital to labour ratio of production. By removing the manufacturer, another margin is also removed. The economies of scale simply transfer to the materials retailer, and their scale would dwarf that of any manufacturer. Those who profit more conspicuously will be those who control economic resources, and those few who are bright and knowledgeable enough to come up with innovative ideas out of which large profits will be made, and those to whom I am referring are essentially you, the readers of this book. This will be much more than investing in the right fledgling company, so that your next ten generations can spend their time snapping up Van Gogh's for the price of hospital wings. What most entrepreneurs share is the conviction that this technology is the next big thing—big enough, many argue, to be this century's most disruptive invention. Whether it results in an ever-increasing wealth gap or an entirely new economic paradigm is mainly up to us.

36

The Future of 3D Printing - How Far Could All This Go?

A concept home 3D printer envisioned by the IDI-Lab graduate design team in Zhejiang

Even the most cursory glance shows that the 3D printing industry is growing at a frightening pace, and four trends are immediately visible:

1. The prices of the technology are falling fast, both for high end

industrial machines, but we are also seeing the first wave of affordable (even though the phrase 'low end' does not do them justice) machines that are suitable for home users.

2. The open source community is a now a huge influence that never existed on such a scale when the first home computers were introduced back in early eighties. The introduction of, at viral speed, new personal and professional 3D printers is highly accelerated due to the modern nature of almost instantaneous internet connections.

3. The largest bottleneck is going to be convenient 3D software for making great digital designs easily and quickly.

4. 3D Printing services are already playing an important role in creating innovative new businesses and exciting new business opportunities.

We have all seen the breathless predictions of 'desktop manufacturing, one in every household!' While this technology is obviously here to stay, for many the value proposition of actually owning one, rather than renting a tiny slice of somebody's much more expensive machine over the internet, seems about as mainstream as the economics of owning a high quality large format photo printer or an entire machine shop. Ownership is certainly something that some professions would certainly consider, and definitely something that a hobbyist would want access to; but not necessarily the right option for everybody.

Most towns would benefit from a high-end printer, charging customers relatively modest sums when they need something like a discontinued dishwasher part. Perhaps this is how the industry will develop, and production will become much more localised. Every neighbourhood will have a small fabrication shop that can produce an enormous variety of products at a moment's notice. This is similar to advent of digital photography and home printing that many thought signalled the death of high street photo shops. Consumers still choose to print photos taken on their smartphone and camera at a shop, but prefer the high quality glossy finish to anything they could manage on their low-cost home printer.

People do not usually keep large-scale copiers at home. If they need a document, they simply bring an original from home and run a copy, just as they will with 3D printers. Moving manufacturing to the consumer, to the end of the supply chain, is a major cultural paradigm shift that might take some time to displace the current mindset. If we consider fast food for example, it does not take much to make a burger, but people still go out to McDonald's simply for the sake of convenience. Even when a fab lab can be shrunk to the size of a suitcase, most people will probably content themselves with what is offered at the future equivalent of Wal-Mart, just as they do with what is broadcast on the TV networks. In reality, places like quick print shops will take up the slack. By using this as a bulk usage service, the cost of the machines will be viable, and we will all be using it as a service.

Consider the similarity to printing glossy 6x4 photos at home. It is certainly possible, but it remains much easier to have them printed down at the mall for a quarter of the price of buying the paper. In fact, there seems to be a growing trend of houses and families that do not have 2D printers at home these days. When I had a printer, the majority use was for school assignments, but even schools are moving towards electronic assignment submission. Anybody that is banking on every house having a 3D printer in the living room might want to take a quick retrospective look at Kodak and their recent problems, before they completely commit themselves.

The office supplies chain, Staples, has already jumped on this bandwagon by announcing that they will be making in-store 3D printers available in Belgium and Holland at the beginning of 2013. We are speculating that this service is being rolled out in Europe first rather than the highly litigious States due to potential copyright issues. The Staples announcement differs from other 3D printing services in a number of ways: Firstly, the company has decided to use Mcor laminated object manufacturing technology based on paper rather than plastic printing. The company claims that paper prints cost less than a fifth of the price of their plastic counterparts. Secondly, the company operates over 2,300 stores in twenty-six countries throughout North and South America, Europe, Asia and Australia. This major high street presence is very different from other 3D printing services, and means that customers will be able to collect their products rather than having them shipped over long distances.

Home 3D printing will certainly take place in the longer term, it's just a question of exactly when. Even the transition steps will be extremely exciting. Will your grandma have a 3D printer by the end of 2013? Maybe not, but she does have another piece of personal fabrication equipment in her living room—a sewing machine. In this day and age, she might also have a microwave, a blender and mixer in the kitchen, and so the step up to a 3D printer is not completely infeasible.

Before every home has a 3D printer, I personally am looking forward to the day when every education facility has one. So far, a large chunk of existing 3D printer sales have been to schools, colleges and universities. Never mind individual homes having one of these machines, if each high school had a 3D printing and CNC requirement added to the Home Economics course, then that would certainly spell trouble for factories world-wide. CNC machining is pretty damn cool and far more mature—but 3D printing has even more to offer when we consider its ability to create pre-assembled products, materials with complex internal structures that make them stronger and lighter than milled pieces. If we were to put the tools to design and make just about anything (e.g. 3D printers, TechShops, Maker Sheds, FabLabs) at the fingertips of every child, not only would the economy change, but the entire world would be a significantly different place. Enabling and empowering a generation of "makers" will serve to spur the creative juices of an entire new crop of product designers who know exactly how to, and what to, create. Imagine how different society would be if manufacturing were to become cool again, instead of being downplayed in favor of 'services' and 'financial engineering'. Putting 3D capture, modeling and manufacturing technologies into the hands of students will unleash the next generation of entrepreneurs and demonstrate, in a very tangible way, that education in STEM (Science, Technology, Engineering and Math) subjects is not only interesting, but incredibly fun as well. Letting students "feel" their digital models, through haptic-touch enabled devices, then printing physical representations of those creations, will unlock imaginations and unleash incredible creativity.

So, unlike many other pundits, I do not for the time being, predict a 3D printer in every home. I do foresee a rapid proliferation of 3D scanners, perhaps a simple app, or maybe a small stepper motor device so that any camera or phone for that matter can create accurate .stl files. With suitable algorithms, not only will it digitally model the item, it will optimize its volume so that parts print with the highest efficiency, creating only the least possible waste. Why print any more than is necessary, when software can efficiently hollow out unnecessary interiors or ergonomically improve an item to a user's pre-stated preference? Once armed with an algorithmically optimized digital model, then the customer simply emails it off to the local print shop.

In the same way that eBay and Amazon made hard-to-find items much more easily available to people in remote locations, this might be one of the first trends that we see with 3D printers. Just think how useful this would be on remote Pacific islands, deployed military forces or eventually, lunar base camps.

It is interesting to note that up until now, companies well outside the traditional printing arena are manufacturing all the 3D printers on the market. The 2D desktop printer giants are still holding their cards close to their chest, watching the game develop. Their previous strategies have already created a great deal of enmity among consumers. 3D printers, partly because of the terrible experiences with 2D printers, do not impress everybody. As one anonymous forum poster vehemently complained, "I thought home printers were going to revolutionize printing. I was going to print out my own books, but with 3 decades to get good, all we have still is crappy printers, paper jams, computer stalling, print jobs frozen and super expensive ink that still has not gone down in price. I bought a laser printer, but still get paper jams, piece of crap!"

The big players may be waiting for what they see as being an opportune moment to move into the sector, but the current exponential pace of growth might signify that they have already missed their chance in all three markets: industry, office and home. Another surprising factor is that the leading suppliers of 3D printers are currently in Europe and not the USA or Southeast Asia. China is already losing its manufacturing dominance. As the early tax and land benefits given to the large multinationals are beginning to expire and labour costs continue to rise, companies are moving away to significantly cheaper locations. The country has so far failed to make the jump from low end to high-end manufacturing and, looking at the terrible state of education it is unlikely that this will ever happen. For anybody that has ever done business with Chinese factories, the ability to produce independently in your home location will be such a relief from all the lies, cheating and corruption that is an integral part of doing business in the PRC.

In the next phase, biological materials and components will join plastics and metals, which will broaden the engineering possibilities even further. One interesting view of the future is already in full operation at the campus of Virginia Tech. The DreamVendor is essentially a 3D printer vending machine, and it allows students to fabricate prototypes for their academic, and even personal, design projects. The faculty thinks of it as a vending machine with an infinite inventory. Simply insert an SD card that contains 3D printer code and DreamVendor then prints a 3D part and dispenses it when it is finished. For the time being, they are not asking people to pay to use the machines, but being located in an academic building is not the same as being in the mall. While it is probably great for public relations, I wonder how long it will be before some young nerd decides to print out a complete set of parts for his new RepRap.

How long will it be before we can turn our thoughts into actual 3D objects? Not as long as you might think according to Tinkerthing founder Brian Salt. The visionary team is already working to build tomorrow's intuitive interfaces of the mind, to literally generate real objects by thought. After working on the development of the first 3D engine on the ARM 9 chipset, and more recently collaborating with blue chip medical companies and the British military on virtual reality visualizations and simulations, Brian has some radical ideas about the future of 3D modelling. In a recent media interview, he spoke about interfacing directly to the imagination.

"Our first prototype will utilize the EmotivEPOC, a high resolution neuro signal acquisition and processing wireless neuroheadset to collect signals from the brain. Our software will allow the user to evolve 3D models with the power of thought, which will then be created in ABS plastic using a MakerBot."

Just imagine how incredible it would be to imagine a thing and have it appear, ready made. The aim at ThinkerThing is to create the software to interface the latest neuro-technology equipment with the latest in 3D printing machines to make objects with the power of thought. This might still seem like science fiction, but, amazingly the technology needed to make this a possibility is already in existence today, all that is missing is a creative approach to build the interface between mind and machine. Here is how Salt puts it. " As any parent will tell you a child's imagination is boundless. My own son, Noah, currently lacks the motor skills to use a pencil well, yet he finds it easy and intuitive to navigate a touch tablet interface. What if we could create interfaces directly to the imagination, allowing the creation of real physical objects from thought." What indeed?

With the possibilities that lay before us in this new age of technology, we must always look to the past for lessons and parables. Isaac Newton once used the phrase; "If I have seen further, it is by standing on the shoulders of giants." A humble way of saying that his intellectual leaps were only possible because of the work of others before him. The giant at the top of the beanstalk, however, wanted to consume Jack, the curious young fellow. Open source, hacking, filesharing and the many other democratic uses of technology are the giants upon whose shoulders we can see the future. Copyright, mass production, centralized control of knowledge and production are the giant at the top of the beanstalk that threatens to consume us all.

PART IV

Appendices

Appendices

Forums, Blogs and Wiki's
Further Reading
1. Articles and eBooks
2. Physical Books
TV and Video
Miscellaneous Software
3D Printing Related Fiction
Distributed Networking
Understanding Miniature Scales
3D Printing Personal Wish Lists
Gift List for a 3D Printer

Forums, Blogs and Wiki's

http://www.reprap.org/wiki/Main_Page

The RepRap Wiki is an excellent place to start. The RepRap was the very first of the low-cost 3D printers, and the RepRap Project soon kick-started the open-source 3D printer revolution. It has become the most widely-used 3D printer among the global members of the Maker Community. Since many parts of RepRap are made from plastic and RepRap prints those parts, RepRap self-replicates by making a kit of itself—a kit that anyone can assemble given time and materials. It makes objects from a cheap plastic made from corn starch, so is well within school budgets. It also means that—if you have a RepRap—you can print lots of useful stuff, and you can print another RepRap for a friend...

One interesting function of the site is an interactive map that lists DIY printers and laser cutters all over the world. It is surprising that there are people scattered all over the map and yet so far, not one member in China. Considering that the PRC is touted as the workshop of the world, I wonder if they are going to be left behind when economic clout has more to do with good design, than cheap labor, non-existent health and safety and zero pollution regulation.

The RepRap Forums (http://forums.reprap.org/) (not to be confused with http://www.reprap.pl/ which is the Polish language specialist site) is an absolute treasure house of information. There are so many interesting sections including "Look what I made!", "Let's design something! (I've got an idea ...)", "So, I took apart this printer ...", "Hello, I need something designed for money, as well as 'For Sale' and 'Wanted' sections". There are loads of 'Working Groups' and even a good selection of foreign language User Groups.

The eMaker Forum (http://www.emakershop.com/forum) was created to encourage the growing community of fabbers and reprappers to collaborate in making printed parts and designs available to all. The Mendel-Parts Forum (http://www.mendel-parts.com/new_forum/phpBB3/) is a similar forum with nearly 3,000 registered members.

Fab@home (mailto:Fab@home) is a platform of printers and programs which can produce functional 3D objects and which will change the way we live. It is designed to fit on your desktop and within your budget. Fab@Home is supported by a global, open-source community of professionals and hobbyists.

There are at least two useful Flickr groups showcasing the work of 3D printers.

Flickr RepRap Group has fifty-four members:
http://www.flickr.com/groups/684136@N23/

Flickr Art of Printing failure Group has 57 members:
http://www.flickr.com/groups/3d-print-failures /HYPERLINK
"http://www.flickr.com/groups/3d-print-failures%20/"
(http://www.flickr.com/groups/3d-print-failures /)

Buildlog.net goes way beyond DIY 3D printers and into CNC mills, laser cutters and assembly bots. This is the site that you might prefer if you have a very practical engineering bent and prefer action to lots of armchair discussion.

http://www.buildlog.net/forum/ucp.php?mode=register"g.net/foru
m/ucp.php?mode=register
(http://www.buildlog.net/forum/ucp.php?mode=register)

As well as being an interesting blog, Fabbaloo has one of the best resource pages on the web. This is a very well-organized links page that covers many important subjects. If you cannot find something in this short ebook then the Fabbaloo resource page is the next logical place to search. Subjects covered include, About 3D Printing, Hobby Printers, Commercial 3D Print Services, Popular Books, Crowdsourcing, Artists, Commercial Software, Free Software, Web-Based Tools, Printable 3D Models, Scanners, Accessories and Blogs.

http://fabbaloo.com/3d-resources

Once you become more interested in the subject of printers, their resolutions and their capabilities, then you might, as I did, find a micron to millimeters conversion table to be invaluable.

http://www.metric-conversions.org/length/microns-to-millimeters-table.htm

While there are many blogs out there looking at the development of 3D printing, my current favorite is Scoop.it (http://www.scoop.it/). This site is curated by Kalani Kirk Hausman and is a social content creation tool. Users can curate information about any topic they want. That falls somewhere between a content management system, a bulletin board system, and a weblog.

http://www.scoop.it/t/3d-printing-and-fabbing

3Ders.org provides latest news and developments in the field of 3D printing technology, and information on 3D printers. In addition, they have a very comprehensive directory of nearly one hundred printers all with feature descriptions and price comparisons. A very useful page.

http://www.3ders.org/index.html

http://www.3ders.org/pricecompare/3dprinters/

Instructables, launched back in August 2005, specialises in user-created and uploaded do-it-yourself projects, which other users can comment on and rate for quality. While the site's scope goes far beyond 3D printing, it is a fantastically useful resource, focusing on step-by-step collaboration among members to build a variety of projects. Instructions are accompanied by visual aids including photos, diagrams, video and animation to help explain complex terminology and mechanisms in clear and understandable terms. They are written in such a way that they easily allow other members to replicate, and share with the rest of the community. Instructables employs a full-time staff, and has a volunteer group made up mainly of "Pro" members who pay about $2 to $4 a month. One of the highlights of the site are the monthly contests, each one with a unique category and often featuring very attractive prizes from large corporate sponsors. In August 2011, Instructables was aquired by Autodesk.

www.Instructables.com

Make Magazine

Make is an American quarterly magazine first issued in January 2005, marketed at people who enjoy making things and features complex projects that can often be completed with cheap materials, including household items. Rather than Home DIY such as bedroom furniture and kitchen remodeling, it focuses more on projects that involve computers, electronics and robotics. It is also available as an e-zine and Texterity digital edition on the Web. Cory Doctorow is a regular columnist for the magazine, and Bruce Sterling was a regular columnist for the magazine's first eighteen issues. The Primer section is a frequent feature teaching skills in areas as diverse as welding, electronics and mould making. The magazine has also launched a number of public annual events called Maker Faires, the first being held at the San Mateo Fairgrounds in 2006. It included over one hundred exhibiting *Makers*, hands-on workshops, demonstrations and DIY competitions, and has since spread to Austin, Detroit, New York and more recently Cairo and Lagos.

In addition to all the above, I found the Hackaday site, The Slashdot forums and the Guardian newspaper online sites very useful when researching this book. 3D printing is a very hot topic and any news stories related to the subject are soon repeated on hundreds of different sites. What made these three sites different were the rich communities associated with each one, and the wide variety of opinions and comments that they generated.

Further Reading

Despite the fact that 3D printers have been around for at least thirty years, it is only in the last couple that the real breakthroughs have transpired, finally bringing $100,000 machines down to just a few hundred dollars. It is for this reason that there are not yet many books or documentaries devoted to the subject. As I have found, it is difficult to compile reliable information, when the situation is changing so fast. Even so, many things are available that are worth reading and watching and you will probably find more as your research continues.

1. Articles and eBooks

It Will Be Awesome if They Don't Screw it Up: 3D Printing, Intellectual Property, and the Fight Over the Next Great Disruptive Technology by Michael Weinberg

An excellent discussion of the swathe of problems that is likely to face the development of 3D printers. A must read for anybody keen on becoming professionally involved in the field.

http://www.publicknowledge.org/it-will-be-awesome-if-they-dont-screw-it-up

"Rise of the Replicators"

This interesting article, from 2010, focuses on the home-brew side of the market and introduces many of the important industry terms and personalities. Again, important background reading for those just getting started.

http://www.newscientist.com/article/mg20627621.200-rise-of-the-replicators.html?full=true

"The Printed World"

Three-dimensional printing from digital designs will transform manufacturing and allow more people to start making things. This is a very useful introductory piece, with an equally useful explanatory article of how the processes actually work.

http://www.economist.com/node/18114221/print".economist.com/node/18114221/print

http://www.economist.com/node/14299512

"The Future of 3D Printing" by Janice Karin."
This piece is from the aptly named site Thefutureofthings.com. More great background as well as some equally useful 'Interviews with Three 3-D Printing Companies.'
http://thefutureofthings.com/articles/11106/the-future-of-3d-printing.html

"The Technology Liberation Front"
Despite being more than a year old now, and being a little bit out of date in terms of the fast moving technology, this article is still worth a read for its discussion of what the future holds in terms of future capabilities, regulations and coming controversies.
http://techliberation.com/2011/06/10/3d-printing-the-future-is-here/

Additive Manufacturing, 3D Printing, and the Coming Stock Market Boom by Dr. Alexander Elder
Dr. Elder's book is a short but easy-to-read volume that focuses on long-term financial investment in this fast growing sector. The author has created a true eBook complete with embedded video links so that readers can actually see how 3D printers work. There are two long but uncomplicated sections on the basics of the technology and the machines themselves, and then the remainder discusses possible stock market plays. This could be a very useful book once you are making a good income with your 3D printer and you want to reinvest your profits. Addictive Manufacturing, 3D Printing, and the Coming Stock Market Boom (http://www.amazon.com/Additive-Manufacturing-Printing-Coming-ebook/dp/B008NF34XO)

"3D Printing, IKEA and the Lessons to Be Learned From the Music Industry"
A very interesting piece by an author that is obviously well ahead of his peers in this field, and therefore well worth a read, especially if you are interested in the legal quagmire that lies just ahead of the 3D printing industry.
http://www.huffingtonpost.co.uk/luke-hebblethwaite/3d-printing-lessons_b_1601106.htm

2. Physical Books

Fab: The Coming Revolution on Your Desktop—from Personal Computers to Personal Fabrication by Neil Gershenfeld

Gershenfeld manages MIT's Center for Bits and Atoms and predicts that computers will soon upgrade from PCs to PFs, or personal fabricators. Instead of shopping for existing products, a programmable PF will make it possible for users to design and create their own objects. Gershenfeld discovered the interest in such cybercrafting back in 1998, when he offered a course entitled How to Make (Almost) Anything course, and was inundated with applicants, all of whom were interested in "fulfilling individual desires rather than merely meeting mass-market needs." After discussing some of those students' unique creations, Gershenfeld offers a history of how things are designed and made, from the Renaissance to industrialized automation, and then goes on to provide an overview of the technology and its social implications this science involves. The book contains over 150 explanatory illustrations. Gershenfeld's extrapolation of these futuristic wonders is a visionary tour of technology, tools and pioneering PFers, even though it is now a good ten years out of date. In addition, it often seemed unfocused, with Gershenfeld rambling from one point to another without a logical transition. If you enjoy the topic, the book will certainly be interesting.

Fabricated: The New World of 3D Printing is a new paperback from Hod Lipson and Melba Kurman that is being released by Wiley at the beginning of 2013. The authors are well established experts on 3D printing. Lipson coordinates a lab at Cornell University, which has pioneered research into the subject, while Kurman is a technology analyst with a proven track record in game–changing technologies. Their book is based on detailed research and dozens of interviews with experts from a broad range of industries, Fabricated promises to be an informative, engaging and fast–paced introduction to 3D printing now and in the future.

Disruptive Technologies is currently being written by Anarkik3D CEO and founder Ann Marie Shillito. It will be published by A. & C. Black in early 2013.

Make magazine published its first 3D printer buyer's guide at the very tail end of 2013. This is very brave move on behalf of the editorial staff, considering how many new models of 3D printer are being announced every month. Undoubtedly a good start, but a book that that will need updating even more often than this one. At the time of writing, the book had not yet been launched, but there was a very appealing desciption on the Amazon pre-order page:

> *The 3D printing revolution is well upon us, with new machines appearing at an amazing rate. With the abundance of information and options out there, how are makers to choose the 3D printer that's right for them? MAKE is here to help, with our Make: Ultimate Guide to 3D Printing. We brought 16 of the top printers to our headquarters and hosted a weekend-long printer shootout staffed by the editors of MAKE and a number of luminaries in the field. We documented out-of-box experiences and subjected the printers to a number of print and torture tests. This issue presents our findings for you in a clear, concise manner.*

TV and Video

In terms of video, I am still looking for a documentary dedicated solely to the technology of 3D printers. The devices are often featured on science news shows, but rarely feature in any great detail. An exception is the excellent TED Talk series that is freely downloadable from the web.

Here are a few to start with:

Klaus Stadlmann: The world's smallest 3D printer
What could you do with the world's smallest 3D printer? Klaus Stadlmann demos his tiny, affordable printer that could someday make customized hearing aids—or sculptures smaller than a human hair. (Filmed at TEDxVienna.) Klaus Stadlmann was pursuing his PhD at Vienna's Technical University when a broken laser system gave him some unexpected free time to think. Instead of working on his thesis, he decided to build the world's smallest 3D printer.
http://www.ted.com/talks/klaus_stadlmann_the_world_s_smallest_3

d_printer.html"lks/klaus_stadlmann_the_world_s_smallest_3d_printe
r.html
(http://www.ted.com/talks/klaus_stadlmann_the_world_s_smallest_
3d_printer.html)

Lisa Harouni: A primer on 3D printing
TEDSalon London Spring 2011

2012 may be the year of 3D printing, when this three-decade-old
technology finally becomes accessible and even commonplace. Lisa
Harouni gives a useful introduction to this fascinating way of making
things—including intricate objects once impossible to create. Lisa
Harouni is the co-founder of Digital Forming, working in "additive
manufacturing"—or 3D printing.
http://www.ted.com/talks/lang/en/lisa_harouni_a_primer_on_3d_pr
inting.html

Dale Dougherty: We are Makers
America was built by makers—curious, enthusiastic amateur
inventors whose tinkering habit sparked entire new industries. At
TED@MotorCity, *Make* magazine publisher Dale Dougherty says we
are all makers at heart, and shows cool new tools to tinker with, like
Arduinos, affordable 3D printers, even DIY satellites. A technology
and publishing enthusiast, Dale Dougherty founded *Make* magazine
and created the world's largest DIY festival, Maker Faire.
http://www.ted.com/talks/dale_dougherty_we_are_makers.html

Paola Antonelli previews "Design and the Elastic Mind"
MOMA design curator Paola Antonelli previews the ground-breaking
show "Design and the Elastic Mind"—full of products and designs
that reflect the way we think now. Antonelli is on a mission to
introduce—and explain—design to the world. With her shows at
New York's Museum of Modern Art, she celebrates design's presence
in every part of life. "The idea of being able to build things bottom
up, atom by atom, has made [scientists] all into tinkerers. And all of a
sudden scientists are seeking designers, just like designers are
seeking scientists."
http://www.ted.com/talks/paola_antonelli_previews_design_and_th
e_elastic_mind.html

Lee Cronin: Making Matter Come Alive

Before life existed on Earth, there was just matter, inorganic dead "stuff." How improbable is it that life arose? And—could it use a different type of chemistry? Using an elegant definition of life (anything that can evolve), chemist Lee Cronin is exploring this question by attempting to create a fully inorganic cell using a "Lego kit" of inorganic molecules—no carbon—that can assemble, replicate and compete.

With his research group, Lee Cronin is investigating the emergence of complex self-organizing chemical systems—call it inorganic biology. http://www.ted.com/talks/lee_cronin_making_matter_come_alive.ht m
Currently, the only DVD that I know of relating to the subject of 3D printing is the following:

Rapid Prototyping Solutions (with 3D CAD/ ProE, the Zcore, the Stratasys Fused Deposition Modeling (FDM), the 3D Systems StereoLithography, (SLA), and the Helisys Laminated Object Manufacturing (LOM) methods with in-depth practical demonstrations)

Edited by Professor Paul G. Ranky, PhD, NJIT
Filmed and edited by the staff of the world famous research group which hosts the EPSRC Centre for Innovative Manufacturing in Additive Manufacturing in Nottingham, England. This is a fifty-three minute documentary that was released way back in 2005 and yet still costs an enormous $79.99. At the time of writing, I am still trying to obtain a review copy, as I am very interested in giving this DVD a full review, based on the excellent reputation of Nottingham University and its proximity to highly relevant manufacturers such as Games Workshop.

http://www.amazon.com/Prototyping-Deposition-StereoLithography-Manufacturing-demonstrations/dp/B000CPGYGW
If you plan to go use your printer to enter the custom toy market then a few TV shows might be useful in terms of background research;

The Toys That Made Christmas
In December 2011, Robert Webb took a light-hearted look back at

playthings of the past, offering fortysomethings the chance to reminisce about the days before PlayStations, laptops and iPods. It was a more innocent time when Fuzzy-Felt and Spirograph brought out the artist in everyone, girls spent hours with Barbie and boys were engrossed in trying to bolt together their impossibly fiddly Meccano models—to name just four of the toys mentioned

100 Greatest Toys

If you can put up with the smarmy insincerity of Jonathan Ross, then 100 Greatest Toys is a 2.5 hour countdown of a nation's favourite toys and games. From Action Man to Yahtzee, and from Barbie to Trivial Pursuit, inventors and toy-makers tell the inside stories of their creations and success. To fully explain the impact of these toys and games, the children of yesteryear—today's celebrities, authors, actors and journalists—reveal exactly what it was that made them love a particular toy.

James May's Toy Stories

This show provides interesting background material for those unfamiliar with vintage brands. In the first six episodes, he attempts to prove that traditional, old-fashioned toys are still relevant by pushing them to the limit in spectacular, supersize challenges.

1. James takes model airplanes to a new level when he tries to make a full-size Spitfire out of Airfix. The venture soon hits problems when it becomes clear the giant 36' pieces may not be strong enough, and nobody knows how they will fit together.
2. James tries to make a garden entirely out of Plasticine and then enters it at the Chelsea Flower Show. He persuades thousands of members of the British public to help make the thousands of Plasticine flowers he needs, but will it be enough to persuade the guardians of the world's most prestigious horticultural event to let him make a garden with no real flowers in it?
3. James joins forces with Edwina Currie to build a full-size bridge from nothing but Meccano. Top engineers pitch incredible designs, but the project soon careens out of control when the Meccano does not arrive and James realises the structure will take longer to build than he imagined. A last-minute accident also means that James's bridge may never

see the light of day.

4.   James May continues his quest to show what is possible with old-fashioned toys by using them on a scale never seen before. James attempts to build the biggest Scalextric track in the world, nearly three miles long, on the site of Britain's oldest grand prix track at Brooklands in Surrey. The track will have to go through people's gardens, over ponds and rivers and even negotiate a business park. Who will win the race of the century, the plucky locals or the team of Scalextric experts?

5.   With thousands of people and over three million Lego bricks, James attempts to do what no one has ever managed—to build a two-storey house out of this colourful toy.

6.   James attempts to build the longest ever model railway track—a whopping ten miles long. He builds it in Devon, linking two towns, Barnstaple and Bideford, which last had a train service over forty years ago. Thousands of people turn out to help, but nature and the odds look to be against the plucky little engine in what is certainly James's most ambitious idea yet.

The Toy Hunter

In the US, a new show featuring Jordan Hembrough, a toy dealer and collector with more than twenty-five years of experience in the business, provides an interesting introduction to the subject. The renowned toy fanatic takes toy picking to a new level as he visits collections from some of the most popular cities on the East and West Coasts. Toy Hunter premiered on the Travel Channel in August, 2012, and has been renewed for a second season with six new episodes added to the freshman season. The show was produced by Sharp Entertainment, and the episodes are very much in the vein of Pickers or Oddities, but entertaining and educational all the same.

Miscellaneous Software

For the last ten years, I have found the Extreme Picture Finder (EPF) software to be one of my most useful research tools, especially when seeking out new product niches. First produced by Extreme Internet Software back in 2001, the company focuses on creating image processing and multimedia content distribution software for everyday use. The founder is a graduate of Kharkiv State Polytechnic University of Radio Electronics and always provides first class support and updates for his products. Over the years, I have built up a personal library of over a hundred thousand images in more than a thousand different categories. I much prefer this method of collection to services such as Google or Bing images, as I can just set my searches running and then view them off line. EPF has a much broader range of search than either of the bigger online engines and always provides me with inspiration that I would never have otherwise expected.

3D Printing Related Fiction

It would seem that this field is moving so fast that we are becoming reliant on science fiction writers to see what is just around the corner.

Long before now, this technology was the idea of science fiction writer Zenna Henderson, in her short story "The Anything Box"—be careful what you wish for! Modern Science fiction writers have been quick to pick up the baton.

Cory Doctorow thinks the copyright war in the last twenty years of internet policy turns out only to have been a skirmish, and in the coming century the war will be against the general purpose computer.

His 2007 short story collection *Overclocked: Stories of the Future Present*, published by Thunder's Mouth, a division of Avalon Books includes the 3D printers and MakerBot themed story "Printcrime". His novel "Makers" offers us an imagined world of printed objects and an emergent culture of 3D makers who directly challenge many of the core assumptions of industrial society.

Doctorow is a regular contributor to Boing Boing where he often comes up with interesting pieces such as "3D printer jargon in action." He also wonders, "Will 3D plans for bongs become illegal, too?" Thingiverse recently had its first modular bong design uploaded, raising the question: if it is illegal in some jurisdictions to own or sell a bong, will it become illegal to own or sell the 3D design for printing a bong on your desktop 3D fab?

Neal Stephenson's novel *The Diamond Age* revolves in large part over efforts to overcome the restrictions on nanotech-powered "matter compilers," intended to prevent users from compiling weapons or harmful substances. While the novel is critically acclaimed, it is let down by the setting. Much of it was supposed to take place in Shanghai, where I was living at the time, and while he wrote competently about 3D printers, the background was nothing like the Shanghai that I knew or could imagine.

One of the very first treatments of self-replicating machines was written way back in 1955 by Philip K. Dick and titled "Autofac". Set a number of years after the apocalypse, only a network of hardened robot "autofacs" remain in operation to supply goods to the human survivors. Once humanity has recovered enough to want to begin reconstruction, the autofacs are targeted for shutdown since they monopolize the planet's resources. Unfortunately, the ability to control the autofacs was lost in the war. This leaves the future of humanity, and the planet, in uncertainty as the autofacs consume every resource they can attain to produce what they perceive as needed. The story involves the human survivors as they try to steal the supplies they need and search for a way to take the power of production back into their own hands.

While many authors have done a lot of interesting writing in this area, I am most impressed by the work of Bruce Sterling as an insight into what the future might hold. In his novella *Kiosk, (Ascendencies: The Best of Bruce Sterling)*, the main character, Borislav, is a humble, limping man from a cold, Eastern European country who owns a street kiosk selling 3D printed tchotchkes. A young girl called Jovanica is a regular customer—returning day after day with her pocket-money to buy 3D printed barrettes, hair clips and scrunchies—she is the trend setter of the area. She picks out the coolest hair toys and leads the next hair toy craze - with Borislav's kiosk being the only supplier.

> *The fabrikator was ugly, noisy, a fire hazard, and it smelled. Borislav got it for the kids in the neighbourhood. One snowy morning, in his work gloves, long coat, and fur hat, he loudly power-sawed through the wall of his kiosk. He duct-taped and stapled the fabrikator into place. The neighborhood kids caught on instantly. His new venture was a big hit. The fabrikator made little plastic toys from 3-D computer models. After a week, the fab's dirt-cheap toys literally turned into dirt. The fabbed toys just crumbled away, into a waxy, non-toxic substance that the smaller kids tended to chew. Borislav had naturally figured that the brief lifetime of these toys might discourage the kids from buying them. This just wasn't so. This*

wasn't a bug: this was a feature. Every day after school, an eager gang of kids clustered around Borislav's green kiosk. They slapped down their tinny pocket change with mittened hands. Then they exulted, quarreled, and sometimes even punched each other over the shining fab-cards. The happy kid would stick the fab-card (adorned with some glossily fraudulent pic of the toy) into the fabrikator's slot. After a hot, deeply exciting moment of hissing, spraying, and stinking, the fab would burp up a freshly minted dinosaur, baby doll, or toy fireman.

The 'Kiosk' story has already been the inspiration for real world developments. With its Kiosk project, Antwerp-based design studio Unfold explores a future scenario in which digital fabricators are so ubiquitous that we see them appear on street corners, just like fast food is sold on the streets of New York City. The rapid prototyping kiosk enables customers to "get a custom made fix for your broken shoe, materialize an illegal download of Starck's Juicy Salif orange squeezer that you modified for better performance, or quickly print a present for your sister's birthday".

Perhaps the most inspiring piece of Streling's work that I have ever come across was this excerpt from a speech that he gave at the Computer Game Developers Conference, back in March 1991, in San Jose, California, entitled: "The Wonderful Power of Storytelling." More than twenty years on, it seems as relevant to 3D printing entrepreneurs now as it did to computer programmers back then.

Follow your weird, ladies and gentlemen. Forget trying to pass for normal. Follow your geekdom. Embrace your nerditude. In the immortal words of Lafcadio Hearn, a geek of incredible obscurity whose work is still in print after a hundred years, "woo the muse of the odd." A good science fiction story is not a "good story" with a polite whiff of rocket fuel in it. A good science fiction story is something that knows it is science fiction and plunges through that and comes roaring out of the other side. Computer entertainment should not be more like movies, it shouldn't be more like books, it should be more like computer entertainment, SO MUCH MORE LIKE COMPUTER ENTERTAINMENT THAT IT RIPS THROUGH THE LIMITS AND IS SIMPLY IMPOSSIBLE TO IGNORE!

I don't think you can last by meeting the contemporary public taste, the taste from the last quarterly report. I don't think you can last by following demographics and carefully meeting expectations. I don't know many works of art that last that are condescending. I don't know many works of art that last that are deliberately stupid. You may be a geek, you may have geek written all over you; you should aim to be one geek they'll never forget. Don't aim to be civilized. Don't hope that straight people will keep you on as some kind of pet. To hell with them; they put you here. You should fully realize what society has made of you and take a terrible revenge. Get weird. Get way weird. Get dangerously weird. Get sophisticatedly, thoroughly weird and don't do it halfway, put every ounce of horsepower you have behind it. Have the artistic *courage* to recognize your own significance in culture!

Okay. Those of you into SF may recognize the classic rhetoric of cyberpunk here. Alienated punks, picking up computers, menacing society.... That's the clichéd press story, but they miss the best half. Punk into cyber is interesting, but cyber into punk is way dread. I'm into technical people who attack pop culture. I'm into techies gone dingo, techies gone rogue—not street punks picking up any glittery junk that happens to be within their reach—but disciplined people, intelligent people, people with some technical skills and some rational thought, who can break out of the arid prison that this society sets for its engineers. People who are, and I quote, "dismayed by nearly every aspect of the world situation and aware on some nightmare level that the solutions to our problems will not come from the breed of dimwitted ad-men that we know as politicians." Thanks, Brenda!

That still smells like hope to me...

You don't get there by acculturating. Don't become a well-rounded person. Well-rounded people are smooth and dull. Become a thoroughly spiky person. Grow spikes from every angle. Stick in their throats like a puffer fish. If you want to woo the muse of the odd, don't read Shakespeare. Read Webster's revenge plays. Don't read Homer and Aristotle. Read Herodotus where he's off talking about Egyptian women having public sex with goats. If you want to read about myth don't read Joseph Campbell, read about convulsive religion, read about voodoo and the Millerites and the Munster Anabaptists. There are hundreds of years of extremities; there are vast legacies of mutants. There have always been geeks. There will always be geeks. Become the apotheosis of geek. Learn who your spiritual ancestors were. You didn't come here from nowhere. There are reasons why you're here. Learn those reasons. Learn about the stuff that was buried because it was too experimental or embarrassing or inexplicable or uncomfortable or dangerous."

Distributed Networking
One important result of 3D printers is going to be the greater importance of distributed networks, and this subject is well worth reading up on. I would recommend that you start with Wikinomics.

Wikinomics: How Mass Collaboration Changes Everything by Don Tapscott and Anthony D. Williams
This book explores how some companies in the early twenty-first century have used mass collaboration (also called peer production) and open-source technology, such as wikis, to be successful. Chapter 6 is especially relevant even though it does not go into the kind of detail for which most of us are looking.

> *Global Plant Floor recognizes that manufacturing has become more open and able to support mass customized products. This is essential for new products to get to market effectively.*

Crowdsourcing: Why the Power of the Crowd Is Driving the Future of Business by Jeff Howe

> *In his prescient 2006 article in Wired, Jeff Howe coined the term "crowdsourcing" to describe how the Internet has enabled large, distributed teams of amateurs to do work that was previously the domain of isolated experts or corporations. Linux and Wikipedia are only two of hundreds of examples of this phenomenon. Howe's article in Wired focused on two innovative companies who had successfully harnessed the power of crowdsourcing: iStockphoto, a community-driven source for stock photography, and InnoCentive, where corporations offer cash prizes for solving their thorniest research and development problems. Two years later, Howe has*

expanded his article into a 300-page book.

Abundance: The Future Is Better Than You Think by Peter H. Diamandis and Steven Kotler

> *We will soon be able to meet and exceed the basic needs of every man, woman and child on the planet. Abundance for all is within our grasp. This bold, contrarian view, backed up by exhaustive research, introduces our near-term future, where exponentially growing technologies and three other powerful forces are conspiring to better the lives of billions. Since the dawn of humanity, a privileged few have lived in stark contrast to the hard scrabble majority. Conventional wisdom says this gap cannot be closed. But it is closing—fast. Diamandis will address how progress in artificial intelligence, robotics, infinite computing, ubiquitous broadband networks, digital manufacturing, nanomaterials, synthetic biology, and many other exponentially growing technologies will enable us to make greater gains in the next two decades than we have in the previous two hundred years. We will soon have the ability to meet and exceed the basic needs of every man, woman, and child on the planet. Abundance for all is within our grasp. Diamandis explores how four emerging forces—exponential technologies, the DIY innovator, the Technophilanthropist, and the Rising Billion—are conspiring to solve our biggest problems.*

The Mesh: Why the Future of Business Is Sharing by Lisa Gansky

In this painstakingly researched, fun to read book, Gansky has outlined a trend that has been around but often overlooked. The internet has turbocharged our ability to share. It has created a platform for business models based on community use of expensive objects and services. We are now coming into an era where easy access to shared and personalized goods and services is going to be an integral and ubiquitous part of the new economy. In an increasingly crowded, economically uncertain, and environmentally damaged world, people are becoming increasingly wary about the financial and personal burden of buying and owning stuff. Aided by social media, wireless networks and data crunched from every available source, people are moving towards sharing goods and services at the point of need. I especially liked VC David Hornik's comments, "Gansky's book is an important read for anyone who cares about the planet or is looking to make a ton of money."

Of course, no discussion of the subject of the future economics should be considered without at least some input from Kevin Kelly, the original founder of *Wired* magazine.

Any of his books are well worth reading, but this article is particularly relevant to the future of 3D printing.

http://www.kk.org/thetechnium/archives/2008/01/better_than_fre.php

An alternative starting point might be his 1994 book, *Out of Control*. This work was way before its time, and word has it that it is one of those unusual books that sells better each year. Described as a 'sprawling odyssey' that provokes and rewards readers across a wide range of disciplines. Former publisher and editor of *Whole Earth Review*, then executive editor of *Wired*, Kelly's works are an essential starting point for anybody that wishes to understand and exploit the trends of the future.

Kim Eric Drexler is an American engineer best known for popularizing the potential of molecular nanotechnology (MNT), from the 1970s and 1980s. His 1991 doctoral thesis at Massachusetts Institute of Technology was revised and published as the book Nanosystems: Molecular Machinery Manufacturing and Computation, which received the Association of American Publishers award for Best Computer Science Book of 1992. He was the first person to come up with the term "clanking replicator" to distinguish macroscale replicating systems from the microscopic nanorobots or "assemblers" that nanotechnology might one day become make possible. He also coined the term grey goo.

No discussion of replicators and 3D printers would be complete without discussing the possibility of a von Neumann space probe. This concept was named for the Hungarian American mathematician and physicist John von Neumann, who rigorously studied the concept of self-replicating machines that he called "Universal Assemblers" and which are now often referred to as "von Neumann machines". If a self-replicating probe finds evidence of primitive life (or a primitive, low-level culture), it might be programmed to lie dormant, silently observe, attempt to make contact (this variant is known as a Bracewell probe), or even interfere with or guide the evolution of life in some way. While von Neumann never applied his work to the idea of spacecraft, theoreticians since then have done so. This has obviously provided very fertile ground for science fiction writers who have expanded this idea into many different areas.

Understanding Miniature Scales

Understanding the various scales of miniatures can be a little bit confusing at first, as there seem to be so many. Even so, if you are considering printable miniatures, it is essential that you appreciate the difference between each of the scales, and their importance to collectors.

Scale model is often a catch all phrase for an item that depicts reality in smaller or larger scale. People who prefer a particular scale will refer to collecting 1/18 scale diecasts, rather than scale model cars. Railroad scales are referred to by name, rather than calling an HO locomotive a Scale model train. The term scale model is so loosely applied that it now tends to stand for toys, or items built from boxed sets of pre-cast modeling parts.

With metrication in the United Kingdom, United States manufacturers began to use the metric system to describe miniatures, as opposed to the previously popular imperial units, so that their tabletop wargaming models would be compatible.

Scales of 20 mm, 25 mm, 28 mm, 30 mm, 32 mm, and 35 mm are the most common for role-playing and tabletop games. Smaller scales of 2 mm, 6mm 10 mm, 15 mm, and 20 mm are used for mass-combat wargames. Painters and collectors commonly use larger figures of 54 mm or more. Just to complicate matters further, the use of scale is not uniform and can deviate by as much as 33 percent. A manufacturer might advertise its figures as 28 mm, but their products may be over 30 mm tall. A contributing factor is the difference in methods used to calculate scale. Some manufacturers measure figure height from the feet to the eyes rather than the top of the head. Therefore, a 6-foot (1.83 m) figure in 28 mm scale would be 30 mm tall. As a result, 15 mm figures can be variously interpreted as 1/100 scale or 1/120.

A further complication is differing interpretations of body proportions. Many metal gaming figures are unrealistically bulky for their height, with an oversized head, hands, and weapons. Some of these exaggerations began as concessions to the limitations of primitive mold-making and sculpting techniques, but they have evolved into stylistic conventions. The large head, disproportionate models are referred to as 'heroic', a term used as a suffix to the intended scale. In the table below, figure height alone (excluding base thickness) is the feature from which approximate scale is calculated.

Sometimes scale is given as a ratio, (i.e., 1:300 or 1.300) or a fraction (i.e., 1/300). The number on the right of the pair indicates how many units (inches or centimeters) on the original are equivalent to one unit on the replica. For example, with a 1/300 scale miniature, if the miniature is one inch long, then the original was three hundred inches in length. One scale inch is equivalent to approximately 1/200th of an inch, 0.005 inches and 0.127 millimetres. One scale foot is equivalent to approximately 12/200th of an inch, 0.06 inches and 1.524 millimetres. One scale yard is equivalent to approximately 1/36th of an inch, 0.18 inches and 4.572 millimetres.

Scale became more important in the 1970s as people sought more accurate and interchangeable pieces for their collections. Early examples or antiques may vary widely from a scale size. Many railway model scales have gone out of production as the hobby changed from carpet railroads to smaller modern tabletop layouts. As height and fashion changed across history, miniatures changed as well. An antique doll that seems small today may accurately represent someone from her period.

0.27	Some naval miniatures come in this scale	1/6000
0.34	Certain naval miniatures are available in this scale	1/4800
0.35	Some starships available in this scale	1/4600
0.41	A few starships available in this scale	1/3900
0.54	European manufacturers produce naval	1/3000

	miniatures in this scale, just slightly smaller than 1/2400 scale. Also used occasionally for starships	
0.67	Commonly used for naval miniatures (WWI, WWII, modern)	1/2400
1.29	Some German naval miniatures are in this scale	1/1250
1.34	Also used for naval miniatures, especially for pre-20th century ships. (In the modern periods, most gamers now use 1/2400 scale due to price and playing area size.)	1/1200
1.8	Some Fighting Sail era ships available in this scale	1/900
2.0	This is a very small scale and is often used for gaming in tight spaces or with large numbers of player pieces. At this scale, each miniature often represents an entire unit (a group of men, squadron of cavalry, battery of artillery). Recommended for those who want to depict large, epic battles in a limited table space, or who have less time for painting. Popular scale for Victorian science fiction (VSF) games	1/805
2.3	One manufacturer offers rules in this scale, to be used for the paper ship kits he produces. Several ranges of plastic ships are also available in this scale	1/700
2.5	Naval miniatures	1/650
2.7	Naval miniatures	1/600
3.7	Some aircraft available in this scale	1/432
5.6	The popular scale in North America for modern combat, often involving armored vehicles. Periods include WWI, WWII, and contemporary	1/285
5.92	The NATO/EU standard scale for sand-table wargames involving micro armor. Closely related to 1/285 scale and generalized as "6 mm" figure scale. European manufacturers traditionally offer modern armor and infantry in this scale, slightly smaller than 1/285 scale. Aircraft and	1/300

	space fighter miniatures are also available in this scale	
6.0	Miniatures in this scale have the advantage of being inexpensive. The small size also means there is less visible detail to paint. In this scale it is possible to put armies on the tabletop which give the impression of masses of infantry. Figures available for fantasy, historical, and science fiction	1/268
6.2	The US standard for large-scale historical armor battles involving micro armor. Also popular in other genres, such as ancient, fantasy, and sci-fi. Closely related to 1/300 scale	1/285
7.0	Z scale (model railroad scale)	1/220
8.0-9.14	The standard for old 1970-1980 large-scale display plastic aircraft, a large majority of diecast aircraft, and science fiction plastic kits. Also popular in other genres, such as ancient, fantasy, and sci-fi. Figure scale is 8mm generally squared off to 1/160 - 1/200 scale	1/200 - 1/182
10.0	A newer scale, growing in popularity, especially for World War II and science fiction gaming. Roughly equal to N scale railroad trains. Notable manufacturers include Pendraken Miniatures, Magister Militum, Minifigs UK and Old Glory. Large enough to show detail but small enough to fit a large army on a tabletop	1/161
12.0	Aircraft kits in metal and plastic are available in this scale. A newer scale, growing in popularity, closely related to 10 mm. Roughly equal to 1/144 scale and N scale model mini armor	1/144
15.0	The most popular scale used for historical wargames set in the modern era, such as Flames of War or Axis & Allies Miniatures. Also widely used in ancient-era wargaming, such as De Bellis	1/107

	Multitudinis, De Bellis Antiquitatis, and Fields of Glory. but not used in fantasy role playing games. Ranges roughly from 1/100 scale to 1/122 scale. This is TT scale in miniature railroading. Also used for fantasy, science fiction, and 20th Century "skirmish-level" games	
16.1	Plastic kits of mechs (robotic fighting machines) are available in this scale. Modern military vehicles also come in this scale, in metal and plastic	1/100
18.5	Same as HO scale (model railroad scale - "HO" is "half O" scale, or 1/87.2). Several popular lines of pre- assembled and painted armored vehicles are available in this scale	1/87
20.0	Very popular with WWII Wargamers and is equivalent to the HO Model Railroad scale which gives a lot of options for purchasing diorama materials made for railroad models	1/91.4
21.2	Same as OO scale (British model railroad scale, alternative to HO scale). Plastic miniatures and kits are available in this scale for aircraft, ground vehicles, and soldiers	1/76
23.0	Another popular scale is 1/72 sometimes also called 20mm, but closer to 23mm. Mostly used for historical gaming in part do to a wide selection of 1/72 scale models	1/72
25.0	Traditionally popular for pre-20th Century wargaming, though most historical gamers have now switched to 15mm. Excellent scale for display games. Continues to be popular for fantasy wargaming, historical skirmish-level games, science fiction, and for use with role-playing games. Same as railroad S gauge	1/64
28.0	The "large" 25mm figures are sometimes listed as being 28mm	1/58
30.0	Older scale and not used very much in modern	1/54

	times. It is a good match for S Scale model railroads Common for pre-1970s wargaming figures; modern minis may be up to 35 mm. Close to S scale model railroads	
32.0	Idiosyncratic to Mithril Miniatures	1/57
33.5	Popular scale for plastic aircraft kits. Some display figures available in this scale. Also a railroad scale (P48 gauge)	1/48
37.0	Traditional O gauge (railroad). Not a wargaming scale	1/43.5
40.0	Some American Civil War figures available in this scale.	1/40
46.0	Popular scale for plastic kits of armor. Occasionally used for modern gaming	1/35
50.3	Same as I scale (model railroad scale). Also used for display models	1/32
54.0	Traditional "toy soldier" scale, no longer a common scale in miniature wargaming. However, it has been making a comeback in recent years - the large figures are said to be more convenient for older gamers. This scale is also popular for display (non-wargaming) figures	1/30
80.0	These and larger scales are not used for wargaming miniatures, but instead are figures which are painted and displayed as a hobby unto themselves	1/20
90.0		1/18
100.6		1/16
178.9		1/9

Converting Between Scale Types

To theoretically convert ratio scales into height scales - and assuming here that height scales measure to "eye height" while ratio scales measure to "head height" - divide 1610 by the scale. For example,

1/285 figures are pretty much the same scale as [1610 / 285 = 5.65] 6mm figures. The reverse is also true: to obtain ratio scale, divide 1610 by the height scale. Thus, 25mm figures are equivalent to 1610 / 25 = 64.4, or 1/64 scale (which is within spitting distance of 1/72 scale, another common scale). This means that 15mm toy soldiers are probably about 16.5mm tall overall, which makes them closer to 1/110 scale than 1/120. N-gauge figures (1/160) are about 11.25mm tall to the top of the head, which makes them about 10mm scale toy soldiers.

Where does the Magic Number 1610 Come From?

To obtain the magic number, all you need to come up with the "eye height" of the average person, measured in millimeters. The number we use is 1610 mm (about 5' 3"). In the simplest case, we take real life - 1/1 ratio scale, eye height of 1610 mm - and multiply 1 x 1610 = 1610. Therefore, 1610 is the constant. For a manufacturer who measures height scale to top of the head, rather than to eye level, Simply the height of the average man in millimeters - 1730 (5' 8").

Doll House Miniature Scales

The Doll House Miniature Scale that is referred to here is mostly is called 1/12 scale. This dollhouse scale is the most popular in the miniature dollhouse world; when a dollhouse miniature is referred to in general conversation this is the scale most often and usually assumed to be the scale of the discussion. Half inch scale (half inch to the foot or 1/24 scale) is fast growing in popularity throughout the art of dollhouse miniatures. 1/48 is a smaller dollhouse scale sometimes called 1/4 scale (1/4 of the regular 1/12 scale). Playscale or 1/6 is the scale used for fashion dolls. A 1/12 scale toy dollhouse for inside a 1/12 scale dollhouse would be 1/12 x 1/12 or 1/144 scale. In addition, there are some common model scales created by particular toy makers. Lundby, a Swedish company famous for their range of sturdy play dollhouses used a scale between 1/15 and 1/18 for their items.

Gauge

Railway modelers not only have to deal with scale, but with gauge, which is the measurement of the space between tracks. Railway modelers sometimes divide themselves into Narrow Gauge and Standard Gauge groups. Narrow Gauge in real railways are typically 3 ft. 6 in. (1067mm) between the rails and are used a lot for private industrial railways or railways in mountainous areas. Standard Gauge railways have 4 ft. 8 1/2in. (1435mm) between the rails and are the most common of the world's commercial railroads. There is an enormous range of miniature railroad scales in both main gauges. Even within named scale groups such as HO there may be huge variation in the ratio. HO may vary in size from 1/72 to 1/90 depending on the manufacturer. Z scale at 1/220 and N scale at 1/160 are the tiniest model railways. The largest for indoors are G gauge/scale at 1/22 to 1/25, often used in garden railroads. Outdoors even larger scales are the ride-on steam trains you see in amusement parks. Some half scale 1/24 dollhouse builders use G scale railway components in their dollhouses, as the scales are similar.

Finescale

More accurate scale miniatures are called finescale, a term that appears mainly in dollhouse and model railroad miniatures. Finescale miniatures are accurately detailed to exact scale.

Model ships may be a standard scale for gaming, 1/2400, or sized to be placed on a mantelpiece, something modelers call FTB or Fit the Box Scale, a scale whose parts can be packed easily by a company.

Collectibles in Mixed Scales

Some collectables use different scales within the same range. One popular series of Christmas villages has buildings which are approximately HO scale (1/87) or S railway scale (1/64) in size with trains in O scale (which varies from 1/43 to 1/48). O is a common size for Christmas and toy trains. The same village may have cars and other vehicles slightly larger than O scale and people who are G scale (1/20, to 1/25). Mixed scales make it hard to purchase pieces from other ranges to match your set unless you know what scale they are.

Proportion Without Scale

While architectural miniatures and miniatures built to be exact scale examples for furniture or ship building may be accurately scaled down to the thickness of the paint, the majority of items we call miniatures are not built to any particular scale. Scale model builders sometimes refer to these as TLAR scale, for That Looks About Right. Collectible cottages, famous building models, tourist miniatures, Christmas ornaments, miniature books and many decorative miniatures fit the TLAR category.

Translating millimeters to inches

One inch = 25.4 millimeters so it is easy to sense how large a humanoid figure would be in these various scales. In the 25/28mm scale a human would be about 1 inch tall which equals 6 feet in size. In the 54 mm scale a humanoid would be a little over two inches tall which equals 6 feet in size.

3D Printing Personal Wish lists

Here is a 3D printer question that I hear repeatedly; "If I have one of these machines, what can it make that is so useful?" Undoubtedly, this really depends on the individual, but I can already think of lots of goodies that I would like to have printed out in the privacy of my own home. I have tried to keep the rest of this book as realistic as possible, but this is my chance to let my imagination soar. All of the previous sections have been extremely careful in my research, ensuring that everything is verified and double-checked. I make no apologies for the pure fantasy of the material that follows. Perhaps you have a similar wish list in mind. I have put together two lists here, one of my top ten stocking fillers, smaller items that should be relatively easy and quick to print, as well as a big ticket list of projects that make my mouth water just thinking about them. Let's take a look at the smaller goodies first.

Stocking Fillers

I still have quite a lot of CDs and jewel cases, as I am sure you do too. Can somebody please come up with some printables to help me upcycle these items into something more useful than a bicycle reflector or a wind chime?

When I was still a boy, I can vividly remember an uncle who had served in the Royal Navy, and spent a lot of time in Hong Kong and the Far East. Of all his exotic souvenirs, the one that fascinated me the most was a Chinese puzzle box, an enigma that would stump me every time I visited his home. It did not matter how many times he showed me the secret, I had always forgotten how to open it by my next visit. All these years later, I would now love to see something similar, utilising the full capabilities of a 3D printer to create complex, and yet almost invisible mechanisms. In Japan, they are known as Himitsu Bako or personal secret boxes. They do exist in contemporary culture, with one example being the puzzle box from the movie *Hellraiser*. These are undoubtedly stylish items, constructed as they are from mahogany and etched brass, but at only three inches in height, they are of little practical use except as a stash box. What I am looking for is a box similar to the one featured in the *The Gift*, the visually stunning online film that was made for Philips from DDB London, RSA Films and director Carl Erik Rinsch, and which won the inaugural Grand Prix in the film craft category at Cannes. Now that is what I call a puzzle box.

Another favourite toy from my youth was that classic children's game, the Bucking Bronco. I saw this again recently and was disappointed by the roughly formed parts and the monochrome accoutrements. Now that we are well into the twenty-first century, I would like to see an updated version of this classic toy. I was thinking a *Star Wars* version featuring maybe a Tatooine Bantha or preferably a Tauntaun. This was the Luke Skywalker's mount on the ice world of Hoth, as featured in *The Empire Strikes Back*, and I can just imagine it being loaded up with all kinds of blasters, light sabres and other *Star Wars* gizmos. Just please don't anybody tell all those spoilsport lawyers.

When I am not writing, I spend a lot of time out hiking, often exploring ancient historical routes such as the Tea Horse Road and the Opium Trails. Unfortunately, I seem to spend an awful lot of the time picking up the detritus of other less responsible tourists. Please can somebody design and print me a rugged but light telescopic litter picker. Ideally with a trigger mechanism akin to an automatic umbrella (or maybe even a light sabre) so that I can keep it in a holster, instead of having to go rummaging through my day pack every time I see somebody's discarded cigarette pack or empty plastic bottle. A durable but dexterous claw, and preferably an auto retract mechanism, making it easier to bag the offending items. I enjoy keeping the trails clean, but I am getting older and do not want to put my back out stooping to pick up some other lazy sod's garbage.

Although I do not yet have a pair of Google's new iGlasses, I will be a lot more keen to invest in the technology if some bright spark out there can develop a printable digital glove, with which I can virtually manipulate all the data that is served up to me. Something nice and lightweight please, ideally custom printed to my own specific measurements. If I need to have some magnetic finger implants so that I can register force feedback, then that is a sacrifice that I would be willing to make, but this keyboard technology that I am using now is well over a hundred years old, and I desperately want to move into the current millennium.

I read recently about some German hackers that made 3D copies of police handcuff keys. Two students, Will Langford and Matt Keeter, made master keys, without access to the originals. Some reports claim that they were master keys that can unlock anything from baggage padlocks to police shackles. My inner 007 would love to have a nice set of lock picks, preferably nicely concealed in an ordinary looking credit card, so that they are not accidentally discovered by customs, causing some rather embarrassing questions at border control. I could also use a pair of printed handcuffs, for the next time I visit Shanghai. I have one particular lady friend in Pudong that has a tendency to turn all 'sa jiao' and pouty, like a true PRC princess, whenever she does not get her own way. A nice gaga pink pair, with her name custom printed on the back in svarowski crystals, would be great for those intimate occasions when I have to reprimand her bad behaviour with a light spanking, just to remind her who is boss.

Back in 1981, Jerdon Industries of Richardson, Texas produced an awesome looking "Model 357 Magnum, The Authentic Western Gun Hair Dryer." It was incredibly cool, with a finish that resembled intricately inlaid silver and even came with a white leather holster. It had three heat settings, Style, Dry, and Quick Dry, and it is such a desirable piece that those still in existence now fetch $300 or $400 a piece on eBay. Although I have looked at having some reproductions made in China, I would not trust most of those jokers not to scrimp on the internals, leaving me with a product that gives a deadly jolt rather than a simple blow dry. In addition, both Europe and the US have ridiculously complex safety codes for the manufacture of such items. Therefore, can someone just design me a case that I can print off at home, which I can then use to upgrade my cheap twenty dollar dryer into a piece of classic Americana?

Despite boasting an extensive collection of historically significant baseballs and basketballs, even super-lawyer, Harvey Specter displays them on simple plastic dimple stands that can be picked up at just a fiver for twenty. Given the capabilities of 3D printers, I would like to see some intricate stands, like those that the Imperial Chinese used to display their finest porcelain. Ming dynasty scholars would display their very best pieces on equally ornate stands, carved from rare and exotic hardwoods with names like purple sandalwood, yellow rose wood and even phoenix tail wood. While these tropical timbers are now on the verge on extinction, I would like to see the tradition of beautiful display stands return, perhaps even utilising what some people refer to as gaian or sacred geometry.

While I do not have an iPhone, I might very well consider buying one if I could print out an iPhone Theater add on. Conceived by Mike Enayah, a designer based in Miami, the iPhone Theater was designed with the iPhone 5 specs in mind and basically scales the iPhone screen to the same size as a movie theater screen. It is perfect for train rides and flights. It resembles a retro virtual reality device, but it actually offers a mini movie watching experience, with a pair of headphones and an attachment that holds the user's iPhone in order to provide a more visually immersive experience. It lifts up when not in use and is adjustable to allow for optimal vision distance. Perhaps the limitations of smart phones would make a pair of straight video glasses a better option. In terms of specifications, I would like a 92" virtual screen between ten and twelve feet away. (The Sony HMZ-T1 features two 0.7inch 1280 x 720 resolution (HD) OLED panels to project a 750 " theatre screen from a distance of twenty meters away.) Dual screens to support 3D movies, in 1080 HD resolution if possible, and the option to read documents, and play music in the background. Ten or twenty GB of local storage to cope with the latest blue ray rips, and a good three or four hours of battery time as a minimum.

I have always enjoyed activities that involved speed and movement through self-propulsion. I always loved bicycles for example, and have recently found great enjoyment in grass skiing. As a youngster I spent many happy hours on roller skates, lining up trolleys in the local supermarket car park, to practice my jumping skills. This was long before the introduction of in-line skates, and ever since then I have been waiting for someone to reinvent the roller skate wheel. With the arrival of 3D printers and their ability to print very complex structures, I am looking forward to someone building an Omni directional pair of skates using the Mecanum wheel. Sometimes called the Ilon wheel after its Swedish inventor, Bengt Ilon, this is a wheel that can move in any direction. The US Navy bought the patent from Ilon in the eighties and put researchers to work on it in Panama City. In 1997 Airtrax Inc. paid the US Navy $2,500 for rights to the technology, to build an Omni-directional forklift truck that could manoeuvre in tight spaces such as the deck of an aircraft carrier. Omni wheels are similar to Mecanum wheels and have revolutionised the very nature of the wheel. They are often used in small robots, giving them the ability to move in all directions.

Big Ticket Items

1. My first priority is power generation, to off-set the consumption of my printer. I have seen domestic wind turbines, but I am looking for a design that is more suited to a small home, where aesthetics plays a role in addition to functionality. I was hoping for some custom designed airfoils, perhaps some horizontal carousels that can collect updraft as well as breeze. Alternatively, I would like to try some kind of electricity producing kite, perhaps using torque to power 3D printed gears. Dogs were used extensively to power machinery in the medieval period, and I would like to see this practice resurface, especially in pounds and kennels where the canine guests can have a good exercise as well as providing the establishment's electrical energy. While I would probably have the oversized hamster wheel fabricated in metal, can somebody please design a gearing system that I can use with it to power a generator?

2. I recently discovered the work of Jean Pain and his discoveries concerning bioenergy and pyrolitics (wikipedia.org link (https://en.wikipedia.org/wiki/Jean_Pain)) His set ups were relatively bulky, and so I am looking ardently for a 3D printed device that can capture similar amounts of energy and transfer it to my needs. Preferably, something like a wormery but with an adaptation that produces energy rather than just liquid fertilizer.

3. Orreries are some of the most beautiful artifacts to come out of the Renaissance period, and yet many people still have no knowledge of them whatsoever. Their intricate gearings could be easily printed out in one sweep and the bodies themselves printed with accurate topographical features. Most orreries have been two dimensional in representation, but I see no reason why a printer could not design a version that moves in all the spherical planes. I would definitely print one of those. I was not entirely surprised to see that one imaginative artist has already had similar thoughts. A contributor known as 'IMVU-Whystler', has already printed a terrestrial orrery complete with proportionate Mercury, Venus, Earth, the Moon and the Sun on an Objet machine. It will be interesting to see what the open source community

can come up with on their Repraps and Rostocks.
http://imvu-whystler.deviantart.com/art/3d-Printed-
Terrestrial-Orrery-135923200

4. I watched a short video segment of the EADS guys and their
    printed bicycle with great interest. It was a piece of the
    British show *Inside Out West* in 2011 and is available here on
    youtube
    (http://www.youtube.com/watch?v=hmxjLpu2BvY).   The
    result was more like an early hobbyhorse with wheels, rather
    than the streamlined racers that we already have today. Of
    course, I am looking forward to the day when high quality
    bikes can be printed, but I am also itching to print out one of
    those human powered flight cycles. There is already a
    MakerPlane project to make it cheap and easy to build an
    airplane. Being able to print airplane parts will still cost a
    pretty penny, but it will be a heck of a lot cheaper than buying
    them individually. The printed plane will be a single-engine
    sport aircraft that can seat two, that only takes twenty hours
    of instruction and a few tests until you are licensed to fly
    alone. The folks behind the MakerPlane expect to have a
    working prototype up sometime in 2014. I know that some
    guys would prefer a James Bond type gyrocopter (and I am
    sure that those too will quickly drop in price following more
    advanced drone technology), but I would prefer to print out
    the an updated version of the Japanese Coolthrust or the
    University of Maryland's latest Gamera human powered
    helicopter. Once one of the two existing Kremer prizes
    (https://en.wikipedia.org/wiki/Human_powered_flight
    (https://en.wikipedia.org/wiki/Human_powered_flight)) has
    been awarded then hopefully we will start to see some really
    practical designs. The Sunseeker Duo is billed as the world's
    first two-passenger solar aircraft but is actually a motor
    glider. Launched in the fall of 2012 as a Kickstarter project,
    the team responsible did not seem to understand the
    motivations of their potential backers or even their future
    customers. Only ninety-six Backers pledged $15,198 out of a
    $70,000 goal, partly because the rewards were unattractive,
    but also because the design was lacking so many innovations.
    For example, backers pledging $50 or more were to receive
    an A4 size Sunseeker Duo print signed by project
    coordinator. Whoop-de-doo! $75 would have got you an

embroidered patch. I have commissioned many custom patches in my time, and can tell you that an 8-inch patch does not cost 75 cents to actually manufacture, let alone 75 dollars. While $100 got you a T-shirt, $250 gained you exclusive access to the Sunseeker-Blog and $500 entitled you to a DVD about the Sunseeker's history. The $1,000 pledge reward was so ridiculous that I have to quote it here. "Big pledges deserve big rewards. As a Gold Supporter, you will receive a desktop model of the Sunseeker Duo with base." Maybe their next project should be a book about how to fail dismally on Kickstarter. Anyway, while the concept was interesting, it was missing way too many features. It needed an inflatable float landing gear to takeoff/land on water, as well as headlights for night landing, so that users can fly all day, then land at sunset, hopping from lake to lake. A rig at the back of the passenger pod to connect a propane-powered generator would also have been a good back up idea.

5. How long do I have to wait to print my own Segway? I refuse to pay $5,000 or more for one of these things and there do not seem to be many Chinese copies zipping about that I can find. I want to print all the bits, except maybe the engine, plus I want to be able to print spares and accessories. Surely 3D printers will have finally come of age when we are all printing our own Segways.

6. I know that vacuum forming is more efficient, but I would really like to print some imperial storm-trooper outfits for my friends and myself. At $1,000 a time for the current examples available on eBay, I would like to find a way to be able to print these amazing suits of armour at a discount price. If I could make an 80 percent saving, it would be well worth having George Lucas and his SWAT trained litigation team on my tail.

7. When is somebody going to design and print a gravity engine? I really do not mind if it uses telescopic ball slides, counter weights or even magnetic spheres as long as it works effectively. That means over-unity at the very least, which is going to challenge the current laws of perpetual motion, but 3D printers are meant to be genuinely revolutionary anyway. Forget Picard and his hot cups of Earl Grey, this is a wish list, and so I want at least to be changing the basic laws of physics.

8. OpenROV is an open-source robotic submarine for

exploration and education that could drastically change the future of ocean exploration. www.kickstarter.com/projects/openrov/openrov-the-open-source-underwater-robot

The brainchild of Eric Stackpole, who wanted an easy way to explore a cave that was rumored to contain sunken treasure near his home, amateur and professional engineers and scientists from over fifty countries have now contributed to this design. Structurally, OpenROV is designed to go to one hundred meter depth and the interface is hosted as a webserver that allows you to control its movements with your computer's keyboard and see its feed on your screen, just like playing a video game. The only downside of this project is that a fully assembled OpenROV currently costs $1,200.

9. Underwater gliders differ slightly from conventional autonomous underwater vehicles (AUVs), in that they utilise an innovative buoyancy-based propulsion system that can extend ocean sampling missions from hours to weeks or months, and to thousands of kilometers of range. They use small changes in buoyancy in conjunction with wings to convert vertical motion to horizontal, following an up-and-down, sawtooth-like profile through the water, and thereby propelling themselves forward with very low power consumption. The most recent models are capable of harnessing energy from the thermal gradient between deep ocean water (2-4 °C) and surface water (near atmospheric temperature) to achieve globe-circling range, constrained only by battery power on board for communications, sensors, and navigational computers. On December 4, 2009, one of these gliders, RU-27, became the first to complete a transatlantic journey, traveling from New Jersey to the coast of Spain in 221 days. In August 2010, a Deep Glider variant of the Seaglider achieved a repeated 6,000-meter operating depth. At present a wide variety of glider designs are in use by Navy and ocean research organizations and typically cost $100,000. I would like to see the same exponential progress that has been achieved with aerial drones applied to underwater gliders, specifically in an open source project that brings down size and cost within the reach range of hobbyists and amateur environmentalists. The ArduPilot Open Source software/hardware, with its built in sensor

stabilization, GPS navigation, programmable 3D waypoints, in-flight reset, and programmable actions, would seem to be ideal for this purpose. It would need to have a user-friendly interface that could bring environmental data to the public for "crowd-sourced" dissemination and use social media platforms to serve as publicly accessible online "cloud" repositories of time-series datasets. On board sensors could perform a range of useful tasks from monitoring water quality conditions and alerting authorities when conditions are ideal for harmful algal blooms to occur, to acting as a submersible metal detector on the lookout for sunken Spanish galleons. It could do anything from pollution monitoring to species identification in Antarctica. "The potential for marine biotechnology is almost infinite," says Curtis Suttle, professor of earth, ocean and atmospheric sciences at the University of British Columbia. "It has become clear that most of the biological and genetic diversity on Earth is—by far—tied up in marine ecosystems, and in particular in their microbial components. By weight, more than 95% of all living organisms found in the oceans are microbial. This is an incredible resource." I personally would like to see a function that can also identify Japanese whaling ships and send location details to groups such as the Sea Shepherds.

10. My own personal submarine. A natural progression would be the DeepFlight Super Falcon, a winged submersible designed by Graham Hawkes that allows travel to the deepest parts of the ocean. Hawkes is a former civilian ocean engineer designing submersible vehicles for both the oil industry and those in the scientific research sectors. You have probably seen his work in the James Bond film *For Your Eyes Only*, or James Cameron's *Aliens of the Deep*. It is capable of a maximum cruise speed of 6 knots (11 km/h;) with a payload of 230 kg (510 lb), or two persons. Of course, what use is a personal submarine if you have nowhere to store it? While I was not able to attend the The Seasteading Conference 2012, held at San Francisco's Le Méridien, I am fascinated by the entire concept. Seasteads are permanent, stationary structures specifically designed for long-term ocean living, and when it comes to jumbo size printing projects, I am definitely looking forward to having my own sovereign

community out in the open ocean. I realise that a full-sized seastead is well beyond the capability of the current generation of 3D printers, but surely they would be ideal for experimenting with scaled down prototypes. Back in 2009, forty-one designs were submitted to compete for a $1,000 seasteading prize along with four additional $250 prizes for specific categories. To be honest, I found most of the designs a little disappointing, perhaps due to the lack of publicity and relatively low prize funds. The majority seemed to be post modern Tokyo-esque nightmares where we will all be hamsters living in archival housing. Still a lot can change in just a few years and I am sure that if the competition is repeated in the next few years, we would see a much higher standard of entries. Perhaps the Chinese government would like to sponsor the contest, so that they can begin populating some of the thousands of remote uninhabited rocks to which they are suddenly laying claim.

Gift List for a 3D Printer

Even if my own wish list does not pan out in the foreseeable future, maybe I should take another tack. Instead of putting these machines into the hands of lunatics that only want to print out firearms, I would like to see 3D printers being put to work by some of the more creative individuals with whom we currently share the planet. I am sure that you have your own contenders for whom these folks are, but this is my book, so here is my list. Of course, I would love to hear your own nominations for those imaginative individuals out there that might put these new machines to best use. Anyway, until I have the means to buy ten printers and start handing them out gratis, this is going to remain strictly a thought experiment, but I still encourage you to join in.

1. Tomas Saraceno is a visionary artist who aspires to bridge the gap between art and science. Knowledgeable in the principles of physics, chemistry and architecture, he has made use of high technology to design cities in the air. He had already experimented with the possibilities of passive solar energy, and built and flown the largest geodesic balloon ever built. Saraceno's vision proposes a network of habitable structures that float in the air. Will the social intercourse of humans, we may ask, improve with altitude? A true follower

in the footsteps of Buckminster Fuller.

2. James Acheson is a British costume designer. Acheson worked on *Doctor Who* in the 1970s, and has also worked on the *Spider-Man* films and designed the titular costume for *Daredevil*. He has won three Academy Awards for Best Costume Design: *The Last Emperor, Dangerous Liaisons and Restoration*.

3. John Mollo is a specialist in European and American military uniforms and author of several books on the subject. This led him to costume design, first being an advisor for the movie *Charge of the Light Brigade* in 1966 and later a costume designer, his first film being *Star Wars* in 1977. It was Mollo that was responsible for the iconic designs of the Imperial Stormtroopers and Darth Vader, as well as creating the wonderfully atmospheric eeriness that made Alien one of the best science fiction movies in history.

4. Bill Mollison is widely known as the father of modern permaculture. He is an incredibly knowledgeable naturalist, whose writings will inevitably become bibles when we finally decide to do something about the resolving the rapid deterioration of our planet. He is also a noted curmudgeon, and would probably provide compelling arguments that would counter almost everything that I have written in this book. With a perspective that is often well away from mainstream thinking I am sure that Mr Mollison could find uses for a 3D printer that nobody else would even dream of.

5. Trevor Baylis OBE is an English inventor, best known for inventing the wind-up radio. Rather than using batteries or external electrical source, the radio is powered by the user winding a crank for several seconds. This stores energy in a spring, which drives an electrical generator to operate the radio receiver. He invented it in response to the need to communicate information about AIDS to the people of Africa. He has been openly critical of TV shows such as *Dragon's Den* and *The Apprentice*, complaining that they "mock, bully and demean" inventors and other creative individuals.

6. Syd Mead, is a "visual futurist" and concept artist, best known for his designs for science-fiction films such as *Blade Runner, Aliens* and *Tron*. The following sentence is one of his most memorable quotes, "I've called science fiction reality ahead of schedule. His books, including *Oblagon, Sentinel* and *Kronlog*

have quickly become collector's items.

7. James Ng (pronounced Ing) is currently the world's leading oriental steampunk artist, most famous for his Imperial Steamworks series and is regular favorite at science fiction and fantasy conventions all over the world.

8. Jem Stansfield is an inventor and television presenter, most famous for his appearances on shows such as *Scrapheap Challenge*, *Planet Mechanics* and *Wallace and Grommet's World of Invention*. He has also worked on special effects for the movies *Lost in Space*, *The Avengers* and *Van Helsing*. Among his inventions are a compressed-air powered motorcycle, and boots that walk on water (for which he won a New Scientist prize).

9. Alan Moore is an English writer primarily known for his work in graphic novels (a term he coined and help popularise), including *Watchmen* and *V for Vendetta*. Frequently described as the best graphic novel writer in history, Moore is just my kind of contrarian, as well as being an occultist, a ceremonial magician, a vegetarian and an anarchist. A good overview of his thoughts and philosophies can be gained from looking at his wikiquote page, (http://en.wikiquote.org/wiki/Alan_Moore) and is just the kind of person that would push 3D printers into the realm of something that the rest of us could never have possibly imagined.

10. Dean Cameron is an ecologist living in Queensland, Australia and is the inventor of a number of award-winning innovations including the Joinlox, a mechanical fastening system and the Biolytix Filter, a sewage treatment system that mimics the intricate conditions of nature. I was lucky to spend a week or so with Dean and his family in a refurbished temple at the height of Yunnan's mushroom picking season back in 2011. He has a computer-filled invention den, partly open to the elements, in which he does his serious work, and I would love to see what amazing prototypes he could come up with if he had a 3D printer among his tools.

About The Author

Christopher follows the favourable climate throughout Asia, from the all year round sunshine of the Himalayan Plateau, to the snowbird beaches of Southern Thailand. He is currently exploring the spectacular Opium Trails of North West Guangxi for a forthcoming hiking guide, but can be contact by email at: christopherdwinnan@gmail.com.

He is also the author of:
Adventures in 3D Printing: *A Exploratory Primer for Makers, Inventors and Entrepreneurs.*

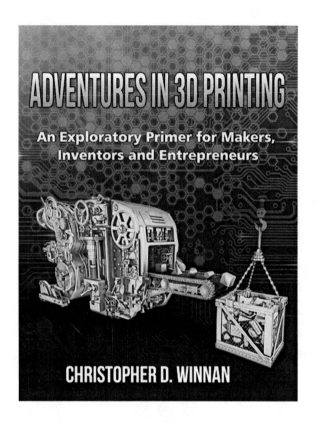

Other books by Christopher D. Winnan

88 Easy Ways to Improve Your English - *Longman (Chinese only)*

Frommers' China - *Frommers' Complete Guides*

China: Yunnan Province - *Bradt Travel Guides*

Intercontinental's Best of China - *Intercontinental*

FORTHCOMING IN 2014

An International Buyer's Guide to the Wholesale
Markets of Guangzhou

Lijiang Twilight - *A Tibetan Vampire Tragedy*

Opium Trails - *A Victoriental Steampunk Travelogue*

Around the World in Eighty Documentaries

Image Retrieval Information

History repeats itself?
http://meerface.com/2012/01/3d-manufacturing-at-home/

A High End Objet1000 Printer
http://www.kurzweilai.net/next-years-3d-printers

The Reprap and its Proud Father
http://www.howitworksdaily.com/technology/how-do-3d-printers-work/attachment/adrian-bowyer-with-reprap/

The Form 1 from Formlabs
http://www.engadget.com/gallery/form-1-3d-printer/5316918/
The Rostock Design

http://reprap.org/wiki/Rostock_mini

The Pwdr 3D Printer
http://www.prsnlz.me/blogs/rpblog/3d-printing-with-powder-at-the-entry-level/

3D printed remixes of masterpieces commissioned by the metropolitan museum of art
http://www.designboom.com/weblog/cat/16/view/21771/3d-printed-replicas-of-met-masterpieces.html

The turning gears on this object were printed rather than assembled. Courtesy of Zcorp
http://www.rapidreadytech.com/2012/03/designing-for-3d-printing/

The Meshup Teabunny
http://blog.ponoko.com/2012/10/22/uformia-meshup/

The Prusa Reprap
http://reprap.org/mediawiki/images/thumb/f/f2/Longboat_Prusa.jpg/190px-Longboat_Prusa.jpg

An open source home 3D printer set up
http://replicatorinc.com/blog/2009/03/3d-printers-always-be-closing/

The Cube by 3D Systems
http://on3dprinting.com/2012/05/11/3d-systems-ceo-3d-printing-will-be-as-big-as-the-ipad/

3D Printed Amplifiers
http://www.3ders.org/articles/20120210-8-cool-iphone-amplifiers-created-using-3d-printer.html

Your imagination is the only limitation
http://blog.ponoko.com/2010/07/29/personal-portable-3d-prinHYPERLINK

We are the makers
http://www.makerbot.com/blog/2012/01/09/introducing-the-makerbot-replicator/

Dodecahedron lamp made by California artist Bathsheba Grossman
http://www.3ders.org/articles/20111119-5-stunning-3d-printed-lamps.html

The O.P.U.S. V
http://blog.makezine.com/magazine/make-ultimate-guide-to-3d-printing/10-coolest-3d-printed-objects/

The O.P.U.S. V Interior View
http://laughingsquid.com/wp-content/uploads/IMGP1095-640x425.jpeg

The 3D Printed Art of Neri Oxman
http://www.partsnap.com/3d-printing-art-by-neri-oxman/

The Multi-Talented Ultimaker
http://lh3.ggpht.com/_XAfAW01Vojc/TPe0UY7-kHI/AAAAAAAAe5o/8MAcEom9N78/s288/image16.jpg

The Birthday of the Grand Moghul Aurangzeb
http://artmundus.wordpress.com/2010/05/09/auranzebs-throne/

Rajahs Paying Tribute
http://travel-culturess.blogspot.com/2012/01/dresden.html

Navy Seal UDT Halo Jumper
http://gray.ap.teacup.com/kazslog/334.html

Deluxe Suit Up Gantry
http://www.phcgames.com.br/?set=02

Mad Cat
http://timdp.members.sonic.net/battletech/MadCatAssembly.html

T08A2 Tank
http://www.tomopop.com/ghost-in-the-shell-tank-figure-hits
-kickstarter-22624.phtml

Paparazzi Drone
http://murdeltas.wordpress.com/category/bunt-gemischt/

Hermit crab shellters by Elizabeth Dema
http://www.tinyhousedesign.com/2008/07/14/

Beauty the Eagle
http://birdsofpreynorthwest.org/beauty-and-the-beak-project/

Chainsaw Attack Survivor
http://i.ytimg.com/vi/y5BYcu1glK4/0.jpg

Evil Face Planter
http://www.thingiverse.com/thing:21191

The work of Samuel Bernier, upcycler extraordinaire
http://www.3ders.org/articles/20120609-samuel-bernier-creates-
designer-lampshade-using-up-3d-printer.html

Even complex working parts are capable of being produced with the
latest generation of home printers
http://www.karakteristiekfotografie.nl/2011/12/magic-3d-
printer/3d-printer-parts-01/

Pyramids for health
http://www.kiranjewellers.co.in/plastic-pyramid-set.htm

Filigree Skull
http://www.ahalife.com/product/1946/3d-printed-filigree-skull/

Cecil Harvey's Dark Knight Armour
http://forums.penny-arcade.com/discussion/154234/science-
fiction-is-becoming-science/p2

Tudor Armour Design
http://www.royalarmouries.org/visit-us/leeds/leeds-

galleries/tournament-gallery/elizabeth-i/almain-armourers-album

Daedric Armour
http://media.beta.photobucket.com/user/omen_the_goth/media/Da edric.jpg.html?filters[term]=Daedric.jpg
Printing parts for humans
http://explainingthefuture.com/bioprinting.html

Inhalers
http://3dprintingindustry.com/2012/10/26/results-from-the-3d-printing-event-challenge/

The Reprap demonstrating its self-replication capabilities
http://www.techrepublic.com/blog/european-technology/reprap-the-3d-printer-thats-heading-for-your-home/229

Reprap Herringbone Gears
http://airwolf3d.com/

The Nurdler
http://paradise.rca.ac.uk/?p=652

The Botmill Reprap Glider 3.0
http://www.3dfuture.com.au/2011/05/glider-3-0-for-us-1395/

Miniature war machine
Left image retrieved from
2011/12/thinks-to-make-3d-

Right image retrieved from
http://www.games-workshop.com/gws/catalog/productDetail.jsp?

The Virtual Handgun
http://geekapolis.fooyoh.com/geekapolis_gadgets_wishlist/8182714

A concept home 3D printer envisioned by the IDI-Lab graduate design team at Zhejiang
http://www.idi.zju.edu.cn/blog/?cat=17

*****

CPSIA information can be obtained at www.ICGtesting.com
Printed in the USA
BVOW03s2118201213

339730BV00016B/532/P